Juli Kendall & Outey Khuon

WRITING SENSE

Integrated Reading and Writing Lessons
for English Language Learners

K–8

Stenhouse Publishers
Portland, Maine

Stenhouse Publishers
www.stenhouse.com

Credits
The authors and publisher thank Ellin Keene for permission to include her "Thinking Strategies Used by Proficient Learners."

Excerpts from *My Name Is Jorge on Both Sides of the River,* text copyright 1999 by Jane Medina. Published by Wordsong, Boyds Mills Press, Inc.
Reprinted by permission.

Library of Congress Cataloging-in-Publication Data
Kendall, Juli, 1949–
    Writing sense : integrated reading and writing lessons for English language learn-
    ers / Juli Kendall and Outey Khuon.
        p.cm.
    Includes bibliographical references.
    Contents: Introduction—Best practices in writing for English language learners—
    Assessing writing for English language learners—Selecting texts
    and choosing mentor authors—Preproduction—Early production—Speech
    emergence—Intermediate—Advanced.
    ISBN 1-57110-442-9
    1. English language—Study and teaching (Primary)—Foreign speakers.
    2. Language and languages—Study and teaching (Primary) I. Khuon, Outey,
    1950– II. Title.

    PE1128.A2K4158 2006
    372.652'1044—dc22   2005057610

Cover and interior design by Catherine Hawkes, Cat & Mouse
Typeset by Cat & Mouse

Manufactured in the United States of America on acid-free paper
11 10 09 08 07 06 9 8 7 6 5 4 3 2 1

For our families

Contents

Acknowledgments

The first time we heard about Ellin Keene and her work with comprehension strategies, we were at a school district literacy coaches' meeting. It was a number of years ago, and as the meeting began, the facilitator passed out a copy of *Mosaic of Thought* to everyone and announced that we would be doing a book study. It was this book, coauthored by Ellin Keene and Susan Zimmerman, that first introduced us to comprehension strategies. From that time on, we've never thought about comprehension in the same way.

Ellin Keene's thinking has expanded our own and led us into using comprehension strategies to help English Language Learners integrate reading and writing. We are incredibly grateful to her, especially since she graciously agreed to let us include the Thinking Strategies Used by Proficient Learners in this book. Without her work about the importance of comprehension throughout the school day, this book would not be possible.

How can we ever thank Philippa Stratton for editing this book? It would be impossible to list all the ways she has helped us, but beyond that she is the perfect person to edit a book about English Language Learners. She has a deep knowledge base that is complemented by her understanding of the importance of language and culture in educating children.

As for everyone else at Stenhouse with whom we work, including, but not limited to, Tom Seavey, Jay Kilburn, Doug Kolmar, Nate Butler, and Chuck Lerch, thank you for continuing to believe in us as writers and teachers.

Ed Garcia, our principal, has helped us refocus on writing. He's a cheerleader for Writing Workshop. He presents mini-lessons on all the aspects of teaching writing and willingly models in classrooms. We are truly fortunate to have such a knowledgeable, instructional leader. Our vice principal, Lucy Salazar, supports us with her knowledge of English Language Learners and her fantastic ability to relate to parents and families. Thanks, Ed and Lucy! We love you both.

We are honored to work with teachers who share their understanding of English Language Learners with us, especially Wendy Wahlen, Kathy Hernandez, Jason Cordero, Saroeung Yoeun, Linda Warner, Puthea Ing, Chansorado Chum, Maria Valenzuela, Anita Gomez, Anne McConaghy, Linaromy Prom, Walter Yang, Lena Phany Chhou, Theavy Lim, and Channary Sei.

I (Outey) am indebted to numerous people who provided me with endless encouragement, friendship, and love. To my former principals, Dr. Randy Ward and Mary Marquez, I owe you both my teaching career. You gave me

Hope is the thing with
  feathers
That perches in the soul

—EMILY DICKINSON

vii

the opportunity to become a teacher for the second time. To Alejandro Morales, David Taylor, Sherrie Quach, Sharon Lazo-Nakamoto, Paul Boyd-Batstone, Joan Shifflett, and Lee Newbauer, I am very touched by your friendship and encouragement. There was never a time that you said no when I needed your help. To my husband, Vandy, and to my sister, Kimly, you are always there for me. In your own traditional Cambodian way, you support my work with love, understanding, and patience.

I (Juli) owe a special debt of thanks to my friend Judy Swanson, who not only raises money by climbing mountains but who also always has the perfect quote. John Norton of the Teacher Leaders Network (http://www.teacherleaders.org) was the one who first got me writing and still continues to stand guard over four years of my reading/writing journals at Middle Web (http://www.middleweb.com). The journals that he so skillfully edited are woven into this book. Two of the vignettes in Chapter 2 first saw the light of day in MiddleWeb journals, as did several of the lessons in Chapters 8 and 9.

Once again, the love and support of my husband, Jim, makes this book, as well as everything else, possible. He spent endless hours taking photos, sorting through them, organizing, and printing. But it's more than that—on a daily basis, he helps me sort out how to go about the business of living. For that I am incredibly grateful.

Our deepest appreciation goes to the students we teach. Our wish is that each of them becomes a lifelong learner, loving reading and writing. It's just like Clara writes in her poem "Advice to Writers":

Look at the sky,

See around,

Dream it,

And write it down.

figure 1.1 (left) Juli confers with kids as they revise their writing.

figure 1.2 (below) Outey introduces students to a new book.

1 INTRODUCTION

Several years ago, we attended a weeklong Writing Institute coordinated by Columbia Teachers College Writing Project and our school district. It wasn't the first time we had been trained in writing, but this time we had a chance to sit together and talk to each other as we learned. During the advanced sections on Writer's Craft, Revision, and Group Structures, we took notes and made plans to implement lessons, confer with student writers, and organize units of study with the teachers we work with as Literacy Specialists.

The whole time we talked about how what we know about developing oral language and teaching English Language Learners (ELLs) could be drawn into lessons about writing. "What do you think about using this book with our kids?" one of us would say, and that would head everyone off into a conversation about stages of language acquisition and appropriateness of the texts used to model writing for lessons. It was a challenge to overcome our own fears and trepidations about teaching writing. For two years, we worked to

The fifth-grade English Language Learners that I work with did better than ever with their writing this year and I think it is due, in big measure, to the integrated strategy instruction— same books and same strategies for reading and writing. It all seemed to make more sense to them.

—JULI KENDALL

1

make it all come together. And then came the year we were told, "Don't worry about writing this year; we'll worry about it next year."

It was after the year of "not worrying" that we read *Writing Through the Tween Years* by Bruce Morgan. In it we discovered the list of Strategies Used by Proficient Learners created by Ellin Keene and her colleagues at the Denver-based Public Education and Business Coalition. It was *Mosaic of Thought*, the book Ellin cowrote with Susan Zimmermann, that introduced us to teaching comprehension in reading. What's different about the proficient learners' list is that it includes writing.

The lessons in this book are based upon Keene's most recent version of these strategies, Thinking Strategies Used by Proficient Learners. We noticed as we worked with them that kids did better than ever in writing. We believe that was due, in big measure, to the integrated strategy instruction—same books and same strategies for teaching reading and writing; for more about this, see Integrating Strategy Instruction in the Appendix. It all seemed to make more sense to them.

Organized by describing what proficient learners do, these strategies, which include writing, integrate insights from reading comprehension instruction. They include the following:

- Determine what is important in the text
- Inferring
- Use prior knowledge to make connections (schema)
- Asking questions
- Monitoring meaning and comprehension
- Fix-up strategies
- Synthesizing information
- Using sensory images (visualizing)

The thinking strategies used by proficient learners opened up a world of possibilities for us. Because they included writing, we saw how they could be the basis for a series of lessons to teach writing to English Language Learners. This tied in perfectly with the renewed emphasis on writing in our school and district, the needs of English Language Learners, and our desire to teach writing well. In *Writing Through the Tween Years*, Morgan (2005) agrees:

> We had to take a hard look at our practices and face our fears that we weren't good enough or didn't know enough to be teaching writing well. It's not easy having confidence as a teacher in these times. (p. 2)

So many teachers find teaching writing very intimidating. Although Juli took easily to it using the strategies, Outey's education and teacher training in Cambodia and her experiences as a writer of Khmer, French, and English led her down a different path. Like so many other teachers, not just those whose first language isn't English or who work with English Language Learners, she faced fears that she wasn't good enough and didn't know enough to be teaching writing well. The thinking strategies used by proficient writers help by giving a structure for planning mini-lessons. They provide teachers with a helpful resource for understanding what writers need to be able to do, as well as confidence that their instruction is headed in the right direction.

For more than twenty years, we've been teaching writing to English Language Learners. We believe that they can build oral language proficiency while they are learning to write. But as writing teachers, we face many challenges: using writer's notebooks with students; choosing literature for mentor texts and choosing mentor authors; modeling using our own writing; organizing and planning lessons; helping students write first drafts; teaching students to revise, not just edit; conferring with students; and finding ways to motivate students to publish works. When we work in classrooms, we see all these things happening. But teachers still find it difficult to do writing instruction with English Language Learners. So that's why we wrote this book—because, in these times, it's not easy having confidence as a teacher, and, we need to base writing instruction for English Language Learners on what proficient learners do.

We see this book as filling the need for teachers who are challenged to teach writing instruction that draws on what good writers do and that uses best practices to support English Language Learners as they take on these strategies. We bring to this book the same point of view that we brought to our *Making Sense* book: the idea that the importance of instruction based on the thinking strategies used by proficient learners is magnified for English Language Learners who are developing oral language proficiency as they learn to read and write.

The Nuts and Bolts of Writing Instruction for English Language Learners

How can English Language Learners learn to write while they are developing oral language? We suggest writing lessons based on the thinking strategies used by proficient writers as an important way to scaffold instruction for ELLs. To be effective, they need to be organized around an analysis of student work and the needs of the learners as writers, an in-depth understanding of Keene's Thinking Strategies Used by Proficient Learners, the writing process, and the stages of language proficiency.

An Analysis of Student Work

We frequently hear, "My kids can't make complete sentences. How can I teach them to write?" As teachers, we find we need to leave behind what the writer cannot do and look at what proficient writers do and then teach students how to do it. We begin by analyzing student work—by simply looking at students' writing samples. We focus on the things they can do—collecting ideas, choosing an idea to write about, writing a first draft. We look at their process of revision. How do they monitor meaning and comprehension? We check how they use fix-up strategies by editing for spelling, punctuation, and grammar. We examine their final drafts to see how they bring it all together. Then we make a list of their strengths as writers.

After analyzing student work, we use the needs of our students as writers to develop writing lessons. The lessons in this book provide examples of how to do this. We use a variety of ways to help students gain access to important writing strategies and skills; included in them are Interactive Writing, the Language Experience Approach, using mentor texts, having kids choose mentor authors, and modeling using our own writing as well as students' writing.

An Understanding of the Thinking Strategies Used by Proficient Learners

As noted earlier, Ellin Keene's Thinking Strategies Used by Proficient Writers frame our thinking in this book. These are the same strategies we use for comprehension lessons (Kendall and Khuon 2005). They also provide the basis for our writing lessons since the goal is for students to become proficient learners and to use the strategies in reading and writing to develop understanding and make meaning. For more information, see Chapter 2, pages 27–36.

The Writing Process

The process of writing is virtually the same for all writers. Writers get their ideas from many different sources. They organize what they have to say (on paper, on a computer, or in their heads). They write a draft. They ask what others think. They revise, making changes and additions to clarify their meaning. They edit for capitalization, punctuation, grammar, sentence sense, and spelling. Then they publish. It's the same for English Language Learners. They need to move through the writing process just like everyone else.

Prewriting   For English Language Learners, as well as other students, this involves providing experiences and comprehensible input that help students build background. Encouraging kids to draw on their prior knowledge and schema by making connections between what they already know and what they are learning helps them develop as proficient writers. Immersing students in literature by reading a variety of texts and genres provides models of writing and mentor authors to inspire students and teach them "how to do it." Writer's notebooks serve as a catalyst for writing by helping students collect and explore their ideas for writing and try out aspects of the writer's craft. Through brainstorming and/or the use of graphic organizers, English Language Learners learn to organize their writing by discussing and visualizing before they start.

Drafting   This offers students the opportunity to get their ideas down. It may be in writer's notebooks, on separate sheets of paper, or on the computer. We offer writers a choice of ways to draft to motivate them to write and to draw on their different strengths as learners. We stock our small-group areas with

c
a
c
a

w
tl
n
c

ens, and markers to encour-
iting often prefer to use a
istration they feel as writers
heir work.

en they are writing a draft,
aloud slowly and listen to
down what they hear and
al attention will be paid to

R
W
ar
re
re
to
pi

nglish Language Learners.
each writers about revision
l. To help our writers, we
g. We encourage them to
small group and to listen
that the partner reread the
n.

tic
wo
La
to
ing
tas
ate

ask themselves two ques-
tter?" Then we have them
derstanding. For English
on the meaning they want
ng, rewriting, and rework-
own partners for revision
ortable working. This cre-
tes writers to revise.

wri
use
pie
enti

ecklist to staple into their
nd 1.4). To teach kids to
trating how to use it on a
work. We go through the
as we work. In this way,

figure 1.3 *Decorated writing folders hold students' work.*

figure 1.4 *Students scaffold their writing by stapling Revision and Editing Checklists into folders.*

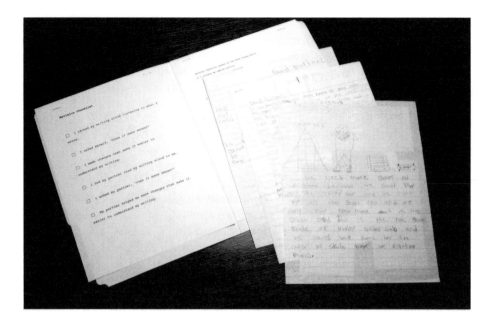

every student understands how to use the list and is accountable for revising their writing as well as that of their peers. They are expected to have worked through this checklist with a partner before asking the teacher for help. Frequent writing conferences with the teacher provide them with opportunities to get assistance, if necessary. For a single-page copy of the following Revision Checklist, see the Appendix.

Revision Checklist

_____ I reread my writing aloud, listening to what I wrote.

_____ I asked myself, "Does it make sense?"

_____ I made changes that make it easier to understand my writing.

_____ I had my partner read my writing aloud to me.

_____ I asked my partner, "Does it make sense?"

_____ My partner helped me make changes that make it easier to understand my writing.

Editing Doing this gets the writing ready to go out into the world. We explain to writers that the purpose of editing is to make writing easy for readers to understand. We use small groups to teach our writers how to use the Editing Checklist and to incorporate what they are learning about grammar and conventions into their editing.

We follow the same procedures as we did with the Revision Checklist. We begin by giving students a copy of the list to staple into their writing folders for easy reference. To teach kids to use the checklist for revising, we first model by demonstrating in a small group how to use it on a piece of our own writing or an anonymous student's work. We go through the entire list, one item at a time, thinking aloud as we work. In this way, every student understands how to use the checklist and is accountable for editing their writing as well as that of their peers. They are expected to have worked through this checklist with a partner before asking the teacher for help. Frequent writing conferences with the teacher provide them with opportunities to get assistance, if necessary. For a single-page copy of the following Editing Checklist, see the Appendix.

Editing Checklist

_____ **I checked my capitalization.**

> At the beginning of sentences
> Proper names
> Titles
> Dialog

_____ **I checked my punctuation.**

> Sentences and periods
> Question marks
> Exclamation points
> Paragraphs (indents)
> Dialog (quotation marks, capitals, commas, paragraphs)
> Underlining

_____ **I checked my grammar.**

> I reread the writing and asked myself, "Does it sound right?"
> I made changes to make it sound better.

_____ **I checked my sentence structure.**

> I reread to see if I used a variety of sentence structures (simple and compound).
> I reread to see if I used different kinds of sentences (declarative, interrogative, imperative, exclamatory).

_____ **I checked my spelling.**

> I used the spell-checker.
> I used the dictionary.
> I asked a friend.
> I asked the teacher.

_____ **I had a partner reread and edit my writing with me.**

_____ **I used the Five Finger Rule for Editing.**

Additional ways to edit provide kids with motivation to check their work. We make use of Grammar Checks; red and green underlining in Microsoft Word; editing with the teacher, with a partner, or in a group; as well as using the Editing Checklist as a scaffold.

We also teach students to use the Five Finger Rule for Editing. Each finger on one hand represents a different editing skill: spelling, capitalization, punctuation, grammar and usage, and sentence structure (see Figure 1.5). It's a simple way to help kids remember how and what to edit, whatever the circumstances. We were pleased to find that they use it frequently to edit their work

figure 1.5 *A copy of the Five Finger Rule for Editing wall chart by teacher Saroeung Yoeun.*

figure 1.5 *A copy of the Five Finger Rule for Editing wall chart by teacher Saroeung Yoeun.*

on writing assessments because it is so easy for them to remember and use. We have found that the rule acts as a scaffold to help kids become more independent with their editing.

Publishing   Publishing offers writers opportunities to take their writing out into the world. There is a wide variety of ways to motivate writers to publish. Taking advantage of class and schoolwide anthologies and literary magazines to collect student writing makes it available to readers in class and school libraries. Readers' theater, poetry cafes, and Open Mike settings encourage kids to orally present their writing—to bring it to an audience. Opportunities for writers to network with other classes and other schools provide feedback about their writing as they participate in online poetry slams and other collaborative writing projects. When kids take their writing, such as picture books, to younger students' classes to share, they get a response from others.

   Not all pieces of writing get published. Writing folders give kids a place to collect the pieces that they choose not to publish. Periodically, they can go back through the writings there to see if there are pieces they want to revise or rework. Examples of student writing folders were shown in Figures 1.3 and 1.4.

The Stages of Language Proficiency

In *Making Sense*, we outlined the stages of language proficiency—descriptions follow—and how they relate to designing lessons and choosing texts for English Language Learners. We also organize our instruction for writing around these stages.

Preproduction   Students at this stage are not ready to produce much language, so they primarily communicate with gestures and actions. They are absorbing the new language and developing receptive vocabulary.

Early Production   At this stage, students speak using one or two words or short phrases. Their receptive vocabulary is developing; they understand approximately 1,000 words. Students can answer "who, what, and where" questions with limited expression.

Speech Emergence   Students speak in longer phrases and complete sentences. However, they may experience frustration at not being able to express completely what they know. Although the number of errors they make increases, the quantity of speech they produce also increases and they can communicate ideas.

Intermediate   Students may appear to be fluent; they engage in conversations and produce connected narrative. Errors are usually of style or usage. Lessons continue to expand receptive vocabulary, and activities develop higher levels of language use in content areas. Students at this level are better able to communicate effectively.

Advanced   Students orally communicate very effectively in social and academic settings, but many may struggle with reading and writing.

Writers and Surprises

When teaching writing, we sometimes encounter surprises. There are some students who have inspired us and whom we remember from year to year. There are some things our students remind us of as we work with them, when they are stuck for words, discouraged, and trying to avoid writing anything. What follows in this section is what we've learned along the way, what we do to help students with writing. This is not like other writing books, many of which are very helpful. It's more individual, more like conferring with writers. Here we share many of the things we know about teaching writing to students who are full of surprises.

Writing has so much to give, so much to teach, so many surprises.

—ANNE LAMOTT
(1994, p. xxvi)

Writers who don't write (Anthony and Edgar)

It occasionally happens that in a group of English Language Learners some students do not write. We believe that allowing students to select their own topics in a low-anxiety, risk-free environment can motivate reluctant writers.

This was the case with Anthony. He refused to write anything until he was introduced to the writer's notebook and encouraged to write whatever he chose. He soon filled pages with retellings based on the plots of his favorite video games. Although he never became a prolific writer and struggled with his attempts on assigned topics, Anthony did write about what he was interested in—video games.

For Edgar, it was time that he needed. Time to read books and talk about what he wanted to write. After struggling with topic selection during a beginning-of-the-year writing assessment, Edgar commented, "It's just too soon to write." It was when he decided that he wanted to be a meteorologist and a weatherman too that his writing really started. He researched the weather as well as jokes that a weatherman would use. Then he practiced writing and rewriting his jokes to get them just right. Encouraging Anthony and Edgar to select topics they cared about helped them develop as writers.

Writers whose writing is difficult (or impossible) to read (Amancio and Gil)

For some reason there are students who find it difficult to write so that others can understand. Their writing appears to be gibberish and yet often the students, themselves, can read it back to help us understand that they know what they want to write. Amancio and Gil's writing was like that. They used no punctuation, misspelled words, and had difficulty making a coherent sentence.

From the beginning of the year, they worked with one goal in mind: their writing would make sense to the reader. One way Juli found to help them was to have them read back their writing as soon as they had finished it. She wrote it down on a separate sheet of paper as each of them read it back. Then she went over their writing, helping them match what they had written with the transcript made. Over time they began to see how important it was for their writing to be conventional so that others could read it. They worked on learning how to spell 100 high-frequency words, using appropriate punctuation, and reading lots of literature and mentor texts. Soon their writing became more comprehensible, and other students were able to read and understand it. Rereading proved to be an important strategy to help them improve as writers.

Writers whose writing doesn't make sense (Patti and Nayeli)

As English Language Learners move through the writing process, it is important for them to ask, "Does it make sense?" This ties in to one of the strategies for how proficient writers monitor meaning and comprehension in their writing. "Writers monitor their composition process to ensure that their text makes sense for their intended audience at the word, sentence, and text level" (Keene).

We use writing partners to help each other with this question. They begin by looking at the word level. For example, Nayeli and Patti were sitting together revising Patti's writing. Nayeli read aloud for several lines and then said, "Look, Patti, this doesn't make sense. You need to add another word to make sense." Next, they took time to look at each sentence. Finally, looking at the whole text, they asked, "Does it make sense?"

This question is critically important for English Language Learners because they need to make the connection between reading and writing. The idea that what they write will make sense to a reader is of utmost importance.

Writers who never revise (almost everyone)

The idea of revision is tough for all of us, adults and kids. We struggle to reread our work and think about what the reader will take away from it and how to make our meaning clearer as well as more interesting. In our teaching, we stress the importance of rereading and having others read your writing to monitor for clarity and impact. This remains an ongoing challenge for all writers, and we constantly look for ways to motivate our writers, and ourselves, to revise.

Drina provided us with a good example of learning to revise. At the end of fifth grade, all the students in her class wrote an essay about elementary school. The class selected one essay to be read by a student at their promotion ceremony. Drina's essay was selected, so she took it home over the weekend to practice reading it.

On Monday, after she had done a wonderful job of representing her class with her essay, her teacher commented, "Wow! That really changed over the weekend." It seems that Drina went home and, while rereading her essay, made substantial changes to the original—all to the better and with the idea of making her writing easier to understand. This had not been her teacher's intention, but the need to read the essay to a group of parents and students had provided her with the motivation to revise.

Writers who edit only a little, if at all (Gladys and Casey)

To help writers who struggle with editing, such as Gladys and Casey, we scaffold the editing task with the Five Finger Rule for teaching kids to edit one thing at a time. The thumb and each of the four fingers stands for one part of the complex task of checking for conventions. The little finger stands for capitalization. The ring finger represents punctuation. Grammar and usage is the middle finger. The index finger stands for sentence variety. Finally, the thumb represents spelling.

This editing strategy starts with our youngest writers and moves along with them. For example, as they learn more and more rules for capitalization, the little finger stands as a reminder that when they are editing, they should check capitalization. The rule encourages them to apply correct conventions to seek clarity and impact for the reader, which is a fix-up strategy proficient writers use.

Writers who take forever to finish (Tony, Jenny, and Carmen)

Some writers never seem to finish and publish what they write. Their drafts and projects drag on and on, and they tire of them before they are completed. Our challenge is to look for ways to motivate them.

Providing motivation has become easy since we discovered a variety of ways for students to publish their work. Using a writing folder or portfolio as a motivator, students select work for Open Mike (an opportunity for students to read or perform their writing much the same as in a coffeehouse), online poetry slams, the school newspaper, classroom anthologies, and reading to younger students.

Setting a deadline, and learning to work toward it, also provides motivation for many reluctant finishers. Setting small goals that lead up to the publication of a piece of writing and learning to plan and budget their time are valuable lessons for students.

Writers who always write about the same topic (Stephen and Jenny)

Once in a while a writer gets consumed by one topic. For some writers, cartoons, movies, and video games fall into this category. For several years, the popular video game Pokemon popped up as a topic over and over again for some students. They wrote personal narratives, poetry, fiction, feature articles, and persuasive essays about this one topic. Helping them find other topics was a real challenge.

One thing that often helped was reading aloud a variety of different authors and genres. This gave them a sense of what else they could write about. In addition, writer's notebooks can be a source of new topics and ideas for these students, especially if mini-lessons encourage them to "give it a try" in the notebooks.

Writers who find it difficult to get organized and come up with ideas (Oscar)

Some writers just seem to have difficulty keeping track of their work. Oscar is one of those writers. He has to hunt around to find a pencil, frequently loses his writer's notebook and needs to start another, and misplaces his drafts. But he also struggles with how to start writing. Here's his story.

Oscar can't get started on his next piece of writing. He always has a hard time coming up with an idea. Even though he uses a writer's notebook to collect seed ideas and spends lots of time thinking, it's still a challenge. Every time Juli asks him what he's going to write about next, he responds, "I have to write more?" So she pulls together four students to do a small-group conference about how to get started with your writing.

Nayeli, Drina, and Bryan are there to share their expertise with Oscar as the teacher acts as a facilitator and encourager. Even after he chooses a topic, Oscar struggles to come up with a strong lead, stumbling over how to begin. This group will help scaffold the task for him. The four students sit together at a table talking about how Oscar can get started. They offer suggestions, give encouragement, and even provide examples of how they might do it.

After all the revising, rewriting, and reworking by the small group, Oscar has a beginning for his story about basketball.

> *The Beginning of Oscar's Story*
>
> It was a hot day at the park. I was playing with Michael Jordan. Then the ball went into the net. Then my two best friends Drina and Bryan said, "Could we play?"
> We said, "Yes!!"
> Bryan said, "Who's that big guy?"
> I said, "It's Michael Jordan."

Writers who struggle, really struggle, with spelling (Henry)

For some writers, spelling is a constant challenge. One way we help writers with spelling is by encouraging them—"Give it a try!" on a sticky note (see Figure 1.6).

figure 1.6 *Students figure out how to spell words by using sticky notes.*

"Can I have a sticky note?" Henry asks. "This is so cool!" Henry's finally gotten the idea that getting a sticky note when he's unsure of a word and trying out his spelling several times will help him visualize the word better. It works for him since he figures out how he wants to spell the word *strength*. His three attempts (*strangth, stranegh, straneght*) show that he's getting much better at approximating spelling.

The following are Outey's comments about spelling:

Why correct spelling? In Cambodia, where I came from, correct spelling was always a focus in writing. Spelling was a mandated subject in school. When we did the spelling test, it was a whole text "dictation," often a page or more, not just a few words. Although I believe in inventive spelling as a way to get the students to produce more writing, I still don't want them to get used to misspelling the words because I am afraid they will internalize it. In a way, I don't want the students to concentrate on the content alone, but also to pay attention to the conventions. To me it is a way to train students to keep multiple tasks in mind. They need to get used to thinking about and performing multiple tasks with ease.

How This Book Is Organized

The writing lessons in this book are structured in the same way as they are in *Making Sense* (Kendall and Khuon 2005). The lessons here are divided into five sections based on the stages of English Language Learners' proficiency:

- Preproduction
- Early Production
- Speech Emergence
- Intermediate
- Advanced

The instructional materials (for example, books, charts, notebooks, etc.) listed in the lessons can often be used flexibly with students with more or less language proficiency. Since every student's needs are individual, always check for understanding with each of them to make sure that the instructional materials are comprehensible and support oral language development.

Within each stage of language proficiency, the lessons are further divided by strategies used by proficient writers.

- Schema (using prior knowledge to make connections)
- Asking Questions
- Visualizing (making pictures in your mind and using sensory images)
- Inferring (reading between the lines)
- Determining Importance in Text (not in beginning stages)
- Synthesizing Information (not in beginning stages)
- Fix-Up Strategies (not in beginning stages)
- Monitoring Meaning and Comprehension (not in beginning stages)

Chapters 5 through 9 begin with a description of students at a specific stage of language acquisition. Then chapters are organized into lessons for younger and older ELLs.

The first section has a vignette of younger students learning about writing and includes lessons for teaching writing based on the thinking strategies used by proficient writers described at the beginning of this chapter. The second section follows the same format for older students. There are also lists of possible anchor texts (Harvey and Goudvis 2000), organized by the strategies, to use with students.

These lessons come from our experience teaching writing to English Language Learners. For more than fifteen years we've collaborated, and teaching students how to improve their writing has been an important part of our work. Each small-group lesson includes two parts: instructional materials and teaching moves.

Instructional Materials (what makes the lesson comprehensible)

- Resources (realia—for example, concrete objects, photographs, illustrations, student work, music, video, technology, field trips)
- Books

- Materials (for example, pencils and pens, paper, markers, sticky notes, charts, graphic organizers, writer's notebooks, writing folders)

Teaching Moves (what the lesson looks like)

- Start Up/Connection (helping students develop background experience and use prior knowledge to connect to the lesson)
- Give Information (explicitly telling students what they are going to learn, why they are learning it, and then teaching them)
- Active Involvement (often occurs during the teaching as students practice what they are learning while the teacher checks for understanding and monitors and adjusts instruction)
- Off You Go (opportunities for students to practice what they have learned, with peers or independently)

The writing lessons in this book give an indication of what English Language Learners can learn about writing as they progress through the stages of language proficiency. As you work through the book, allow the standards for which you are responsible and students' work to guide you. Choose those lessons that match the needs of *your* students.

figure 2.1 (top) Before writing, Bopau and Vichneath record their images and visualizations.

figure 2.2 (center) Outey uses a culturally relevant book as a mentor text.

figure 2.3 (bottom) Juli assists Cindy and Yoanna with writing using primary language support in Spanish.

2 BEST PRACTICES

Teachers often ask, "How do I teach writing to my English Language Learners?" They may have one non-English speaking student, a handful of students at different stages of language acquisition, or an entire classroom full of students who are learning English. They may be pullout teachers working with small groups of English Language Learners (ELLs) or teachers tutoring students after school. It doesn't really matter—the concern is the same. Everyone wants to provide instruction that will help their kids improve as writers.

It is possible for all teachers to provide writing instruction for ELLs by using best practices. The question is, "What constitutes instructional best practices when teaching writing to English Language Learners?" Language acquisition theories point out key practices that can be directly applied to teaching writing; however, there are also other important best practices such as Writing

Workshop, small-group instruction, and the thinking strategies used by proficient writers (see Chapter 1). Although many of these practices are important for all students, they are of particular importance to English Language Learners who are learning to write as they develop language proficiency.

Five Best Practices in Writing for English Language Learners

All students, regardless of their proficiency with English, come to school with a valuable background of experiences and knowledge on which teachers can capitalize.

Include Language and Culture

Classrooms that engage English Language Learners in writing, provide a low-anxiety environment, and are affirming of a child's native language and cultural heritage can have a direct effect on students' ability to learn by increasing motivation and encouraging risk-taking (Krashen 1981, Krashen and Terrell 1983).

To include English Language Learners in the community of learners and let them know their culture is valued and respected, it's important to incorporate kids' home cultures in the classroom. Using folktales and legends from the countries of students is one way to bring culture into the classroom; they can be easily integrated into reading and writing lessons (Kendall and Khuon 2005). Storytelling is another important strategy that can be used to include various cultures. Asking students to tell and/or write a story about their home countries or one that comes from their own experiences can help build confidence and draw on prior knowledge.

In addition to Krashen and Cummins (1981, 2000), there is a wealth of current research that has shown the advantage of incorporating a student's native language into their instruction (Thomas and Collier 1997). One positive effect is that it increases understanding. This is a way to access kids' prior knowledge—an important strategy for developing understanding and making meaning.

Preview/review is one way to incorporate students' native language into their instruction. By briefly previewing lessons in students' native language before instruction in English begins, students are more easily able to access their prior knowledge. By reviewing the English lesson when it is finished, students' native language can be used to clarify their comments and answer questions. This technique is most often used with beginning English speakers.

Teachers who are monolingual and want to support students' use of native languages have several resources they can use. A paraprofessional who speaks the child's language can be used for preview/review and clarification. Parents can work with students at home using their native language to support what kids are learning at school. A peer tutor who speaks the same language as the student can be used to answer questions and clarify information.

Use Culturally Relevant Texts and Materials

Culturally relevant texts and materials are ones that students can connect with, ones that draw on their background and culture (Freeman and Freeman 2004). They do this by connecting to students' lives, not just to their cultural heritage. They draw on students' experiences at home, in the community, and at school and contribute to the students' process of making meaning.

Freeman and Freeman (2004) have developed a series of questions for students and teachers to use to examine cultural relevance. The following questions can also be used by writers to revisit, rework, and revise their own stories and those of their peers:

- Are the characters in the story like you and your family?
- Have you ever had an experience like one described in this story?
- Have you ever lived in or visited places like those in the story?
- Could this story take place this year?
- How close do you think the main characters are to you in age?
- Are the main characters in the story boys or girls?
- Do the characters talk like you and your family do?
- Do you often read stories like these?

Increase Comprehensible Input

Krashen's theory of comprehensible input (Krashen 1981) stresses ways in which teachers can make writing instruction more understandable to their students. These include providing pictures, objects, demonstrations, and gestures and using models of teacher and student writing and other texts to teach writing. As language proficiency develops, other strategies can be added, including building from language that is already understood; using graphic organizers and Thinking Maps; providing hands-on learning opportunities such as inquiry; and using small-group or peer tutoring techniques for composing, revising, and editing.

One way to make writing lessons more comprehensible is to use realia— real, concrete objects—to make connections with vocabulary words, stimulate conversation, and build background knowledge. Realia give students the opportunity to use all of their senses and facilitate writing.

Model Thinking Skills

Cummins's theories of academic language and cognitively demanding communication (1981) suggest ways to develop more advanced, higher-order thinking skills as students' language proficiency increases and they work on writing. These suggestions include asking students more difficult questions as a part of revision and modeling by thinking aloud as you write in front of them or talk about a piece of writing. Teachers can also assist in language development by questioning, listening, and rephrasing during instruction (CREDE 2005).

Provide Opportunities to Work with a Partner, a Small Group, and/or the Teacher

Small-group work facilitated by a teacher and focused on academic goals, such as improving writing, encourages the use of instructional conversations to improve student achievement (CREDE 2005). Strategies that increase opportunities for students to use their language for real purposes in authentic situations encourage kids to communicate and negotiate meaning. This can be done in small groups, working with a partner, or conferring with the teacher. Strategies to encourage communication include cooperative learning, partner work (for example, revision buddies), inquiry- and project-based learning, and one-to-one teacher–student interactions during writing conferences.

Writing Workshop and Small-Group Writing Instruction

English Language Learners benefit from both whole-class instruction during Writing Workshop and small-group instruction in writing. The lessons in this book can be used in both contexts. What makes them work is when teachers know their ELLs as writers and match instruction to their needs. The frequent use of visuals, word banks, and presentation of models, such as thinking aloud, scaffolds instruction and means every lesson can be used with students at several language-acquisition stages.

The lessons included here are carefully balanced to provide enough choice and enough structure to encourage writing during Writing Workshop and small-group instruction. This balance between choice and structure is key so that students are not turned off by writing, an important consideration when working with ELLs. Although the lessons are designed for English Language Learners, they also work well with majority language speakers; the basic lesson design provides a structure that works for all students.

Writing Workshop

Writing Workshop is one way to incorporate best practices while teaching writing to English Language Learners. Many wonderful books have been written about how to teach Writing Workshop. Various authors, such as Lucy Calkins, Donald Graves, Ralph Fletcher, Joanne Portalupi, and Katie Wood Ray, have laid out a strong foundation for workshops as a best practice.

Most often when English Language Learners are included in Writing Workshop it also means that they are included in writing instruction with English speakers. One advantage to this is the development of language. As students share ideas before they write, give each other ideas for revision, develop word banks, and share their writing, the amount of language generated is enormous. Kids at all levels of language acquisition demonstrate growth when they are included as part of a daily Writing Workshop in the regular classroom and the necessary scaffolding is provided.

The lessons in this book can be used as whole-class mini-lessons during Writing Workshop, and then followed by independent writing and teacher/

student conferencing to measure how students are applying the thinking strategies used by proficient writers in their writing.

Writing Workshop Instruction for English Language Learners in Real Time

As she learns more and more about teaching writing, Juli explores the idea of including English Language Learners in Writing Workshop with the whole class. One of the resources she's read is Katherine and Randy Bomer's book, *Teaching for a Better World: Reading and Writing for Social Action* (2001); they propose the following two faces of writing:

> One that in some way is tuned inward to the writer, the writing that is a tool for thinking rather than communicating.

> One that is directed outward toward others—it's the writing you do for readers. (p. 111)

Juli wonders what she can do to help English Language Learners feel a part of the Writing Workshop and get them to put their writing down on paper. And it comes to her that the writer's notebooks are a place to put their thinking. So she looks around for ideas for mini-lessons that will expand the idea of using their notebooks as "a tool for thinking."

In Chapter 7, "Noticing the World, Writer's Notebooks as Tools for Social Critique," Katherine and Randy discuss how teachers might use writer's notebooks as a part of Writing Workshop: "Writer's Notebooks are a tool for noticing the world, and how kids are taught to keep these notebooks influences the sorts of things they pay attention to" (Bomer and Bomer 2001, p. 113).

Their ideas helped Juli form a list of mini-lessons to teach "Noticing the World." She teaches kids that a writer can draw readers' attention to critical incidents and social issues when

- someone is treated unfairly;
- someone abuses power;
- the writer realizes that other people live differently;
- the writer feels anger, pity, compassion, or sympathy toward individuals or for members of particular groups;
- the writer has an idea for something she or he could do with others to make the world better.

When Juli examines her own writer's notebook, she finds entries about a variety of topics. The problem with the soccer field at school seems especially well suited. She decides to share some of her entries with the kids. So she reads the following aloud to the whole class during Writing Workshop mini-lessons, sharing what her thinking was as she was writing.

Entry #1—"The Garden and the Soccer Field"

I'm sitting at the staff meeting and can't believe what they're saying: The reason the district came and sprayed weed killer over a third of the grass on the soccer field is because they're going to put in a community garden. And first, they need to kill the grass. Weed killer! And the kids can't go on any part of the field for two weeks.

This school has only one pathetic, small tree on the whole playground and they take five-twelfths (one class went out and measured it) of the only grass field in the entire neighborhood. A garden is a great idea, but why not a container garden that could be used to beautify the asphalt areas. That's what we need.

Entry #2 (a week later)—"The Letter Writing Campaign"

The grade-level teachers have a meeting to discuss "stuff" and up comes the garden. One suggests that kids could write letters expressing their opinions about the garden so that those "in the know" will know what the kids think about the garden. It even fits nicely into the lessons on writing a persuasive letter.

Everyone agrees, except for one quiet soul.

Entry #3 (two weeks later)—"The Expanding Garden"

What a mess this garden has turned out to be. Now we sit in our Site-Based Decision-Making Meeting voting on whether or not to "extend" it by another seven feet. They really don't seem to care at all what the kids think about this. I just don't understand.

The motion passes 8 to 3, and now the garden has grown by seven feet. I can't even think what to tell the kids. They will be so disappointed.

And the irony of the situation is—a garden is a wonderful thing. There's some sort of a lesson on "point of view" in all of this.

The Kids Share

After Juli shares her entries, she asks the kids to search through their own writer's notebooks for entries about social issues. In her initial mini-lessons, Katherine advises: "Spot the potential for socially engaged writing in your personal writing. Look at your entries through the lens of, *this is not fair. Something needs to be done about this!*" (Bomer and Bomer 2001, p. 114).

The following are some of the entries the kids wanted to share from their writer's notebooks:

Student #1: The thing that I hate about the soccer field is about the garden. Their going to make a garden. That's what bother me. How we're going to play football. I wish that they would not put a garden their. I hope they could put it some where else. I want to play more football. (written by a girl)

Student #2: It bothers me that we can't play in the soccer field. It is boring here. There going to put a garden in the soccer field. It made all the boys and girls mad.

Student #3: The soccer field should not change to a garden because kids play soccer there. They like to play soccer. Even I like to play soccer. It's fun and cool. Gardens are nice and beautiful but I like soccer more. It is really fun to play soccer.

Student #4: I do not like people that do graffiti at school on weekends because they did not pay for the school. And I think people that do that is get in scarry trouble.

Student #5: That they cut the trees of the forest. There's not going to be any more trees for the people and we are not going to have things for people. There's not going to be paper, pencils, wood houses, and other things.

After this, it's off to the part of Writing Workshop set aside for independent writing. Kids divide up in pairs and work to turn their notebook entries into drafts. Juli confers with kids as they work, stressing the importance of writing about what is important to them. This Writing Workshop is a wonderful combination of using real, authentic experiences for reading, writing, listening, and speaking—just what English Language Learners need to learn the language as they are learning to write.

Consider this closing thought about Writing Workshops from the Bomer and Bomer book, *Teaching for a Better World:*

> But part of the learning process ought to include, as its necessary and logical extension, a passion for making the world better. That's not merely a pleasant dessert to be indulged in after the main course of "real learning"; rather, it is having a different idea of "what we are doing here" from the start. (2001, p. 8)

Using Small Groups for Writing Instruction

Small-group lessons can scaffold writing instruction for English Language Learners. When we teach to small groups to meet students' needs, we gradually release responsibility to develop independence and become lifelong learners to them—our ultimate goal.

Small-group instruction can encompass various ways of teaching students how to write as they learn English—reading aloud literature as models, Interactive Writing, the Language Experience Approach, teacher-modeled writing, and much more. The lessons in this book can be used with small groups as a part of a comprehensive literacy program. "What makes them effective is the classroom environment that teachers create to support English Language Learners" (Kendall and Khuon 2005, p. 4). Of course, working with a small group is possible only if children know how to go about their work with some independence.

There are many ways to use small groups for writing instruction. For example, the classroom teacher could instruct during Writing Workshop while other students are working independently or peer conferencing. Another possibility is to collaborate with the school's other ELL teachers. With planning, these lessons might be done with a small group of English Language Learners at the same time other students are doing the same strategy in class with the classroom teacher. The lessons can help the classroom teacher provide scaffolds for writing instruction whether he or she teaches a lesson or uses a push-in/pullout model. Additionally, the lessons can be used as part of an after-school tutoring program for small groups of students.

The following are several reasons to consider small-group instruction for English Language Learners because they provide a number of scaffolds that promote writing proficiency.

Low-anxiety environment
Opportunities for direct teacher-to-student interactions
Guided student-to-student interaction
More on-task behaviors
Easier to check for understanding
Facilitates monitoring and adjusting instruction

Small-Group Writing Instruction for English Language Learners in Real Time

Juli's class discovered a strategy for incorporating small-group writing instruction that really worked for them—Poetry Partnerships. It's the latest thing; surrounded by poems, a dozen or so poetry partners read together and discuss their responses. Then they reread, "like writers" this time, talk more, write some of their own poems, and share. A room full of poets and a willing and eager audience are in attendance, whether they know it or not.

Kathleen Tolan, from the Teachers College Reading and Writing Project, says that doing it this way helps kids improve their writing. During the summer of 2002, she taught "Group Structures in the Writing Workshop" for the LBUSD Writing Institute. The six reasons she gives to use Writing Partnerships during Writing Workshop work well for our kids.

- To have colleagues and support in the lonely business of writing.
- To strengthen the writer's sense of audience.
- To hold students accountable.
- To build up trust between writers.
- To make room for responses, which helps writers rethink what they have done.
- To help students progress as writers by having more conferences.

Juli adds one more reason: To include more small-group instruction for
   English Language Learners.

Concentrating on poetry as a way to learn more about connections between reading and writing in this unit of study, the kids as well as the teacher meet in *Poetry Partnerships*—small groups where two kids work together and the teacher facilitates as they use poetry to make their own reading and writing connections.

1. Kids read poems like readers

They respond to the pieces in the Poetry Packet and other anthologies, asking each other, "What are the purposes for poets as they weave their poems together?"

Juli's class read the poem "Sun" by Myra Cohn Livingston. Then kids met in Poetry Partnerships to discuss the purposes for this poet as she wove her poem together. Here's what they said about the poet's purposes:

Susan and Amanda: "just to talk about the sun and to learn more about the sun"

Blanca and Maria: "to learn the things that it has and to tell us more about the sun"

Richard and Astrick: "to tell us it was made of gas and to show us what she knows about the sun"

Lorena and Marina: "she tells us a little about the sun and she's showing how it looks"

Mary and Miguel: "to tell you how the sun evaporates and moves and stuff and to teach us about the sun"

Johnnie and José: "to entertain"

The class also read "Cultural Celebration" written by the school's office assistant. This poem delights the kids because they know the poet. She left it printed on the whiteboard in their classroom after she taught a computer class.

"Cultural Celebration"

My name is Ruselle.
His name is Antonio.
I am Jamaican.
He is Colombian.
I have medium brown skin.
He has light brown skin.
My eyes are medium brown.
His eyes are hazel brown.
My hair goes to my shoulders and is original curly.
His hair goes to his back and he has more curls.
I am 5'8".
He is 6'2".
I am a lady.
He is a young man.
I work at an elementary school.
He goes to high school.
I'm going to attend Cal State Dominguez Hills.
He's going to attend Cerritos College.
I'm a Lakers fan.
He is a San Francisco 49ers' fan.
We may be different.
But we are still mother and son.

Here's what the kids said about her purposes for writing the poem:

Susan and Amanda: "to talk about her and her son"

Blanca and Maria: "to introduce herself and tell us about how tall she is—all about herself"

Richard and Astrick: "to show somebody even though they are related they still have something different and to tell us what she is doing"

Lorena and Sophanna: "to see how it's different for her son and her"

Mary and Manuel: "tells us about how her son feels and how her son acts"

2. Kids read poems like writers

As they read, the kids watch to see how poets craft their work, asking each other, "What do you notice that the writer did in this poem?" then talking about "how the authors wrote these texts" and "how poets make their writing decisions."

Reading many different poems, the poetry partners focus their discussions on "What do you notice that the writer did in this poem?"

Amanda and Susan: "Not lots of rhyming words, words are slanted (italics), a couple of words on each line, then a long line, then back again. They centered their words. They curved them to make them look like the subject; made it like a story. They had a couple of rhyming words in it."

Maria and Blanca: "No periods; it sounds like a story but looks like a poem. It has short sentences. Sometimes there's a rhyme."

Lorena and Sophanna: "They're kind of giving us a little bit of a drawing with words and pictures."

3. Kids write some of their own poems

As Gerardo and Christian work in a partnership, each of them writes their individual poems while they share the book *I am puppy, hear me yap: The ages of dog* by Roy Blount Jr. They read their poems to each other, to the rest of the class, and easily remain engrossed in their work for an hour.

Poems by Gerardo

Please don't fall.
I can't catch you all.

You're too small.
You act like you're tall
But you're really small.

Poems by Christian

This one I guess will turn out
To be more or less.

Do you have the strangest fear?
I have the strangest atmosphere.

Salvador wanted to sit by himself as he wrote. "The other kids are distracting me," he said. So he moved to a table around a corner.

"My Shoes" by Salvador

I wear my shoes all the time
But when it's nighty night I want
My slippery slippers.

4. Kids "read, post, talk about, and reread texts that students, including themselves, have written"

Poetry partners share poems with each other and with other partnerships. Everyone reads and rereads the poems. Here are a few of our favorites.

"Up! Up! Above the Sky" by Karol

Up above the sky, low from earth
I imagine what's up the world so high
The Stars are bright as the night.
The night is dark
Full of wonders
And the stars appear
One by one a light comes
That takes to the night place.
I'm just a little girl full of wonders
And I'm eleven years old,
And to explore all of the wonderful things
That are up! Up!
Above the world so high,
Imagine how wonderful it would be.
Follow your dream.
If I can I bet you can do it too.

Poem by José

It is hard to breathe without you
I can't believe you broke my heart
Again and left my feelings all broke.
My heart's on pain my heart sank
My life is boring without you
My heart is lonely too.
Please come back to my sweet life,
All the memories that I have of you
I can't let them go away.
It feels like floating in my stomach.
It feels, it feels like butterflies
Are in my stomach.
I love you, I love you
My darling.

5. Using poetry, kids make their own connections between reading and writing

It may be difficult for adults to see connections between reading and writing, but it's easy for Juli's kids.

Amanda: "I think that reading and writing have a connection because reading can help you write better and to know more words. And writing can help you read better and to know more words."

Susan: "If we wouldn't have reading, then we couldn't write anything."

Yesenia: "I think they are connected—you could read and at the same time write about the story. And if you don't have something, how could you read or write?"

Maria: "When you write, you read it. Then you read the words, and you are thinking about the writing. When you read, there's words. And when you write, it has to make sense. So that's why you have to read. You have to read so your writing can make sense."

Blanca: "It's like the same because you use the same words when you are reading and you are writing. If you didn't have books, we couldn't have ideas to write on the paper."

This incorporation of small-group instruction into the classroom using Poetry Partnerships has proved to be very valuable for Juli's classes. Students see the connection between reading and writing much more clearly and also have become more independent in their use of the thinking strategies used by proficient writers.

Thinking Strategies Used by Proficient Writers—Best Practice for English Language Learners

This last year Juli saw some unexpected growth in writing for English Language Learners. How did this happen? What made the difference? The biggest change was that she based writing lessons on the Strategies Used by Proficient Learners developed by Ellin Keene and her colleagues at the Public Education and Business Coalition in Denver. These strategies have a direct correspondence to the reading comprehension strategies; they include the following:

- Determining what is important in text
- Drawing inferences
- Using prior knowledge—schema
- Asking questions
- Monitoring meaning and comprehension
- Fix-up strategies
- Synthesizing information
- Using sensory images—visualizing

These strategies are nothing if not best practice. They clearly delineate what good writers do, and that's what we want for ELLs. With proper scaffolding and attention to language-acquisition levels as well as age of students, they give a structure for planning lessons. They also provide teachers with a resource for understanding what proficient writers need to know and be able to do, and the confidence that their instruction is headed in the right direction. Although much thought has been given to comprehension in reading, these writing strategies expand the idea of comprehension beyond text and look at how kids understand ideas through writing. Ellin Keene (2002) wrote this in the *Cornerstone Literacy Newsletter*:

> I realized that we had missed a fundamental piece of the puzzle we call comprehension. Comprehension is about understanding ideas, not just in text, but throughout the day. The term comprehension is, for teachers, so often associated with reading that we had failed to consider the implications for learning outside reading.

As you browse through the following list, Thinking Strategies Used by Proficient Learners, notice how the same language is used for writing and reading strategies. This strengthens the connection to writing for kids because it corresponds more with the language they are used to hearing in reading comprehension lessons. As Ellin says, it helps them understand how "comprehension is about understanding ideas, not just in text, but throughout the day."

Ellin Keene's Thinking Strategies Used by Proficient Learners

Determining What Is Important in Text

Readers

- Readers identify key ideas or themes as they read.
- Readers distinguish important from unimportant information in relation to key ideas or themes in text. They can distinguish important information at the word, sentence, and text level.
- Readers use text structure and text features (such as bold or italicized print, figures and photographs) to help them distinguish important from unimportant information.
- Readers use their knowledge of important and relevant parts of text to prioritize in long-term memory and synthesize text for others.

Writers

- Writers observe their world and record what they believe is significant.
- Writers make decisions about the most important ideas to include in the pieces they write. They make decisions about the best genre and structure to communicate their ideas.
- Writers reveal their biases by emphasizing some elements over others.
- Writers provide only essential detail to reveal the meaning and produce the effect desired.
- Writers delete information irrelevant to their larger purpose.

Mathematicians

- Mathematicians look for patterns and relationships.
- Mathematicians identify and use key words to build an understanding of the problem.

- Mathematicians gather text information from graphs, charts, and tables.
- Mathematicians decide what information is relevant to a problem and what information is irrelevant.

Researchers

- Researchers evaluate and think critically about information.
- Researchers sort and analyze information to better understand it.
- Researchers make decisions about the quality and usefulness of information.
- Researchers decide what's important to remember and what isn't.
- Researchers choose the most effective reporting platform.

Drawing Inferences

Readers

- Readers use their schema and textual information to draw conclusions and form unique interpretations from text.
- Readers make predictions about text, confirm their predictions, and test their developing meaning as they read on.
- Readers know when and how to use text in combination with their own background knowledge to seek answers to questions.
- Readers create interpretations to enrich and deepen their experience in a text.

Writers

- Writers make decisions about content inclusions/exclusions and genre/text structure that permit or encourage inference on the part of the reader.
- Writers carefully consider their audience in making decisions about what to describe explicitly and what to leave to the readers' interpretation.
- Writers, particularly fiction and poetry writers, are aware of far more detail than they reveal in the texts they compose. This encourages inferences such as drawing conclusions and making critical judgments, predictions, and connections to other texts and experiences possible for their readers.

Mathematicians

- Mathematicians predict, generalize, and estimate.
- As mathematicians read a problem, they make problem-solving decisions based on their conceptual understanding of math concepts (e.g., operations, fractions, etc.).
- Mathematicians compose (like a writer) by drawing pictures, using charts, and creating equations.
- Mathematicians solve problems in different ways and support their methods through proof, number sentences, pictures, and charts and graphs.
- Mathematicians use reasoning and make connections throughout the problem-solving process.

- Mathematicians conjecture (infer based on evidence).
- Mathematicians use patterns (consistencies) and relationships to generalize and infer what comes next in the problem-solving process.

Researchers

- Researchers think about the value and reliability of their sources.
- Researchers consider what is important to a reader or audience.

Using Prior Knowledge—Schema

Readers

- Readers spontaneously activate relevant, prior knowledge before, during, and after reading text.
- Readers assimilate information from text into their schemata and make changes in that schemata to accommodate the new information.
- Readers use schema to relate text to their world knowledge, text knowledge, and personal experience.
- Readers use their schema to enhance their understanding of text and to store text information in long-term memory.
- Readers use their schema for authors and their style to better understand text.
- Readers recognize when they have inadequate background information and know how to create it—to build schema—to get the information they need.

Writers

- Writers frequently choose their own topics and write about subjects they care about.
- Writers' content comes from and builds on their experiences.
- Writers think about and use what they know about genre, text structure, and conventions as they write.
- Writers seek to better recognize and capitalize on their own voice for specific effects in their compositions.
- Writers know when their schema for a topic or text format is inadequate, and they create the necessary background knowledge.
- Writers use knowledge of their audience to make decisions about content inclusions/exclusions.

Mathematicians

- Mathematicians use current understandings as first steps in the problem-solving process.
- Mathematicians use their number sense to understand a problem.
- Mathematicians add to schema by trying more challenging problems and hearing from others about different problem-solving methods.
- Mathematicians build understanding based on prior knowledge of math concepts.
- Mathematicians develop purpose based on prior knowledge.
- Mathematicians use their prior knowledge to generalize about similar problems and to choose problem-solving strategies.

- Mathematicians develop their own problems.

Researchers

- Researchers frequently choose topics they know and care about.
- Researchers use their prior knowledge and experiences to launch investigations and ask questions.
- Researchers consider what they already know to decide what they need to find out, and they self-evaluate according to background knowledge of what quality products look like.

Asking Questions

Readers

- Readers spontaneously generate questions before, during, and after reading.
- Readers ask questions for different purposes, including clarification of meaning; making predictions; determining an author's style, content, or format; and to locate a specific answer in text or consider rhetorical questions inspired by the text.
- Readers use questions to focus their attention on important components of the text.
- Readers are aware that other readers' questions may inspire new questions for them.

Writers

- Writers compose in a way that causes readers to form questions as they read.
- Writers monitor their progress by asking questions about their choices as they write.
- Writers ask questions of other writers in order to confirm their choices and make revisions.
- Writers' questions lead to revision in their own pieces and in the pieces to which they respond for other writers.

Mathematicians

- Mathematicians ask questions before, during, and after doing a math problem.

    Could it be this?
    What happens if?
    How else could I do this?
    Have I seen this problem before?
    What does this mean?

- Mathematicians test theories/answers/hypotheses by using different approaches to a problem.
- Mathematicians question others to understand their own process and to clarify problems.
- Mathematicians extend their own thinking by asking themselves questions they don't have an answer to.

Researchers

- Researchers ask questions to narrow a search and find a topic.
- Researchers ask questions to clarify meaning and purpose.
- Researchers ask themselves:

  What are the most effective resources and how will I access them?
  Do I have enough information?
  Have I used a variety of sources?
  What more do I need?
  Does it make sense?
  Have I told enough?
  Is it interesting and original thinking and does my writing have voice?

Monitoring Meaning and Comprehension

Readers

- Readers monitor their comprehension during reading—they know when the text they are reading or listening to makes sense, when it does not, what does not make sense, and whether the unclear portions are critical to overall understanding of the piece.
- Readers can identify when text is comprehensible and the degree to which they understand it. They can identify ways in which a text becomes gradually more understandable by reading past an unclear portion and/or by rereading parts or the whole text.
- Readers are aware of the processes they can use to make meaning clear. They check, evaluate, and make revisions to their evolving interpretation of the text while reading.
- Readers can identify confusing ideas, themes, and/or surface elements (words, sentence or text structures, graphs, tables, etc.) and can suggest a variety of different means to solve the problems they have.
- Readers are aware of what they need to comprehend in relation to their purpose for reading.
- Readers must learn how to pause, consider the meanings in text, reflect on their understandings, and use different strategies to enhance their understanding. This process is best learned by watching proficient models "think aloud" and gradually take responsibility for monitoring their own comprehension as they read independently.

Writers

- Writers monitor during their composition process to ensure that their text makes sense for their intended audience at the word, sentence, and text level.
- Writers read their work aloud to find and hear their voices.
- Writers share their work so that others can help them monitor the clarity and impact of the work.
- Writers pay attention to their style and purpose. They purposefully write with clarity and honesty. They strive to write boldly, simply, and concisely by keeping those standards alive in their minds during the writing process.

- Writers pause to consider the impact of their work and make conscious decisions about when to turn a small piece into a larger project, when revisions are complete, or when to abandon a piece.

Mathematicians

- Mathematicians check to make sure answers are reasonable.
- Mathematicians use manipulatives/charts/diagrams to help themselves make sense of the problem.
- Mathematicians understand that others will build meaning in different ways and solve problems with different problem-solving strategies.
- Mathematicians write what makes sense to them.
- Mathematicians check their work in many ways: working backward, redoing problems, and so on.
- Mathematicians agree/disagree with solutions and ideas.
- Mathematicians express in "think-alouds" what's going on in their head as they work through a problem. They are metacognitive.
- Mathematicians continually ask themselves whether each step makes sense.
- Mathematicians discuss problems with others and write about their problem-solving process to clarify their thinking and make problems clearer.
- Mathematicians use accurate math vocabulary and show their work in clear, concise forms so that others can follow their thinking without asking questions.

Researchers

- Researchers are aware of what they need to find out and learn about.
- Researchers can identify when they comprehend and take steps to repair comprehension when they don't.
- Researchers pause to reflect and evaluate information.
- Researchers choose effective ways of organizing information— note taking, webbing, outlining, and so on.
- Researchers use several sources to validate information and check for accuracy.
- Researchers revise and edit for clarity, accuracy, and interest.
- Researchers check sources for appropriate references and copyrights.

Fix-Up Strategies

Readers

- Readers use the six major systems of language—(grapho-phonic, lexical, syntactic, semantic, schematic, and pragmatic)—to solve reading problems. When not comprehending, they ask themselves questions such as these:

  Does this make sense?
  Does the word I'm pronouncing sound like language?
  Do the letters in the word match the sounds I'm pronouncing?
  Have I seen this word before?
  Is there another reader who can help me make sense of this?

What do I already know from my experience and the context of this text that can help me solve this problem?

- Readers have and select a wide range of problem-solving strategies and can make appropriate choices in a given reading situation (e.g., skip ahead or reread, use the context and syntax or sound it out, speak to another reader, consider relevant prior knowledge, read the passage aloud, etc.).

Writers

- Writers revise (add, delete, and reorganize) and edit (apply correct conventions), continually seeking clarity and impact for the reader. They experiment with and make changes in overall meaning, content, wording, text organization, punctuation, and spelling.
- Writers capitalize on their knowledge of writers' tools (e.g., character, setting, conflict, theme, plot structure, leads, style, etc.) to enhance their meaning.

Mathematicians

- Mathematicians listen to others' strategies and adjust their own.
- Mathematicians use estimation to determine whether their answer is reasonable.
- Mathematicians use trial and error to build thinking.
- Mathematicians cross-check by using more than one way to do a problem (e.g., check subtraction by adding).
- Mathematicians use tools (e.g., manipulatives, graphs, calculators, etc.) to enhance meaning.

Researchers

- Researchers revise and edit for clarity and accuracy.
- Researchers check sources for updated copyrights and legitimate reliable sources.

Synthesizing Information

Readers

- Readers maintain a cognitive synthesis as they read. They monitor the overall meaning, important concepts, and themes in the text as they read and are aware of ways text elements "fit together" to create that overall meaning and theme. They use their knowledge of these elements to make decisions about the overall meaning of a passage, chapter, or book.
- Readers retell or synthesize what they have read. They attend to the most important information and to the clarity or the synthesis itself. Readers synthesize in order to better understand what they have read.
- Readers capitalize on opportunities to share, recommend, and criticize books they have read.
- Readers may respond to text in a variety of ways, independently or in groups of other readers. These include written, oral, dramatic, and artistic responses and interpretations of text.

- A proficient reader's synthesis is likely to extend the literal meaning of a text to the inferential level.

Writers

- Writers make global and focal plans for their writing before and during the drafting process. They use their knowledge of text elements, such as character, setting, conflict, sequence of events, and resolution, to create a structure for their writing.
- Writers study other writers and draw conclusions about what makes good writing. They work to replicate the style of authors they find compelling.
- Writer reveal themes in a way that suggests their importance to readers. Readers can create a cogent synthesis from well-written material.

Mathematicians

- Mathematicians generalize from patterns they observe.
- Mathematicians generalize in words, equations, charts, and graphs to retell or synthesize.
- Mathematicians synthesize math concepts when they use them in real-life applications.
- Mathematicians use deductive reasoning (e.g., reach conclusions based on knowns).

Researchers

- Researchers develop insight about a topic to create new knowledge or understanding.
- Researchers use information from a variety of resources.
- Researchers enhance their understanding of a topic by considering different perspectives, opinions, and sources.

Using Sensory Images

Readers

- Readers create sensory images during and after reading. These images may include visual, auditory, and other sensory as well as emotional connections to the text and are rooted in prior knowledge.
- Readers use images to draw conclusions and to create unique interpretations of the text. Images from reading frequently become part of the readers' writing. Images from readers' personal experiences frequently become part of their comprehension.
- Readers use their images to clarify and enhance comprehension.
- Readers use images to immerse themselves in rich detail as they read. The detail gives depth and dimension to the reading, engaging the reader more deeply, making the text more memorable.
- Readers adapt their images in response to the shared images of other readers.
- Readers adapt their images as they continue to read. Images are revised to incorporate new information revealed through the text and new interpretations as they are developed by the reader.

Writers

- Writers consciously attempt to create strong images in their compositions using strategically placed detail.
- Writers create impact through the use of strong nouns and verbs whenever possible.
- Writers use images to explore their own ideas. They consciously study their mental images for direction in their pieces.
- Writers learn from the images created in their minds as they read. They study other authors' use of images as a way to improve their own.

Mathematicians

- Mathematicians use mental pictures/models of shapes, numbers, and processes to build understanding of concepts and problems and to experiment with ideas.
- Mathematicians use concrete models/manipulatives to build understanding and visualize problems.
- Mathematicians visually represent thinking through drawings, pictures, graphs, and charts.
- Mathematicians picture story problems like a movie in the mind to help understand the problem.
- Mathematicians visualize concepts in their heads (e.g., parallel lines, fractions, etc.).

Researchers

- Researchers create rich mental pictures to better understand text.
- Researchers interweave written images with multisensory (e.g., auditory, visual, kinesthetic) components to enhance comprehension.
- Researchers use words, visual images, sounds, and other sensory experiences to communicate understanding of a topic (possibly leading to further questions for research).

figure 3.1 *(top) Gabi confers with friends to revise their writing.*

figure 3.2 *(center) Casey paints a portrait of himself before he writes his "All About Me" autobiography.*

figure 3.3 *(bottom) Two students listen carefully as a book is read aloud.*

3 ASSESSING WRITING

Writing is all about making meaning. Teaching writing to English Language Learners (ELLs) can be a challenge because they frequently get confused about what they want to say as they work. The reason we teach them to write using the strategies of proficient writers is because our overall goal is to help ELLs know what they are doing well enough so that they can explain it clearly to their readers.

By using the Thinking Strategies Used by Proficient Learners in their writing, students take on the behaviors of proficient writers. They determine what is important in text by observing and recording their observations. The strategies help the reader draw inferences by making decisions about content, genre, and text structure. They use prior knowledge (schema) to "choose their topics and write about subjects they care about." The ELLs write in such a way that readers form questions as they read. Students monitor meaning and comprehension as they write by asking the question, "Does it make sense?" They use

If you can't explain it clearly, you don't know it well enough.

—ALBERT EINSTEIN

37

Cris Tovani's (2000) fix-up strategies to revise and to enhance meaning. They synthesize information through studying other writers and learning what makes good writing. They help readers visualize by creating strong sensory images in their writing. And a whole lot more.

This book is about getting ELLs to write and to love writing and to become proficient writers. Along the way, we use many different ways to assess our writers.

High-Stakes Testing

One measure of writing proficiency is doing well on high-stakes writing tests, which come in a variety of formats. One format uses multiple-choice questions to determine whether students can revise by combining sentences, by reorganizing sentences within paragraphs, and/or by eliminating extraneous material; and whether they can edit by checking for capitalization, punctuation, grammar, sentence structure, and spelling. Another format has students respond in writing by addressing a prompt. When planning for classes, we look carefully at English Language Learners' scores on high-stakes tests as well as our state's grade-level writing assessments to see what kids do well and what they need to work on. We want to make certain the writing lessons for English Language Learners transfer to the high-stakes tests.

Three-Day Writing Assessment

To get a baseline assessment of students' writing abilities, at the beginning of each year, Juli gives students an initial writing assessment. It's set up as an Assessment/Quick Publishing mini-unit for the first three days. She got this idea from the Teacher's College Writing Institutes she has attended, and using it provides great information about her students as writers.

To get ready she explains to kids that they will spend three days writing and publishing a piece. She tells them she will watch and observe what they do as writers. Then she will use the information she gathers to plan mini-lessons and teacher–student conferences.

Day One, Draft

Juli begins by reading *The Keeping Quilt* by Patricia Polacco. After discussing the book briefly, she introduces this prompt: "Find something in your backpack, wallet, or purse and write about what it makes you think about." She gives them time to discuss their writing ideas with partners before they start. Most kids share with the person sitting next to them.

Kids start writing and most finish their drafts in thirty minutes. Two students have difficulty choosing topics. She has a brief group conference with them about getting started, and then has them talk with each other to see what they can come up with. After about five more minutes, they also start writing.

Juli's job is to observe students as they are writing and to take notes on what she observes. Each student's name goes on a sheet of paper, and she writes comments and observations about all their writing as they work.

When kids ask questions, she doesn't answer them. Instead, she responds, "Writers make their own decisions." One student really struggles with not getting answers to his questions. On the third day when Juli asks the kids how it went, he responds, "Too soon to write."

Day Two, Revise

Revision usually turns out to be the part of writing about which students know the least. Juli begins by explaining that everyone will revise their drafts: "Take a minute and think about everything you know about revising and reworking your drafts. Now, I want you to spend today working on revising your work to make it easier for the reader to understand." She doesn't explain what revision is because she wants to find out what students know.

Kids are asked to reread their drafts, at least once, and then have a partner read their work and make comments. They are given three sticky notes to use as they revise. Juli doesn't tell them what to do with the notes, and no one asks. They seem to have their own ideas about how to use them. Some correct spelling, which is more like editing. Some write notes about their partners' papers. Others use stickies to add additional text to their own drafts. As they work, Juli observes and takes notes on each student's revision process. She also makes notes about whether they seem to understand what revision is and how to revise their work.

This time, there are two students who discuss how to improve their leads, but otherwise the conversations don't focus on one particular aspect of the writing craft. There are also some issues with students about what they wrote not making sense. Juli lets kids work that out for themselves because she wants to see how they do throughout the writing process. One partner gives up the revision task because the paper is so confusing to him, but most students are able to help their partners improve what they've written. Students finish revising within fifteen minutes. This is the shortest day.

Day Three, Edit and Publish

This is the longest day. Juli explains what they will do by saying, "Today is the last day of the three-day writing assessment, so you will be editing your work and writing your final drafts."

First, kids edit their own papers for spelling and grammar. As resources, they can use the Editing Checklist hanging on the classroom wall as well as the Five Finger Rule chart. The lists encourage them to check their work for capitalization, punctuation, grammar, sentence structure, and spelling. Then they recopy the piece to get a final draft that includes their revisions and edits. This takes a good bit of time.

Juli is especially interested in seeing how they work independently, how they manage spelling, and what resources they use to check their spelling. She doesn't respond to their queries about how to spell words. She just says, "Writers make their own decisions." Generally, they ask another student how to spell a word. Several try using dictionaries. Often when they "correct" a word, it's still spelled incorrectly, but they have shown that they recognized there was a problem.

After all is said and done, the observational notes and student writing give Juli a wealth of information about what kids know about writing and what they can do (see Figures 3.4 through 3.7). It also helps her plan the next steps for instruction in mini-lessons and teacher–student conferences.

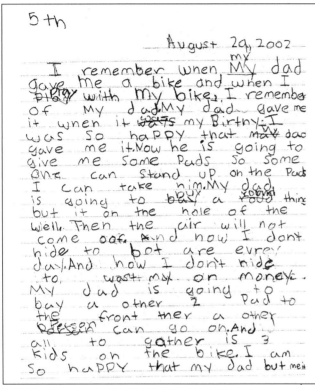

figure 3.4 *Manuel writes about the time his dad gave him a bike.*

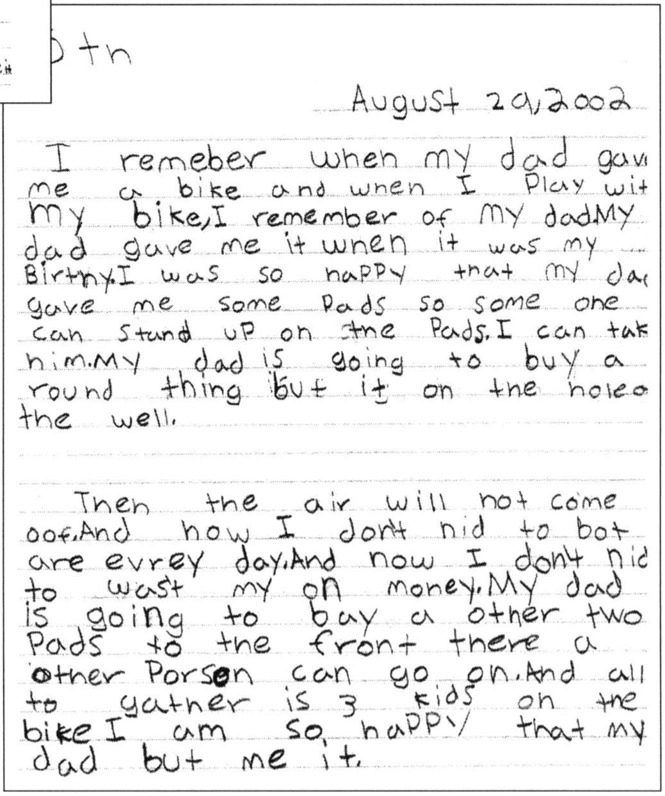

figure 3.5 *Manuel's final draft shows the changes he made during the assessment.*

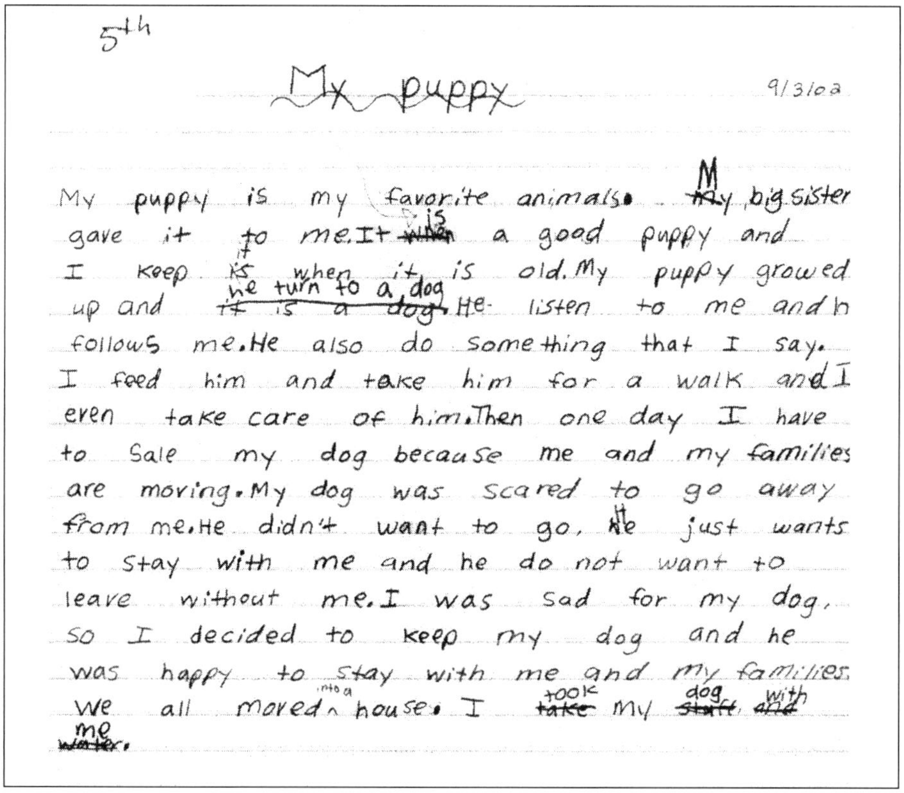

5th

My puppy

9/3/02

My puppy is my favorite animals. ~~my~~ M big sister gave it to me. It ~~was~~ is a good puppy and I keep ~~is~~ it when it is old. My puppy growed up and ~~it is a dog~~ he turn to a dog. He listen to me and h follows me. He also do something that I say. I feed him and take him for a walk and I even take care of him. Then one day I have to Sale my dog because me and my families are moving. My dog was scared to go away from me. He didn't want to go. ~~he~~ He just wants to stay with me and he do not want to leave without me. I was sad for my dog, so I decided to keep my dog and he was happy to stay with me and my families. We all moved into a house. I ~~take~~ took my ~~stuff~~ dog ~~and~~ with ~~water~~ me.

figure 3.6 *Sophanna writes about her puppy for the assessment.*

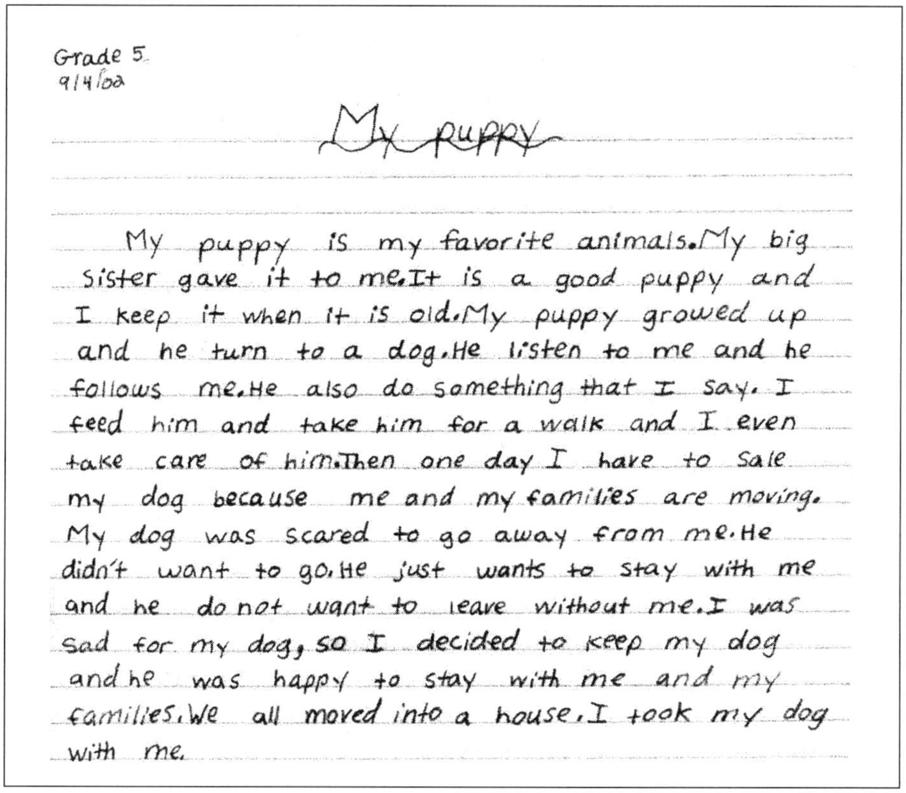

Grade 5
9/4/02

My puppy

My puppy is my favorite animals. My big sister gave it to me. It is a good puppy and I keep it when it is old. My puppy growed up and he turn to a dog. He listen to me and he follows me. He also do something that I say. I feed him and take him for a walk and I even take care of him. Then one day I have to Sale my dog because me and my families are moving. My dog was scared to go away from me. He didn't want to go. He just wants to stay with me and he do not want to leave without me. I was sad for my dog, so I decided to keep my dog and he was happy to stay with me and my families. We all moved into a house. I took my dog with me.

figure 3.7 *The final draft includes Sophanna's revision and editing and is very neat.*

Quick Assessments

From time to time, we do a quick writing assessment to see how kids are doing. We usually give a prompt such as "Write about your favorite book" or "Write down everything you know about_____" or "Write down what you are wondering about_____." Kids have five or ten minutes to write down everything they can. As they are writing, we record our observations and then look at the writing samples.

For the quick assessment writing shown in Figures 3.8 and 3.9, with our notes, we used the prompt "Write about your favorite book." This gives us a window into what our kids are reading, how they write about their reading, and the connections they see between reading and writing.

figure 3.8 *Vichneath summarizes "Little Red Riding Hood" for her Quick Writing Assessment.*

figure 3.9 *This student demonstrates understanding of the mystery stories genre in his assessment.*

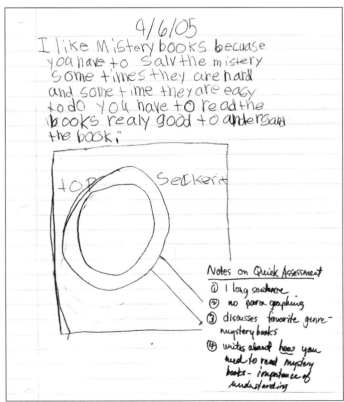

Rubrics, Scoring Guides, and Checklists

Various types of tools also provide ways of measuring students' writing proficiency; descriptions of several follow. They can be used to evaluate students' writing and plan instruction.

The chart "Building an Effective Writing Process Over Time," which can be found in *Guiding Readers and Writers* (Fountas and Pinnell 2001, p. 7), includes criteria for determining whether students are emergent writers, early writers, transitional writers, self-enhancing writers, or advanced writers. The criteria can also be used to determine the next steps to use for writing instruction.

Writing Traits Rubrics (Six Traits Writing) evaluate student writing according to ideas and content, organization, word choice, voice, sentence fluency, conventions, and presentation. Because they look at each of the traits separately, they can be used to target instruction based on students' needs.

Schoolwide, district, and state writing rubrics provide ways to evaluate student writing and then compare it among students, classrooms, grade levels, schools, districts, and so on. To help them make informed

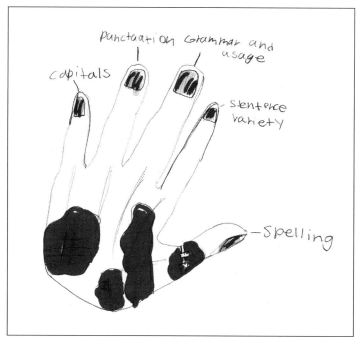

figure 3.10 *Casey draws a chart for the Five Finger Rule for Editing.*

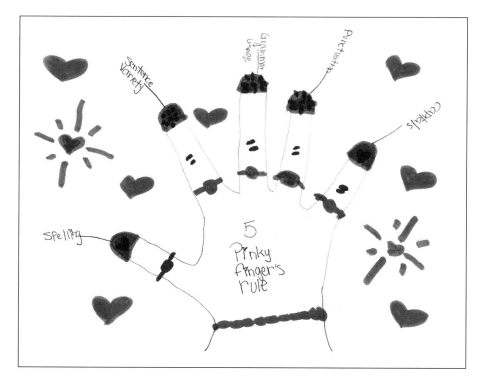

figure 3.11 *Rosa renames her chart the 5 Pinky finger's rule.*

teaching decisions, teachers often work together to look at this student data about writing.

Teacher- and student-generated rubrics, scoring guides, and checklists allow students to have input into their creation. As they work together to design their own evaluation structure, kids become more motivated to write and their interest and proficiency in writing improves. One additional thought—as students' overall participation in school increases through generating rubrics and other ways to evaluate their writing, they are more likely to be motivated to do well. The charts two kids created (see Figures 3.10 and 3.11) to help them remember the Five Finger Rule for Editing are a good example of this. See the Appendix for additional examples of rubrics, scoring guides, checklists, and forms generated with kids.

Kids' Conversations About Writing

Paying attention as kids talk with each other about their writing provides insight into what they are thinking and how they go about writing. These conversations can either be structured, such as peer conferences, or informal kids' discussions.

What we are listening for as kids talk about their writing is that they are taking on the language and vocabulary of writers. Especially for English Language Learners, many of the words a writer uses are new. Helping them to take on the vocabulary as their own and use it with peers encourages a gradual release of responsibility. The following are examples of vocabulary use to watch for:

- Do they talk about writer's notebooks, drafts, revising, editing, and publishing?
- Do they use language that helps writers improve their piece—for example: rereading, revisiting, reworking, changing, adding, and/or deleting?
- Do they talk about conventions for editing such as sentence variety, capitalization, punctuation, and spelling?

When matching English Language Learners up to work with peers, it is important to take into consideration their stage of language acquisition. Giving them the opportunity to work with students who are at a slightly higher stage provides models of language and encourages verbal interaction between students.

Here's a bit of conversation between Drina, Oscar, Nayeli, and Bryan. Oscar is having difficulty with picking a topic and starting a draft.

> "What's your topic?" Drina asks first.
>
> "Basketball," responds Oscar. On further questioning he can't decide whether he wants to write about basketball at school or at the park or in the NBA. Finally, after much negotiation, he chooses the park.
>
> "OK," says Bryan. "Why don't you start with something like, 'Bounce, bounce, bounce!'"

Oscar indicates he likes that but still seems puzzled. "Then what do I write?" he wonders.

Nayeli has some advice. "I think you should include some details about where it is," she says, "and the weather. How about adding, 'It was a hot day at the park.' You can put that as the first sentence and then write 'Bounce, bounce, bounce!'" Now Oscar has the beginnings of a piece of writing.

Then Drina chimes in, "Next write, 'Swish,' as the ball went into the net."

"No," adds Nayeli, "I think you need to rewrite it. Take out the 'Bounce, bounce, bounce!' and put in something like 'I was bouncing the ball.'"

Teacher Observations During Writing

Observing students while they are working provides valuable information about them as writers. It's easy to take anecdotal notes while kids are writing. Notes can be written for individual students on stickies that can be placed in portfolios or on a sheet of paper with dates for the different entries; both of these can be kept by the teacher. An alternative is to keep notes for all students on one page. Anecdotal notes about what they do as they write can be used for planning instruction and conferring with kids about their writing.

We watch for a variety of things while taking notes, including the following:

- Do they get started right away or do they reread in their writers' notebooks first?
- Do they like to write with pencil and paper or on the computer?
- Do they use mentor texts and mentor authors to get ideas?
- How do they organize their work?
- Do they lose papers and so on?
- Do they have conversations with peers about their writing?
- How do they go about revising?
- Do they use the Five Finger Rule for Editing to help them edit their work?

Conferring with Writers

Carl Anderson's question—"How's it going?"—from his book about conferring focuses our writing conferences with kids. Having conversations with kids about their writing while listening to their thinking means that Juli learns a lot about what they know and are able to do. But it needs to be about the writer and not just the writing. Here's what Lucy Calkins says about conferences in *The Art of Teaching Writing*:

If we can keep only one thing in mind—and I fail at this half the time—it is that we are teaching the writer and not the writing. Our decisions must be guided by "what might help this writer" rather than "what might help this writing." If the piece of writing gets better but the writer has learned nothing that will help him or her another day on another piece, then the conference was a waste of everyone's time. It may even have done more harm than good, for such conferences teach students not to trust their own reactions. (1994, p. 228)

An important consideration when conferring with English Language Learners is their stage in the acquisition of the English language. Use words that are easily understood by students. For suggestions, check out The Stages of Language Proficiency section in Chapter 1, Introduction. Also, for beginning English speakers, provide opportunities for a variety of responses such as pointing, nodding, and physically responding during the conference.

The following are a few brief snippets of conversations from conferences with kids about writing feature articles.

Susan's Conference

Juli: How's it going?
Susan: Fine.
Juli: What writing work are you doing today?
Susan: About college football . . .
Juli: What do you need help with today?
Susan: I'm done writing.
Juli: You're done writing. I only see one paragraph. Do you have more notes?
Susan: No.
Juli: OK, let's look at your research and see if there's more information you can use in your feature article. When writers take notes for feature articles, they try to have more than they might use. That way they can be sure to have enough information for their writing. [Juli and Susan went back through her research to find more information she could use for notes for her writing.]

María's Conference

Juli: How's it going?
María: Fine.
Juli: What writing work are you doing today?
María: About snow dogs . . .
Juli: What part of the writing are you working on?
María (pointing to her paper and reading): "They're not just little, but when they train them if they are off the leash they are not dependable."
Juli: I see you are taking notes. Are you finished with your note taking?
María: No, I need a little bit more.
Juli: And what will you be working on when your notes are finished?
María: With another topic.
Juli: Did you know we are going to write a feature article?
María: No.
Juli: Well, after you take your notes on your topic, you're going to write a feature article and you are going to need a good lead to start. Did you want to use one of your touchstone try-its from your writer's notebook?

María: Yes, the one about snow dogs. "Admit it: snow dogs are much better than regular dogs."

Juli: OK. So that's going to be the lead and then you'll use your notes to write your article?

María: Yes.

Juli: Are you ready to get back to your writing work?

María: Yes.

Sophanna's Conference

Juli: How's it going?

Sophanna: Fine, it's going good.

Juli: What writing work are you doing today?

Sophanna: I'm writing "Hound Dogs."

Juli: Actually, I notice that your topic is the English foxhound.

Sophanna: Yes.

Juli: What part of the writing are you working on?

Sophanna: How they run very fast.

Juli: Were you able to come up with a good lead?

Sophanna: Yes.

Juli: Read it for me, please.

Sophanna: "At the time of its inception, coursing the stag with greyhounds was still the favored dog sport of the gentry."

Juli: It sounds to me like you might have taken this sentence right from your research. Is that right?

Sophanna: Yes.

Juli: OK. We'll talk about how you can put those ideas into your own words. Writers need to know how to say things in their own words. But first, didn't you tell me earlier that you were going to use a touchstone try-it for your lead?

Sophanna: Yes.

Juli: OK. Let's find it in your writer's notebook. "The hound dog isn't just a dog. It's also an Elvis Presley song." So, you are going to use this "try-it" lead to help you get started with your writing. Do you want to add it on at the beginning of the writing you are already doing or start again?

Sophanna: Start again.

Juli: In our next conference, we'll talk about how to use notes to help you write in your own words.

Manuel's Conference

Juli: How's it going?

Manuel: Fine.

Juli: What writing work are you doing today?

Manuel: About Dragonball Z . . .

Juli: What part of the writing are you working on?

Manuel: About Goku.

Juli: I see that you have just a few notes and a small amount of writing. Have you finished taking notes yet?

Manuel: I don't think so.

Juli: So, you have a few notes but you need to highlight some more important information and then you can use that to write your feature.

Manuel: OK.

Juli: Show me your research. It looks like you have plenty of research to use for your notes. So, you can keep on looking for information to use in your feature article. Writers know that taking lots of notes makes writing easier. Now, what will you be working on today?

Manuel: Finish my notes.

Juli: Great. I'll check with you again soon to see how it's going for you.

Writer's Notebooks

Writer's notebooks give students an opportunity to live as writers, and act as a springboard for their writing. They also provide us with valuable information about kids as writers and act as a dipstick for assessing writing. In *A Writer's Notebook: Unlocking the Writer Within You*, Ralph Fletcher writes about the role of writer's notebooks: "A writer's notebook gives you a place to live like a writer, not just in school during writing time, but wherever you are, at any time of day" (1996, p. 3).

Our kids begin their writer's notebooks by decorating the cover and then move into the notebook itself. They collect lists of what they like and what they don't like. They paste in photos and artifacts from vacations and family events. They save pages to write down words that fascinate them and that they want to keep close at hand. They try out some of what they are learning during mini-lessons.

A writer's notebook is also perfect for creating opportunities for kids to write and to maintain high expectations for kids as writers. "It gives you a place to write down what makes you angry or sad or amazed, to write down what you noticed and don't want to forget, to record exactly what your grandmother whispered in your ear before she said goodbye for the last time" (Fletcher 1996, p. 3).

Writer's notebooks are a mini-portfolio of sorts because all the writing kids put in them serves to guide instruction (see Figures 3.12 through 3.16). Work is collected over time and revisited, reworked, and revised by kids. How is it possible to assess writing in notebooks? A simple way to do this is to look at the first few pages in a notebook and then move to where the kid is currently writing. In this way, it's easy to see ongoing progress and to determine next steps for instruction.

figure 3.12 *Some students, like Patty, include musical artists and other celebrities on the covers of their Writer's notebooks.*

figure 3.14 *Kids collect favorite words for writing on Word Treasure Box pages.*

figure 3.13 *Others glue on favorite photos and stickers to personalize their notebooks.*

figure 3.16 *A writer's notebook often shows evidence of mini-lessons.*

figure 3.15 *Mary includes a photo of her cousin along with her writing.*

How Do You Know Your Kids Are Getting It?

And what do you do if they don't get it? It all starts with getting kids to write. You won't know whether they are getting it unless you are seeing it.

Step 1   Once kids are writing, the process of initial assessment can begin. By looking at student work, it's easy to see what students are already doing and what they need help with.

Step 2   Goal setting comes next. Use the information gathered from an initial assessment to establish goals that will be attainable. Often we think of this as "no more than 10 percent new material." If we try to teach too much to students before they have mastered essential learnings, it's like water under the bridge—they just don't get it. By teaching one thing at a time, English Language Learners are more able to incorporate the strategies of proficient writers into their work.

Step 3   Now's the time for teaching. Small-group mini-lessons are ideal to scaffold instruction for English Language Learners. They provide the necessary framework to gradually release responsibility to students as they take on more and more of their own learning.

Step 4   Evaluation logically follows instruction. Using rubrics, scoring guides, and checklists allows teachers and students to look back at the writing and evaluate it based on specific criteria. Conversations between students working with partners and students and teachers working in a small group can help clarify criteria and expectations for writers.

Step 5   Reflecting on students' writing provides an opportunity to determine next steps for instruction. Here's a chance to see whether kids are getting what the mini-lessons are teaching. Are they using what's being taught in their own writing? Are they trying to incorporate the strategies of proficient writers and making them their own?

Step 6   Setting new goals follows. Once again, use the information gathered from looking at students' work to establish goals that will be attainable. If the teaching is done in small increments, kids will acquire the knowledge they need to move on to the next steps of instruction. This is a chance to make sure that instruction matches what the kids need. We often think of this as "teach only one new thing at a time." If they just don't get it, it's time to set a goal to reteach. In this way, English Language Learners are more able to incorporate the strategies of proficient writers into their work even if they don't get it the first time.

Step 7   This process continues as kids work on their writing. In this way, the cycle of initial assessment, goal setting, teaching, evaluation, reflection, reassessment, and setting new goals repeats itself. By using the cycle of frequent, ongoing assessment, over time students show growth in writing and take on the strategies of proficient writers.

figure 4.1 *(top) Eric and Vendie browse through books looking for mentor authors.*

figure 4.2 *(center) Jenny uses a book by Gail Gibbons as a mentor text for her writing.*

figure 4.3 *(bottom) Juli and Gladys confer about the mentor author she chose.*

4 SELECTING TEXTS AND MENTOR AUTHORS

We need to put the light-ning of our stories and our heritage into the jars of our children's minds so that they, in turn, can pass them on to future generations.

—FROM THE
BOOK JACKET OF
*WHEN LIGHTNING
COMES IN A JAR* BY
PATRICIA POLACCO

After an initial assessment of writing, the next step is selecting books to use with English Language Learners (ELLs) during writing instruction. Book selection is a very important process; to that end, Katie Wood Ray (1999) recommends the following:

> In order to be able to select texts effectively for your teaching of writing, you need to be able to envision what that text offers your students as writers. The bottom line for why I select a text is that I see something in how that text is written [that] would be useful for my students to also

see. I see something about the text that holds potential for my students'
learning. I am looking for texts that have something in them or about
them that can add to my students' knowledge base of how to write well. I
need to try [to] envision what my students will know and what they will
be able to do as writers after encountering the text I am considering
adding to my collection. (p. 188)

Selecting Texts

With English Language Learners, there are additional considerations for
selecting books for writing instruction. The following paragraphs review some
important ones to keep in mind.

A student's primary language is important for their personal and educational development (Cummins 2000). Books that incorporate and respect the
primary language of students promote learning and encourage kids to build on
their prior knowledge.

Background experiences help writers link new learning to what they
already know. Books that include students' family backgrounds, experiences,
and characters that are the same age and have the same interests motivate
writers by helping them make connections between their lives and school.
Culturally relevant texts "connect to students' lives not just to their cultural
heritage" (Freeman and Freeman 2004).

Consider how the text will support ELLs as they write. What can they
learn from the writer? What can they take away and incorporate into their
own writing? Evaluate the supportive nature of the text. How will the book
help them become proficient writers?

Look at the structure of the language in the book. Does it match the
students' stage of language acquisition? If it requires additional teaching to
provide necessary background knowledge for the vocabulary or its unfamiliar
language structures, think about how to provide kids with the information
they need before reading the text.

Choose books that allow for flexibility when modeling strategy use.
Consider whether the book is appropriate for integrating strategy instruction
into reading and writing. Through integrated strategy instruction, what kids
learn about reading transfers to their writing.

Check on the availability of the text. Some wonderful texts go out of print.
Public and school libraries often have good collections of older stories. Online
used booksellers are also another way to find out-of-print selections.

Additionally, the cost of books can make it prohibitive for teachers to buy
a complete collection for themselves. A grade-level or group of like-minded
teachers can form a book timeshare by purchasing different books individually and then sharing with each other. Another untapped resource for developing a collection of texts to teach writing is a school's media specialist or
librarian. By working together, teachers and media specialists can develop collections of books for teacher use. Our media specialist, Linda Wong, received
a sum of money that needed to be spent quickly. We supplied her with the

bibliography from *Making Sense*, and she was able to order many of the texts so that they would be available for use by other teachers. By working together, books and other materials to teach writing can be shared.

We created our lists from the multitude of wonderful books available to teach strategies. While many of those mentioned in this book were also included in *Making Sense*, there are also some "new to us" texts that we've recently discovered. For example, *A Bird About to Sing* by Laura Nyman Montenegro and *You Have to Write* by Janet Wong talk about what it is like to write and to live as a writer. *Tea Leaves* by Frederick Lipp and *Guji Guji* by Chin-Yuan Chen introduce writers to perspectives from outside the United States.

Helping English Language Learners Choose Mentor Authors

What's all this fuss about learning how to choose a mentor author? What difference does it really make? Mentor authors are an essential scaffold for English Language Learners.

Carl Anderson reminds us: "When we are successful in showing students how to learn from writing mentors, we teach students how to teach themselves" (2000, p. 110). Building independence into writing instruction is crucial to the long-term success of ELLs. We want to show "students how to learn from writing mentors" and "teach students how to teach themselves." The ultimate goal of kids choosing mentor authors is that it encourages independence.

It is important to emphasize that kids should choose their own authors to act as mentors—we don't pick ones for them to use. As Katie Wood Ray notes: "Isoke Nia has challenged us all to remember [that] students need to choose their own writing teachers from the authors they love and whose work they admire" (2002, p. 146). When kids choose mentor authors—those from whom they can learn about writing—they are building on their knowledge of reading like a writer. They begin to notice how writers' lives impact their writing and the genres they choose. They look for aspects of the texts they admire and work to incorporate them into their own writing.

Then too, when kids have chosen mentor authors, it helps us as teachers. We're no longer alone in the classroom trying to teach writing. There are a large number of authors available, as mentors, to help us teach.

Patricia Polacco as a Mentor Author

To help kids choose an author, Juli models with Patricia Polacco, one of her mentor authors. When modeling how to choose a mentor, it's important to pick an author who has written across grade levels and/or genre. Polacco is a good choice because she has written in different genres and her books can be used for many different grade levels. At the end of this chapter is a list of other popular authors whom we recommend as mentors for English Language Learners.

Juli gathers a "ton" of Patricia's books, material about her writing life, and immerses the small group of ELLs in her writing by reading, reading, reading.

Juli models by thinking aloud about what she notices and discusses what Polacco does as a writer. As they talk about her books, Juli and the kids build a chart of what they notice in her writing.

Comments About Patricia Polacco's Writing

- She always uses another word for grandma, *Babushka*. The word is Ukrainian—*Rechenka's Eggs*.
- She puts her husband, Enzo, and other members of her family in some of her stories—*In Enzo's Splendid Garden, My Rotten Redheaded Older Brother*, and *The Keeping Quilt*.
- She gives lots of information about the characters—*Meteor!*
- She often describes grandparents—*Thank You, Mr. Falker*.
- Some of her books take place on a ranch (farm)—*My Rotten Redheaded Older Brother* and *Babushka's Doll*.
- She puts in lots of excitement—*Meteor!*
- She writes poems with rhymes—*Babushka's Mother Goose*.
- She puts her friends in her books—*Chicken Sunday* and *Thank You, Mr. Falker*.
- There's always a problem and a solution—*Chicken Sunday*.
- There's often a sad part. Kids are particularly drawn to *Thank You, Mr. Falker;* "It's the part about not letting go of the grass," they say.

This is the sad part from *Thank You, Mr. Falker* that draws kids' attention:

One evening they lay on the grass together and counted the lights from heaven. "You know," her grandma said, "all of us will go there someday. Hang on to the grass, or you'll lift right off the ground, and there you'll be!"

As a follow-up, Gladys finds a quote as she is reading *Firetalking (Meet the Author)*. In it Patricia talks about her life. Gladys reads Patricia's quote aloud: "I had difficulty reading. Math was and still is almost impossible for me. I knew that inside I was very smart, but at school I felt stupid and slow." Gladys pauses, and everyone gasps. She continues reading, "I had to work very hard to learn things."

It seems that, in the end, the kids who are struggling with reading and writing in English, just like Patricia Polacco did, really do understand how she feels about her work.

Mentor Author Suggestions

Although we let our writers choose their own mentor authors, we do make suggestions and recommendations, encouraging them to check out a variety of writers and their styles. One author who offers a different perspective to writers is Anushka Ravishankar from India. Her *Tiger on a Tree* book received a 2005 New York Book Show Award for Children's Literature and was placed on the 2005 American Library Association (ALA) Notable Children's Booklist. Although educated and trained as a mathematician, she has made a name for herself internationally as an Indian children's writer. Known as the "Dr. Seuss" of India, she has written more than ten poetry, fiction, and nonfiction books.

Books by Anushka Ravishankar

Concept Books

Alphabets Are Amazing Animals
One, Two, Three! (with Sirish Rao)

Nonsense Verse

Anything But a Grabooberry
Excuse Me, Is This India? (with Anita Leutwiler)
Tiger on a Tree
Today Is My Day
Wish You Were Here

Contemporary Nonfiction/Informational Texts

Puppets Unlimited with Everyday Materials (Gita Wolf and Anushka Ravishankar)
Trash!: On Ragpicker Children and Recycling (Gita Wolf and Anushka Ravishankar)

One thing that helps English Language Learners choose mentor authors is knowing what the writers say about writing. The Writers Talk About Writing section in the Resources contains a selection of Web sites where writers reflect on their various views on writing. We share one or two of these writers' comments with our kids from time to time to help them understand what goes on in a writer's mind.

In addition to Patricia Polacco and Anushka Ravishankar, when our writers are ready to choose their mentor authors, we set out piles of books written by the same author for them to browse and read. Most often, they are already familiar with the books. In this way, they can see the writer's range and get a better idea about his or her writing rather than basing a decision on just one book.

Recommended Mentor Authors

The following are a few of the writers we recommend for English Language Learners.

Alma Flor Ada

I Love Saturdays y domingos
Gathering the Sun: An Alphabet in English and Spanish
The Gold Coin

Francisco X. Alarcon

Angels Ride Bikes: And Other Fall Poems
From the Bellybutton of the Moon and Other Summer Poems
Iguanas in the Snow and Other Winter Poems
Laughing Tomatoes and Other Spring Poems

Sandra Cisneros

Hairs/Pelitos
The House on Mango Street
Woman Hollering Creek and Other Stories

Carmen Lomas Garza

Family Pictures/Cuadros de familia
In My Family/En mi familia

Juan Felipe Herrera

Calling the Doves
Grandma and Me at the Flea
Laughing Out Loud, I Fly
The Upside Down Boy

Grace Lin

Dim Sum for Everyone
Fortune Cookie Fortunes
The Ugly Vegetables

Lenore Look

Henry's First-Moon Birthday
Love as Strong as Ginger
Ruby Lu, Brave and True

Pat Mora

A Birthday Basket for Tía
Confetti: Poems for Children
Pablo's Tree
Tomás and the Library Lady

Ken Mochizuki

Baseball Saved Us
Heroes
Passage to Freedom: The Sugihara Story

Naomi Shihab Nye

Come With Me: Poems for a Journey
Salting the Ocean: 100 Poems by Young Poets
Sitti's Secrets

Gary Soto

Chato's Kitchen
Chato and the Party Animals

Neighborhood Odes
The Old Man and His Door
Snapshots from the Wedding
A Summer Life
Too Many Tamales

Janet Wong

Apple Pie 4th of July
Buzz
Hide & Seek
A Suitcase of Seaweed and Other Poems
The Trip Back Home
You Have to Write

Lawrence Yep

Hiroshima
The Khan's Daughter
The Lost Garden
The Rainbow People

figure 5.1 *(top) Outey thinks aloud as she reads to integrate reading and writing strategies.*

figure 5.2 *(center) Students, like this girl, spend time reading before they write.*

figure 5.3 *(bottom) Outey uses Thong's* Red Is a Dragon *as a mentor text.*

5 PREPRODUCTION

This is the beginning stage of language proficiency. To expect English Language Learners to sit down and write a story, a report of information, or a poem is unrealistic. They simply do not have enough English. However, there are many ways they can learn about creating their stories and communicating meaning through writing while they begin to learn English. Interactive Writing (McCarrier, Fontas, and Pinnell 1999), the Language Experience Approach (Carasquillo and Rodriguez 2002), telling stories through drawings, making flap and pop-up books, and using other authors as mentors are all ways to scaffold the writing task for students as they begin to experiment with their own stories and with language.

In Interactive Writing, the teacher and the students work together to compose a text. They talk about what they are going to write with the teacher facilitating the discussion by guiding, modeling, adding, summarizing, confirming, and combining kids' ideas. Once the writing begins, it's all about getting ideas on paper. Teacher and students take turns doing the physical writing. They share a pen or pencil and pass it back and forth as they alternate writing on the paper.

As they work, the teacher encourages them to discuss the content and the process of writing, dealing with the conventions of print and working on grammar, spelling, punctuation, letter formation, and so on. The section that follows this introduction, Younger ELLs in Real Time, contains an example of kindergarteners using *Brown Bear, Brown Bear, What Do You See?* by Bill Martin and Eric Carle to do Interactive Writing.

A major premise of the Language Experience Approach is to help kids understand that anything that can be said can be written and that anything that can be written can be said. The procedure involves experiencing, discussing the experience, recording the experience, and using the record of the experience for reading and writing activities.

The Language Experience Approach begins with the kids and the teacher having a common experience. Then they draw pictures to detail that experience. Next, kids dictate what they want to say about their pictures to the teacher, and he or she writes it down for them. At this stage, if kids dictate, it is usually only one or two words. The development of shared experiences that extend children's knowledge of the world around them assists in building a sense of classroom community, which is so important to the success of English Language Learners. The next chapter, "Early Production," includes an example of a class using the Language Experience Approach to record their common experiences while raising silkworms.

For beginning English speakers, the opportunity to tell their stories—things that happened—through drawing and other art forms is very important. Wordless picture books (for example, *The Red Book* by Barbara Lehman, *Zoom* by Istvan Banyai, *Yellow Umbrella* by Jae Soo Liu, and *Home* by Jeannie Baker) teach students how to convey meaning with pictures. The ideas we teach about drawing stories can be applied to writing as well. Learning to add detail to pictures will apply to adding details to stories, poems, and informational texts as students gain proficiency in English.

For students at the beginning stage of language proficiency who are literate in a language other than English, opportunities for them to write in that language encourage the transfer of literacy skills from other languages to English and support the idea that all of us are writers. It brings them into the classroom community of writers even as they are just beginning to learn English. "Research clearly shows (Cummins 2000) how important a student's primary language is for their personal and educational development" (Kendall and Khuon 2005). Teachers who do not speak the same language as some of their students can use other class members who do know the language as peer tutors, especially for editing and revision.

Younger English Language Learners in Real Time

Joey and Eric sit down at the table during their after-school program to listen to *Brown Bear, Brown Bear, What Do You See?* They are familiar with the story and read along together in sing-song voices. "Brown bear, brown bear,

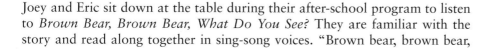

what do you see?" they chant with the text. Their enthusiasm for the story is evident as their voices grow louder and louder. They may be kindergarten students but the repetitive nature of the text, the number of times they have heard the story, and the predictable patterns of colors and animals scaffold the reading for them.

"Now we are going to write our own story about *Brown Bear,*" Juli tells them as Outey takes out large sheets of plain white paper and a box of colored markers. She picks up a marker and says, "You watch me as I do it." She begins by saying, "Brown bear, brown bear, what do you see?" This models how to make a complete idea for the students. Then she picks up another colored marker and starts writing the letters as she slowly says the words. "Brown—what sounds do you hear in the word?" she asks as she slows down her speech. "Brown," she says again slowly. Then she carefully writes each letter at the bottom of the sheet of paper and repeats the word slowly one more time. When she's finished writing the word *brown,* she follows the same procedure with the word *bear.*

"OK, now I want to watch while you try it," Outey says. She's modeled the task, so she's ready for the kids to give it a try. "Let's read what we've written so far, and then think about what comes next." They read the writing and then think aloud about what's next. As they say the word *what* together slowly, listening for the sounds, Joey jumps up to take the marker and write a *w,* then Juli adds the *h* and the *a* and then asks what they hear. Eric knows there's a *t* at the end of *what* so she hands him the marker and he writes it on the paper.

They continue sharing the pen and writing together until they have finished the entire story they want to write. "Brown Bear, Brown Bear, what do you see? I see a black sheep looking at me." Then Joey and Eric illustrate their story.

Over several days they will write more *Brown Bear* stories and put them together to make their own class book. This as well as other writing activities stay in the classroom library and are available for reading independently and with a partner. Kids can also use it as a model to write their own *Brown Bear* books.

Interactive Writing is a wonderful way to support beginning English speakers. The scaffolding it provides is especially helpful to English Language Learners. It gives them the opportunity to demonstrate learning and understanding by taking the pen and writing the letter or word, often without speaking. During this stage, students are developing receptive language, and opportunities to respond physically through interactive writing offer a means of communication that is not oral.

Lessons for Younger English Language Learners

1: Making Connections (Schema)

Writers frequently choose their topics and write about subjects they care about.

Teaching Moves

Start Up/Connection Before reading *Buzz,* introduce students to pictures of things that go buzz. For example, show photographs or realistic pictures of a

bee, an alarm clock, an electric shaver, a lawn mower, a blender, a garage door opener, a small airplane, a clothes dryer, a hair dryer, and/or a doorbell. As you show students the pictures, make the sound, "Buzz," and encourage students to join you.

Give Information Hold up the *Buzz* book. Tell students, "Today we will be reading a book called *Buzz.* It's a story about a little girl who sees all kinds of things that go buzz. After we read the story, we are going to write our own story." As you read the story, stop on each page and point to the item that goes buzz. Encourage students to buzz along with you.

Active Involvement After reading the story, show students the mural and tell them that you are all going to work together to make a *Buzz* story. Draw and cut out things that go buzz and paste them on the mural. Tell them, "Watch me as I do it." Explain that they will draw their own pictures. They can use the pictures and photographs as models. Say, "Now you try it while I watch." After drawing, have students glue their pictures on a mural to make a *Buzz* story for the group (see Figure 5.4). Label the pictures for students, if they wish. Students can also write or cut out the word *Buzz* to go on the mural.

Off You Go Have students use the mural and *Buzz* for rereading and as models for their own writing. Encourage them to do their own *Buzz* books when they have independent writing time.

figure 5.4 *This wall chart for* Buzz *tells the story with pictures.*

2: Asking Questions

Writers compose in a way that causes the reader to form questions as they read.

Instructional Materials

- *Brown Bear, Brown Bear, What Do You See?* by Bill Martin and Eric Carle (big book version)
- Plain 11 × 17" drawing paper
- Markers

Teaching Moves

Start Up/Connection This lesson is based around Interactive Writing—a way to help children who are just learning language attach meaning to print.

Start the lesson by saying, "We've learned all about colors. Let's use the color cards and read the words together." Show the color cards as you say the colors together (for example, red, yellow, green, blue, purple, black, orange, black). "Now let's take a look at the pictures of the animals that we have learned." Show pictures of animals for kids to identify as you say their names together (for example, bear, horse, duck). The book can also be used to review colors and animals.

Give Information "We're going to write a story together. It will have colors and animals in it. Let's read *Brown Bear, Brown Bear, What Do You See?* to see how Martin and Carle wrote their book using colors and animals." After reading say, "Now let's draft our story. Let's use the questions and answers from the book as a pattern to help us." Think aloud, "What will we write first?" Encourage students to contribute their ideas for writing. To begin say, "I think I'll start with—White horse, white horse, what do you see? Watch me as I do it." Pick up the marker and write the first word as you say it slowly so that students can match the sounds with the letters you write.

Active Involvement (Interactive Writing) While you are composing the story out loud with the students, encourage them to volunteer to write the words and letters they know. Prompt them by saying, "Now you try it while I watch." Have them write one at a time using a marker as you and the other children repeat the text the group composed. In Interactive Writing, the teacher fills in the letters and words the students don't know as the group writes together. After the story is written, students can draw illustrations that match the text.

At this stage of language proficiency, students will probably model the text they create directly off of the book they are reading as a model or mentor text (see Figure 5.5 and 5.6). When students do this, they use the words in the story as a framework for their writing. In addition, some students will sit silently watching and listening carefully while others will chime in with words for the text.

figure 5.5 *Teacher and students sharing the pen is an important part of interactive writing.*

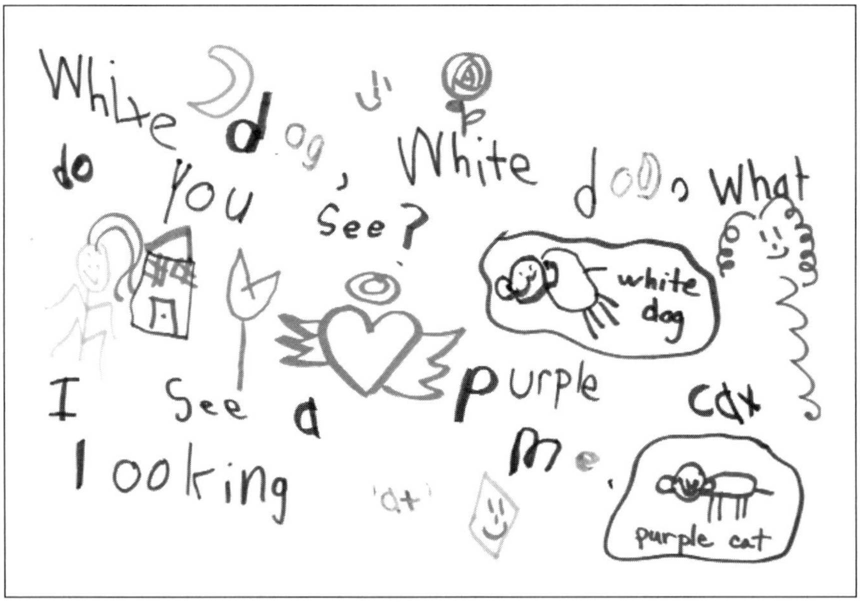

Off You Go "We'll put this story on the walls so you will be able to read it. You can also write your own story about *Brown Bear* and his friends during independent writing." Read aloud other predictable books for kids by Bill Martin and Eric Carle to provide additional models for their writing.

figure 5.6 *Kids enjoy illustrating their interactive writing.*

3: Visualizing (Using Sensory Images)

Writers use images to explore their ideas. They constantly study mental images for direction in their pieces.

Teaching Moves

Start Up/Connection To help students understand what a pop-up book is, go through *Puppy Trouble* several times. Point out the puppy's activities in each picture. Encourage students to pull the flap of each picture and see what happens.

Give Information Explain to students that the group will be making a pop-up book. To help students understand, point to the book and the flaps as you explain. Say, "Watch me as I do it" as you draw a picture and then add a flap. (*Where's Spot?* can also be used as a model for making flaps and pop-ups.) As a model, place your paper as the first page of the book the small group makes.

Active Involvement Have students do their own pictures with flaps. Hand out the materials and say, "Now you try it while I watch." Encourage students to make several different pages with flaps for each book. Encourage them to write something to add to their pictures if possible.

Off You Go Bind the pages together into a book. Read it with students, encouraging them to lift the flaps. Tell them that the flap book will be in the class library and that they can make their own flap books when they are writing. Provide various flap and pop-up books (see Figure 5.7) for kids to read and use as models for their writing.

Instructional Materials

- *Puppy Trouble* (pop-up book version) by Alexandra Day
- *Where's Spot?* (Lift-the-Flap Series) by Eric Carle
- Plain white 8½ × 11" paper
- Half sheets of colored construction paper

figure 5.7 *A variety of pop-up books give kids opportunities to try out using pictures to tell the story.*

Instructional Materials

☐ *One Is a Drummer: A Book of Numbers* by Roseanne Thong
☐ Sheets of colored 4¼ × 11" paper stapled to make 10-page booklets
☐ Crayons, pencils, markers, and white correction tape

4: Inferring

Writers make decisions about content inclusions/exclusions and genre/text that permit or encourage inference on the part of readers.

Teaching Moves

Start Up/Connection Read *One Is a Drummer: A Book of Numbers* with the students. As you go through it, point to the pages and count each of the items the text mentions. For example, "One is a drummer, One is a race, One is a dragon boat that wins first place!" Point to the drummer, the race, and the dragon boat.

Give Information Explain to students that they will each be making a book of numbers. Show them the premade booklets with the sentence frames (One is a _____. Two is a _____.). Tell them, "Watch me as I do it" while you read through each page and draw pictures for each number. Then write the word that you chose for each number in the space. As you write each word, say it slowly and make a direct connection between the sounds you are saying and the letters you are writing (see Figure 5.8). Encourage students to reread each page with you as it is completed.

Active Involvement Give students the opportunity to do their own books. Hand out the premade books and say, "Now you try it while I watch." Provide markers, crayons, pencils, and white correction tape to make changes easier. Help students complete their books. Some students will just use pictures to represent the words, whereas others will draw pictures and attempt to write the sounds they hear in words. Provide whatever support they need to complete their books. It will be different for each child.

figure 5.8 *Kids use Thong's* One Is a Drummer *as a mentor text for their writing.*

Off You Go When students have finished their books, encourage them to exchange with a partner and read each other's books. This helps writers understand that print conveys a message and encourages them to infer meaning.

Books for Teaching Strategies to Younger English Language Learners

Preproduction Stage

Making Connections

Buzz by Janet Wong
Farm Animals (DK Lift-the-Flap book)
Hats, Hats, Hats by Ann Morris
Hide & Seek by Janet Wong
In My Family/En mi familia by Carmen Lomas Garza
One Small Girl by Jennifer Chan

Asking Questions

Brown Bear, Brown Bear, What Do You See? by Bill Martin Jr. and
  Eric Carle
Have You Seen My Duckling? by Nancy Tafuri
Is It Red? Is It Yellow? Is It Blue? by Tana Hoban
Where's Spot? (Lift-the-Flap series) by Eric Hill
Who Says Quack? by Jerry Smith

Visualizing

"Barnyard Dance" from *Rhinoceros TAP, The Book and the CD*, by
    Sandra Boynton
I Spy Treasure Hunt: A Book of Picture Riddles (I Spy books) by
    Walter Wick
Pancakes for Breakfast by Tomie dePaola
Puppy Trouble (pop-up version) by Alexandra Day
Rosie's Walk (big book version) by Pat Hutchins

Inferring

My Friend Rabbit by Eric Rohmann
Old MacDonald Had a Farm, illustrated by Carol Jones
One Is a Drummer: A Book of Numbers by Roseanne Thong
Red Is a Dragon: A Book of Colors by Roseanne Thong
Round Is a Mooncake: A Book of Shapes by Roseanne Thong
Zoom by Istvan Banyai

Older English Language Learners in Real Time

When students are older and are just beginning to learn English, writing presents great challenges. One way to include them as writers while they increase their vocabularies is to allow them to write in their primary language, if they are literate in it. This was what Cindy and Yoanna did when Juli taught a unit of study about personal narrative in their classroom. Since Juli also reads and writes in Spanish, she was able to facilitate this.

At the beginning of the unit of study, both girls were very hesitant to write anything. They sat quietly during independent writing and appeared to be doing nothing at all. But after several days, with encouragement from their teacher and Juli, who both worked with them in Spanish, they began to write in Spanish. Over several weeks, they moved through the writing process along with the other students in the class, but their compositions were in Spanish rather than English. When they completed their first drafts, they worked together to revise their pieces. They conferred in Spanish with the teacher and Juli as they worked on their personal narratives. As they got ready to write final drafts, they edited each other's writing and then made changes in their own pieces.

Yoanna and Cindy chose to write personal narratives titled "Cuando fui a la playa" ("When I went to the beach"). Although their topics were similar, the girls' experiences were very different, and they worked to convey that in their writing.

Through this unit of study, Yoanna and Cindy learned that all of us are writers whether we write in English or in Spanish. They came to appreciate the fact that literacy skills in one language will transfer to another. They also acquired new English vocabulary by participating in an authentic grade-level writing experience that surrounded them with English in a meaningful context.

A teacher who does not speak, read, or write the students' language, and who still wants to allow them to write in their language while they are just beginning to learn English, can encourage this by using peer tutors or adult

volunteers who speak the students' language to facilitate their writing. The purpose of doing this is to allow students to express themselves in writing, even if it is not in English. In this way, they can participate as members of the community of writers in the classroom.

Lessons for Older English Language Learners

1: Making Connections (Schema)

Writers frequently choose their topics and write about subjects they care about.

Teaching Moves

Start Up/Connection Go through *Family Pictures* with students. Stop on each page and point out and label many of the objects. Encourage students to interact with the book and each other.

Give Information Tell students that they will be drawing their own family pictures. Begin by saying, "Watch me as I do it." Demonstrate for students as you draw a picture of your family doing an activity together. Think aloud about what you are drawing as you work.

Active Involvement Give each student paper and pencil and say, "Now you try it while I watch." Encourage students to go back to the book to look at the pictures as they draw their own.

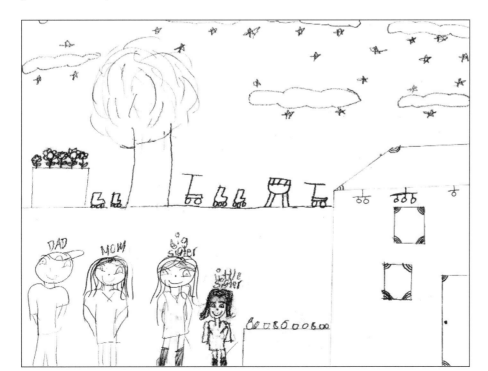

figure 5.9 *Yoanna incorporates the names of her family into her picture.*

figure 5.10 *Cindy uses Carmen Lomas Garza as her mentor author.*

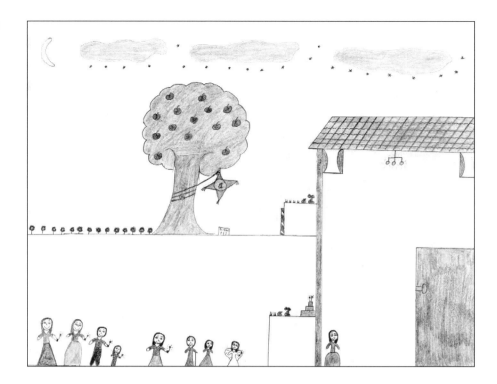

Off You Go When students have finished, they can decide whether they would like to do additional pictures of their families' activities. Pictures can be saved and text added later as students learn more English (see Figures 5.9 and 5.10).

2: Asking Questions

Writers compose in a way that causes readers to form questions as they read.

Teaching Moves

Start Up/Connection Play the tape, *How Many Days to America?*, for students as the small group listens. Hold the book and point and gesture toward the parts of the pictures as they are mentioned on the tape to help students understand. To integrate strategy use, see the comprehension lesson for this story in *Making Sense* (2005, p. 32).

Give Information Explain to students that you are going to draw a story about how your family came to America. Say, "Watch me as I do it." Fold a sheet of the white paper into six equal boxes. Number the boxes in sequence, one through six. Using the flow map, draw pictures of how your family came to America in the numbered boxes, putting the story in sequence.

Active Involvement Hand out paper to students and show them how to fold it into six boxes and number the boxes in sequence to make a flow map. Say, "Now you try it while I watch." Have students draw a sequence of pictures

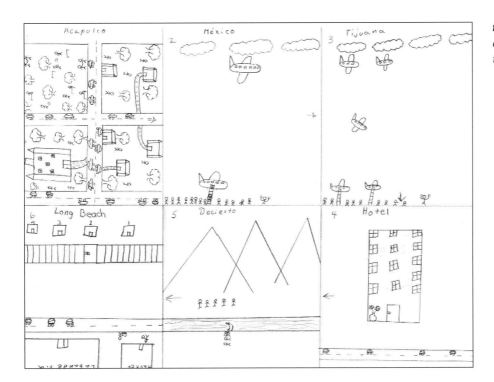

figure 5.11 *A flow map helps one student tell the story of her trip to America in sequence.*

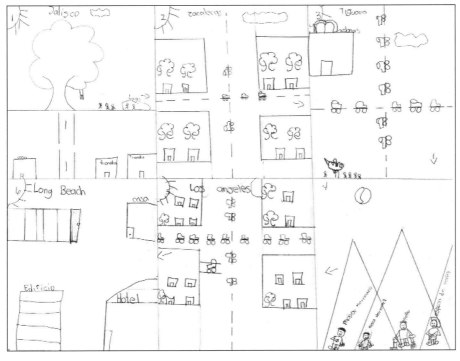

figure 5.12 *Another student shows how her family traveled from Jalisco.*

telling the story of how their families came to America (for example, see Figures 5.11 and 5.12). Use *On the Go* to encourage students to draw the different modes of transportation they used. Have students share their stories with each other.

Off You Go Provide additional opportunities for students to listen to the *How Many Days to America?* book's tape. Encourage students to use flow maps to tell other stories and sequences of activities such as science experiments and field trips.

3: Visualizing (Using Sensory Images)

Writers use images to explore their ideas. They constantly study mental images for direction in their pieces.

Teaching Moves

Start Up/Connection Begin by showing students the *Yellow Umbrella* and playing the music on the CD. Go through the book slowly, pointing out the umbrellas, the rain, and the different settings on each page. This allows students to understand that it is a wordless picture book.

Give Information Tell students that you are going to play the CD music while they "read" through the book. Follow the directions for listening listed on the inside front cover. It takes about eight minutes to read through the book with the CD. Encourage students to be quiet so that they can hear the music and think about the story. Have students watch while you draw a picture of a rainy day. Focus on the setting, adding umbrellas, rain, and other important details to help students understand your story.

Active Involvement Hand out paper and markers to encourage students to tell their own rainy day stories through pictures (see Figure 5.13). Continue to play the CD so that students have the music as a background while they draw.

figure 5.13 *Using a perspective from above, a student tells the story of umbrellas on a rainy day.*

Off You Go Place the book and CD in a listening area so that students can hear it again. You can also add the *How Many Days to America?* book and tape from the previous lesson (2: Asking Questions) to the listening area. Continue adding books with tapes and CDs to expand students' choices.

4: Inferring

Writers make decisions about content inclusions/exclusions and genre/text that permit or encourage inference on the part of the reader.

Teaching Moves

Start Up/Connection Read through *Yo! Yes?* with students several times. Encourage them to read along with you after the first time. This helps students understand how the author uses pictures and a few words to encourage us, as readers, to infer what is happening.

Give Information Explain to students that sometimes authors tell their stories with very few words. Demonstrate how to make a small book like *Yo! Yes?* Tell students, "Watch me as I do it." Fold a paper in quarters to make a four-page booklet. On each page draw two characters. Show how they are having a conversation using only one or two words. Use the book as a model and refer to different pages as you work.

Active Involvement Hand out a sheet of paper to each student. Show them how to fold it in quarters so that it makes a four-page booklet. Say, "Now you try it while I watch." Students can refer to the book as they work. Also encourage them to interact with each other if they are comfortable doing this.

Off You Go While students work on other writing projects, encourage them to try using conversations between their characters to help readers infer what is happening (see Figures 5.14 and 5.15). This helps them understand that meaning can be conveyed with body language and just a few words.

figure 5.14 *Raschka's* Yo! Yes? *acts as a mentor text for Yoanna's story.*

figure 5.15 *Cindy incorporates frequently used expressions along with pictures to tell her story.*

Books for Teaching Strategies to Older English Language Learners

Preproduction Stage

Making Connections

Family Pictures/Cuadros de familia by Carmen Lomas Garza
Gathering the Sun: An Alphabet in English and Spanish by Alma Flor Ada
On the Go by Ann Morris
Shoes, Shoes, Shoes by Ann Morris
Tools by Ann Morris

Asking Questions

Diving Dolphins (DK Readers Series) by Karen Wallace
Four Hungry Kittens by Emily Arnold McCully
How Many Days to America? by Eve Bunting
An Ocean World by Peter Sis
Rockets and Spaceships (DK Readers Series) by Karen Wallace

Visualizing

Can You See What I See? (I Spy books) by William Wick
Home by Jeannie Baker
June 29, 1999 by David Weisner
Sector 7 by David Weisner
Snow Music by Lynn Rae Perkins
Tuesday by David Weisner
Yellow Umbrella by Jae Soo Liu
Re-Zoom by Istvan Banyai

Inferring

A Day, A Dog by Gabrielle Vincent
Don't Let the Pigeon Ride the Bus! by Mo Willems
Free Fall by David Weisner
The Mysteries of Harris Burdick by Chris Van Allsburg
The Red Book by Barbara Lehman
Time Flies by Eric Rohmann
Yo! Yes? by Chris Raschka

figure 6.1 *(top) Outey listens as Hollysun rereads his Language Experience Approach dictation.*

figure 6.2 *(center) Yoanna and Cindy work as partners to write lists.*

figure 6.3 *(bottom) A small group listens as Outey reads Peek! A Thai Hide-and-Seek.*

6 EARLY PRODUCTION

It is important that English Language Learners be able to take risks and experiment with new language in a low-anxiety setting at the early production stage of language proficiency. Mini-lessons about writing expand receptive vocabulary, and classroom activities encourage students to use words they understand. Books with predictable patterns, such as *Mice and Beans* by Pam Muñoz Ryan, *Hush! A Thai Lullaby* by Minfong Ho, and *Just a Minute: A Trickster Tale and Counting Book* by Yuyi Morales, provide a structure that helps to scaffold the development of oral language and writing.

The Language Experience Approach can be used with students at various levels. The procedure involves the following:

- Experiencing
- Discussing the experience
- Recording the experience (with pictures and print dictation)
- Using the record of the experience for reading and writing activities

73

It is a wonderful way to scaffold writing for kids at the early production stage. The approach encourages students to draw illustrations of experiences such as investigating a topic on the Internet (for example, hatching chicks), conducting a science experiment, or going on a field trip. Then, using their own language, they dictate about the illustrations. The purpose is to scaffold the writing task for students by showing them that what can be said can be written. In addition, rereading their stories shows them that anything that can be written can be read. In this way, they come to understand the connections between reading and writing.

Younger English Language Learners in Real Time

Raising silkworms is a spring tradition in Southern California kindergarten classrooms. Outey and Juli will never forget the time they used the Language Experience Approach with a class that was raising silkworms. On the first day, kids watched as the teacher brought in Ziploc bags full of silkworm eggs, several shoe boxes, and sections of egg cartons. The class members collected mulberry leaves from a large tree that grew in the kindergarten play yard and provided plenty of food for the growing worms. Students tore the leaves into dime-size pieces and added everything to the shoe boxes. In went the silkworm eggs, the sections of egg cartons where cocoons would be spun, and the chopped up mulberry leaves.

Over several weeks, students observed the development of the silkworms. Each day they added fresh leaves and watched to see how the size, color, and behavior of the caterpillars changed. This shared experience of raising silkworms extended the kindergarteners' knowledge of science and developed their sense of community.

To support the children's concept development and vocabulary growth, the teacher carefully introduced new words, such as *eggs, hatches, caterpillar, silkworms, mulberry leaves, larva, pupa, cocoon, adult,* and *moth*, at the appropriate times. Students watched as the eggs hatched and tiny black caterpillars began to eat the leaves. Every day kids observed how they were growing and changing. After several weeks, the caterpillars began to spin their silk cocoons.

When the day finally came that the moths ate their way out of the cocoons, students gathered around to see them emerge. It was an amazing experience to watch as the moths squeezed their way out of the white and yellow cocoons and spread their wings wide to dry.

Once the silk moths emerged and began laying eggs, kids took turns working in small groups to draw the life cycle of the silkworms. Everyone got a box of crayons and a large sheet of white paper that was divided into six rectangular sections. The sections were numbered from one to six to encourage sequencing of the events. Kids drew pictures of what had happened from the time the eggs went into the shoe boxes up to when the silk moths were laying their eggs. Their drawings recorded their responses to the experience.

The experience of raising silkworms that the kids shared provided them with the opportunity to grow as a community of learners. This is valuable for English Language Learners (ELLs) because through interacting about common experiences they negotiate the meaning of what they are learning as well as practice new vocabulary and use of oral language in a nonthreatening, risk-free environment. All of this encourages the acquisition of language, and the shared experiences extend kids' knowledge of the world around them while building a sense of classroom community.

After they drew their pictures, Outey and Juli talked with students one at a time and asked them to tell about their pictures. They prompted the kids by asking, "Remember when we . . . ?" They encouraged students to respond by pointing and gesturing to their drawings. They asked questions like "Where are the eggs?" Juli prompted students by saying, "Point to the cocoons. How many do you see?" When students responded verbally, it was usually with exclamations like "Moth out!" and "More eggs!"

As they dictated, Outey and Juli labeled students' drawings with their new vocabulary. There were egg and caterpillar and moth drawings everywhere when the students displayed their work on the classroom bulletin boards.

By labeling students' drawings with their own words, Outey and Juli used the Language Experience Approach to teach students that writing conveys a message. Through this approach, students demonstrated an emerging awareness that thoughts and ideas can be expressed in written language, and they demonstrated an emerging ability to report factual information using pictures. This simple activity also introduced students to the connection between reading and writing. As they reread their work, students learned that the pictures they drew gave clues to the meaning of the words used to label their drawings.

Lessons for Younger English Language Learners

1: Making Connections

A writer's content comes from and builds on his or her experiences.

Teaching Moves

Start Up/Connection Share pictures and stories about families and grandparents with students. *Families* provides pictures of families from around the world participating in a variety of activities. Encourage students to share photos of their own families with the small group. To integrate strategy use, see the comprehension lesson for this story in *Making Sense* (2005, p. 40).

Give Information Read aloud *Mice and Beans* with students. Look at each picture carefully, pointing and labeling items and characters and talking about the relationship between Rosa María, the grandmother, and the importance of her youngest grandchild's birthday. *The Wednesday Surprise* and *A Birthday Basket for Tía* deal with the same subject and can also be used.

Active Involvement After reading and discussing the story with the students, tell them: "You are going to use what you know from your own experience with your family to help you get ideas. First you are going to draw a picture that tells the story of the birthday of someone in your family. Then you will tell us about the story in your picture, and finally, write the story." Have students

Instructional Materials

- *A Birthday Basket for Tía* by Pat Mora
- *Families* by Ann Morris
- *Mice and Beans* by Pam Muñoz Ryan
- *The Wednesday Surprise* by Eve Bunting
- Writer's notebooks
- Drawing and writing paper

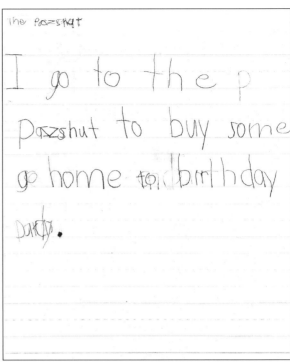

figure 6.4 *(left) Hollysun draws a picture of his birthday party, including the pizza.*

figure 6.5 *(right) After drawing, he writes a story about his picture.*

watch as you do it. Encourage them to talk with each other about what they notice as you are drawing.

After the drawing is finished, tell students the story you drew as you point to the different details in your picture. This oral retelling of the story is very important for beginning writers. It helps them understand that what is in the picture is what they are going to write. It also gives them a chance to rehearse their stories aloud before they write them down. Finally, write out your story for students. Discuss how what you are writing matches what you drew in your picture.

Off You Go When you are finished modeling your drawing and writing, tell students, "Now you try it while I watch." Give them the opportunity to use their writer's notebooks or a sheet of paper to get down their ideas (see Figures 6.4 and 6.5). First have them draw a picture, then have them retell the story from their pictures to a partner, and finally, have them write it down. As they work, encourage students to talk with each other about the family experiences they are using for their drawing and writing.

2: Asking Questions

Writers monitor their progress by asking questions about their choices as they write.

Teaching Moves

Start Up/Connection Provide students with comprehensible input by experiencing a video about chicks hatching. We use Mick and Bob Brown's *Chick,*

Instructional Materials

- *Chick, Chick, Chick,* a video by Mick and Bob Brown
- *Chickens* by Diane Snowball
- *Egg to Chick* by Millicent Ellis Selsam and Barbara Wolff
- Chickenscope 1.5 Explore Embryology (http://chickscope.itg.uiuc.edu/explore/embryology/)
- White 8½ × 11 paper, markers, and crayons

Chick, Chick video, which features natural sounds without commentary. To provide more information, we also use the Chickenscope 1.5 Explore Embryology Web site, which illustrates the day-by-day development of a chick. This helps students build background before the lesson.

Give Information To provide mentor texts for informational writing, read students *Chickens* and *Egg to Chick*. Think aloud as you read and point out how the authors wrote the information about chicks developing in eggs and hatching. Point out that authors who write informational texts often use questions and answers to give information. Use examples from the text such as "Are the chickens ready to hatch after four days? No."

As you read through the books, encourage students to share with a partner what they notice about how the author uses questions to write about how chicks develop in eggs and how chicks hatch. Tell students that they can use questions in their own writing to give information. Keep a list of Powerful Words, including important vocabulary, that students can refer to when they are writing independently.

Important Words About Eggs and Chicks

chickens	chick	develop	wet
eggs	nest	peck	crack
rooster	lay	shells	dry
hen	hatch	beaks	grow

Active Involvement Use the following directions to have students use the Language Experience Approach to record what they learned about how chicks develop and hatch.

1. Hand out sheets of white paper divided into six sections and crayons and markers.
2. If it helps students, have them sequence the stages of development using the numbers one to six or the number of days—one number in each of the six boxes.
3. Encourage students to draw their pictures of the development of the chicks in sequence in the numbered boxes.
4. As they draw, have them dictate their stories.
5. Write their stories next to their pictures, keeping the language as close to what the child says as possible. When you record their dictated stories exactly as they tell them, it makes it possible for the children to reread their language experience stories.

Off You Go Then, give students the opportunity to draw and write informational texts in their writer's notebooks. Provide a copy of the list of important words, copies of the books about chick development, as well as students' language experience stories, for them to refer to as they work.

figure 6.6 *This language experience story documents the student's use of English.*

figure 6.7 *Some vocabulary confusion between the words* seashells *and* eggshells *shows up in this language experience dictation.*

After students have written an informational text (see Figures 6.6 and 6.7), have them share with a partner by reading their stories and answering questions. Also, keep the list of Powerful Words and the teacher's writing available for students to use as models for other informational texts they may choose to write.

Instructional Materials

- *There Was an Old Lady Who Swallowed a Fly* by Simms Taback
- White paper, scissors, markers, and crayons

3: Visualizing (Using Sensory Images)

Writers use images to explore their ideas. They constantly study mental images for direction in their pieces.

Start Up/Connection Read through *There Was an Old Lady Who Swallowed a Fly* with students. Show them how the author, Simms Taback, used holes in the pages to help him explore his ideas. Allow them to examine the book looking for various animals.

Give Information Tell students that they are going to be making their own stories using holes in the pages to explore their ideas. Make it clear that the purpose of "hole" books is to help students find a variety of ways to communicate ideas while their oral language and writing are developing. Model this for students by saying, "Watch me as I do it" as you draw a picture, cut a hole, and write text to go with it. Then add another page underneath the first one, drawing so that the hole in the top paper helps convey the meaning of the story.

Active Involvement Explain to students that they are going to make their own hole books. Give them paper, scissors, markers, and crayons so that they can work on their own ideas. Tell them, "Now you try it while I watch." Help them cut a hole in the paper and then talk about what they want to put in the hole. Be available to answer their questions as they work. Encourage them to explore their own ideas for how they can use hole books to communicate them. When they are finished, staple the two pages together to make a single hole book.

figure 6.8 *By using "hole" books kids discover a way to communicate ideas while their oral language and writing skills are developing.*

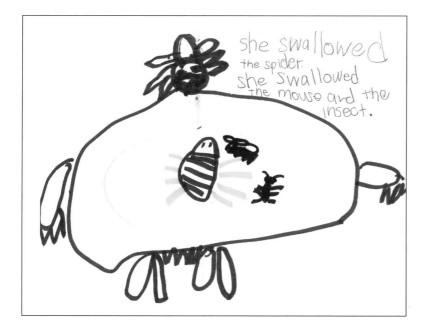

figure 6.9 *This student explores new ways to tell a story.*

Off You Go After students complete their hole books (see Figures 6.8 and 6.9), have them share their stories with each other. Continue to make it possible for students to make hole books as they work on writing about their ideas. This encourages them to communicate ideas while they are learning English.

4: Inferring

Writers make decisions about content inclusions/exclusions and genre/text that permit or encourage inference on the part of readers.

Teaching Moves

Start Up/Connection With students, read *Hush! A Thai Lullaby*. Discuss the different animals in the story and identify any that may be unfamiliar—such as the water buffalo. Encourage students to infer what is happening in the story by carefully checking the illustrations.

Give Information Talk with students about how the author, Minfong Ho, makes decisions about what to include in her story. Point out the different animals and the different illustrations that help readers infer what is happening. Remind students that authors don't just tell us what is happening; they use pictures and words to show us.

figure 6.10 *Kids write their interactive story on chart paper.*

Active Involvement Explain to students that they are going to write a story together with you. Read through *Hush!* one more time, talking about how Minfong Ho helps readers infer what is happening. After reading say, "Now let's draft our story. Let's use the pattern from the book to help us." To make sure students can identify the pattern, reread the first two pages of the story.

Help the group choose an animal for the story as well as what sound the animal makes and what it's doing. (The animal we chose was a yellow baby chick. The sound it made was "Peep, peep." For what it was doing, the kids chose pecking.) Think aloud, "What will we write first?" To begin say, "I think I'll start with 'Hush! Who's that . . .?' Watch me as I do it." Pick up the marker and write the first word as you say it slowly so that students can match the sounds with the letter you write. As you work together, encourage students to contribute their ideas for what to write.

Active Involvement (Interactive Writing) As you are composing the story out loud with students, encourage them to interact with each other as they work to write their story together and spell the words. Have volunteers take turns writing words and letters they know. Prompt them by saying, "Now you try it while I watch." Have them write one at a time using a marker as you and the other children reread the text the group composed.

In Interactive Writing the teacher fills in the letters and words the students don't know as the group writes together. Keep white stick-on correction tape close at hand to fix errors. After the story is written, students can draw illustrations that help readers infer what is happening (see Figure 6.10).

At this stage of language proficiency, students may model the text they create directly off of the book they are reading as a mentor text. When students do this, they use the words in the story as a framework for their writing.

Off You Go Tell students, "We'll put the paper with the story we wrote up on the wall so you will be able to read it. You can also write your own story during independent writing time."

5: Monitoring Meaning and Comprehension

Writers read their work aloud to find and hear their voices.

Teaching Moves

Start Up/Connection Spend some time reading aloud with students. Discuss how important it is for writers to be able to read their writing aloud and to hear their voices. Reading their writing out loud is especially important for English Language Learners. It provides them with authentic opportunities to practice their oral language and to give themselves feedback on their writing. As they read their writing aloud, point out different ways writers make their voices heard—through dialog, powerful words, point of view, and so on. Examples of author's voice can be found in the books in this lesson's Instructional Materials.

Give Information Tell students that when an author writes, he or she has a voice, just like you have a voice when you talk. Explain to students that everyone will be reading a piece of writing to someone else. The reason for doing this is to listen to yourself as you read and to see whether you can hear your author's voice. Your partner will also let you know whether she or he can hear your voice.

Say to students, "Watch me as I do it." Then read a short piece of your writing for them. Stop frequently and ask, "Can you hear my voice?" If not, ask students for suggestions and model how you change your writing to make it have more voice (for example, add dialog, Powerful Words, etc.).

> **Instructional Materials**
> - *Bear Wants More* by Karma Wilson
> - *The Cow That Went Oink* by Bernard Most
> - *The Little Mouse, the Red, Ripe Strawberry, and the Big Hungry Bear* by Don and Audrey Wood
> - *Peek! A Thai Hide-and-Seek* by Minfong Ho
> - Student writing ready to be published

Juli's Writing

A long time ago when I was six, my father taught me how to roller skate. "This will be fun!" I thought to myself as I strapped on my skates. I didn't have any idea what was going to happen.

We didn't have fancy stuff like Rollerblades or kneepads—just some hard-soled shoes, a pair of skates, a skate key, and a white pillow strapped to my back end. It was old school!

"This is fun!" I thought to myself as Daddy held my hand and I skated down the sidewalk. And then he went inside.

I clung tightly to the side of the waist-high rock wall as I started off on my own. I barely moved, two steps, and then ka-boom! Down I went on the concrete. I pulled myself back up again. Two more steps and ka-boom! again.

Over and over and over, I tried to get it. Finally, I just sat down and cried. "This is not fun," I sobbed quietly to myself.

Active Involvement Encourage students to try reading finished pieces of writing to partners. Provide a risk-free environment by allowing students to choose their partners and where they would like to sit while they read. Provide an opportunity for the partners to give each student feedback. As they listen to the writing, ask them to think about the question "Can you hear my voice in my writing?" Have them point out any places that are confusing.

Off You Go Encourage students to read to a partner whenever they are working on their writing. Keep a low-anxiety, risk-free environment for students to read with partners. As they listen to each other, ask them to give their partners suggestions about how to change the writing so that it has more voice.

Instructional Materials

- ☐ Copy of kids' Interactive Writing from Lesson 4: Inferring
- ☐ Copies of unedited anonymous student's writing
- ☐ Copies of writing for each student

6: Fix-Up Strategies

Writers revise (add, delete, and reorganize) and edit (apply correct conventions), continually seeking clarity and impact for readers. They experiment with and change overall meaning, content, wording, text organization, punctuation, and spelling.

Teaching Moves

Start Up/Connection With students reread the chart of Interactive Writing they did for the preceding Lesson 4.

Discuss the process for Interactive Writing and how everyone works together to get the story down and pays attention to the use of conventions. Use Interactive Writing to point out examples of the use of capitals, punctuation, grammar and usage, sentence variety, and spelling.

Give Information Explain to students that the purpose of conventions is to help the reader understand the writing. Refer to the Interactive Writing chart for examples. Explain that editing is checking for capitals, punctuation, grammar and usage, sentence variety, and spelling. Talk to them about how writers use editing to make their writing easier for readers to understand.

Active Involvement Show students a sample of writing done by an anonymous student. (We used the sample in Figure 6.11 that was done by a kindergartener with teacher assistance.)

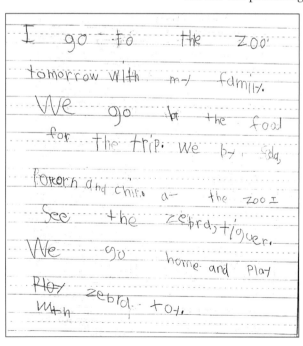

figure 6.11 *Vendie's writing sample before editing.*

I go to the zoo
tomorrow with my family.

We go by the food
for the trip. We by soda,
popcorn and chip. at the zoo I
see the zebra tiguer.
We go home and play play with zebra toy.

Work together as a group to edit the writing sample. First, discuss the use of capitals. (This writer left off a capital at the beginning of a sentence.) Then talk about punctuation. Ask them for suggestions. Be sure to point out the need for commas in a series. For grammar and usage, point out that the writer needs to add an *s* at the end of *chip*. Also explain that the spelling for *by* needs to be changed to *buy* because of the meaning of the word.

Provide individual copies of the writing sample for students. Have them sit with partners as they make editing changes on their copies. Monitor as they work to make sure they find the necessary changes (see Figure 6.12), and adjust the instructions if necessary.

Off You Go As students do first drafts of their own writing, have them work with a partner to make changes that will help the reader understand. Encourage them to check for capitals, punctuation, grammar and usage, sentence variety, and spelling in their own writing and that of their peers.

figure 6.12 *An individual student's copy of Vendie's writing as edited by using correction tape.*

Books for Teaching Strategies to Younger English Language Learners

Early Production Stage

Making Connections

A Birthday Basket for Tía by Pat Mora
Families by Ann Morris
Mice and Beans by Pam Muñoz Ryan
The Ugly Vegetables by Grace Lin
Yoko's Paper Cranes by Rosemary Wells

Asking Questions

Bedtime in the Southwest by Mona Hodgson
Chickens by Diane Snowball
How Do Dinosaurs Get Well Soon? by Jane Yolen
The Wednesday Surprise by Eve Bunting
Which Witch Is Which? by Judi Barrett

Visualizing

all the small poems and fourteen more by Valerie Worth
Creatures of the Earth, Sea, and Sky: Poems by Georgia Heard

Joseph Had a Little Overcoat by Simms Taback
There Was an Old Lady Who Swallowed a Fly by Simms Taback
The Wheels on the Bus by Paul Zelinsky

Inferring

Bear Wants More by Karma Wilson
The Cow That Went Oink by Bernard Most
George and Martha Back in Town by James Marshall
George and Martha Encore by James Marshall
George and Martha Round and Round by James Marshall
George and Martha Tons of Fun by James Marshall
George and Martha: The Complete Stories of Two Best Friends by James
  Marshall
Hush! A Thai Lullaby by Minfong Ho
The Little Mouse, the Red, Ripe Strawberry, and the Big Hungry Bear by
  Don and Audrey Wood
Peek! A Thai Hide-and-Seek by Minfong Ho

Older English Language Learners in Real Time

It never fails that science experiments provide classroom excitement. Juli was working with a small group of fifth graders to develop their oral language in English and provided opportunities for them to write using the Language Experience Approach in science. The group was investigating the question, What are the stages in a plant's life cycle?

To explore the question, students grew plants from fast-growing radish seeds. The objective was to have the plants go through a complete life cycle to produce new seeds in about forty days. Juli had students begin by filling a small flowerpot with soil. Then they placed four fast-growing radish seeds in the pot, spaced evenly apart near the rim. They covered them lightly with soil, carefully watered them, and using a dropper, added liquid houseplant fertilizer to the soil.

Next, they placed the flowerpots near a window with the blinds open to give them as much light as possible. They checked the soil every day, making sure to keep it moist but not wet. When the seeds began to sprout, students gave each tiny plant a different number to help keep track of its growth. They wrote the number on the pot near each plant.

In their science notebooks, they made charts for recoding height as the plants grew. Every time they came to work in their pullout group, they measured and recorded each plant's height. Then students made a line graph that showed each one's growth. As the plants grew, they drew pictures of them at different times and then dictated their observations to Juli. She wrote their comments next to the drawings in their science notebooks. In this way, kids used the Language Experience Approach to help them "write" about science. When the plants were about two inches (5 cm) tall, students used a red marker to make a dot on the stem just below the leaves. Each time they measured and recorded the distance between the soil and the dot, they did it at the same time of day.

But then came the excitement. The directions told them to help the plants form flowers by using cotton swabs to transfer pollen from the flower of one plant to the flower of another plant. Then they were to record their observations. Problem was—no flowers! The little radish plants just didn't bloom.

In a moment of desperation, Juli turned to an author for help. Two books by Gail Gibbons, *The Pumpkin Book* and *From Seed to Plant*, saved the day. Juli used the illustrations and the simple text to help students understand the life cycle of a plant and how the experiment might have ended. It was a great example of the importance of flexibility and the need for plenty of resources. In the end, the students learned a valuable lesson and were able to share their language experience charts, drawings, and stories about the experiment with others in their class.

Lessons for Older English Language Learners

1: Making Connections

A writer's content comes from and builds on his or her experiences.

Instructional Materials

- *Just a Minute: A Trickster Tale and Counting Book* by Yuyi Morales
- Writer's notebooks

Teaching Moves

Start Up/Connection Before reading, take a picture walk through *Just a Minute*. Talk about the illustrations and how they help you understand what is happening in the book. Bring students' attention to the counting pattern in English and Spanish, the use of the cat and the skeleton (*calavera*) in each of the illustrations, and the nature of a trickster tale (that someone is fooling someone else). Show students examples from the text to help them understand.

Give Information Read *Just a Minute: A Trickster Tale and Counting Book* with the small group. As you go through the book, have students share their thinking with partners. Tell them that authors use their experiences and what they know from their lives to write.

Active Involvement Have students work with partners to look for examples in the book of how the author, Yuyi Morales, used her experiences in her writing. One set of examples could be all the different work that Grandma Beetle had to do (sweep one house, boil two pots of tea, make three pounds of corn into tortillas, etc.). Point out the different jobs to students and have them share their own experiences with partners. Another example of how she used her experiences might be the character Señor Calavera (the skeleton). Have students share with each other and then they can share what they discussed with the group.

Off You Go As students have opportunities to write, remind them that they can use their own experiences and what they know to write their stories. Encourage students to keep a list of things they like and know about as well as their experiences in their writer's notebooks. On their lists students can include such things as animals, movies, TV shows, favorite foods, living in other countries, going to school in other countries, their families, books,

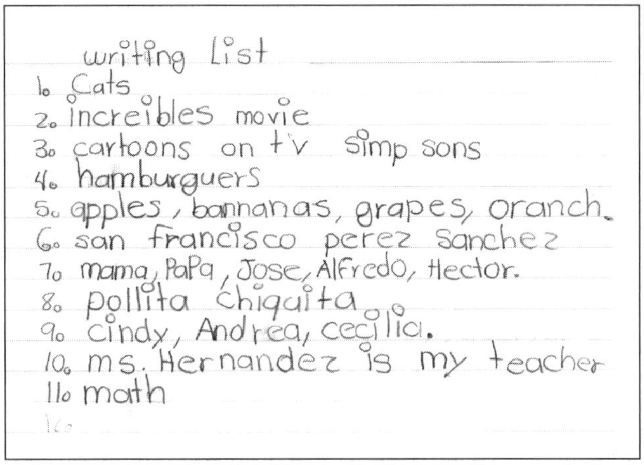

writing List
1. Cats
2. increibles movie
3. cartoons on tv simp sons
4. hamburguers
5. apples, bannanas, grapes, oranch.
6. san francisco perez sanchez
7. mama, PaPa, Jose, Alfredo, Hector.
8. pollita chiquita
9. cindy, Andrea, cecilia.
10. ms. Hernandez is my teacher
11. math

figure 6.13 *A student's list of writing ideas written independently.*

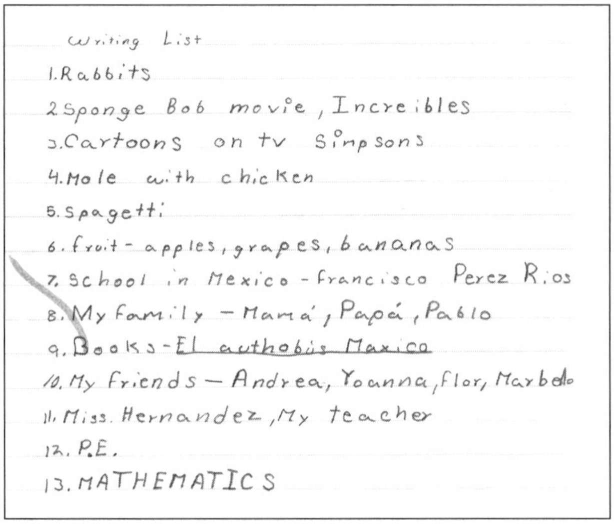

Writing List
1. Rabbits
2. Sponge Bob movie, Increibles
3. Cartoons on tv Simpsons
4. Mole with chicken
5. Spagetti
6. fruit - apples, grapes, bananas
7. School in Mexico - francisco Perez Rios
8. My family - Mamá, Papá, Pablo
9. Books - El authobús Maxico
10. My friends — Andrea, Yoanna, flor, Marbelo
11. Miss. Hernandez, My teacher
12. P.E.
13. MATHEMATICS

figure 6.14 *A list of writing ideas written with a partner.*

friends, teachers, and school subjects like P.E. (see Figures 6.13 and 6.14). This provides them with a source of easily accessible writing ideas based on their own experiences, and it eliminates the "I don't know what to write about" lament.

Instructional Materials

- *Actual Size* by Steve Jenkins
- *Red-Eyed Tree Frog* by Joy Cowley
- *What Do You Do When Something Wants to Eat You?* by Steve Jenkins
- *What Do You Do With a Tail Like This?* by Steve Jenkins

2: Asking Questions

Writers monitor their progress by asking questions about their choices as they write.

Teaching Moves

Start Up/Connection Talk to students about questions and how they help us learn information. Show students examples of questions from books like *What Do You Do With a Tail Like This?* and *Red-Eyed Tree Frog*. To integrate strategy use, see the comprehension lesson for this story in *Making Sense* (2005, p. 46).

Give Information Explain to students that some books are written to answer questions. Read through *What Do You Do When Something Wants to Eat You?* with students. Point out how each of the different animals has a

figure 6.15 *Student writing in response to "What do you do if you don't want to go fishing?"*

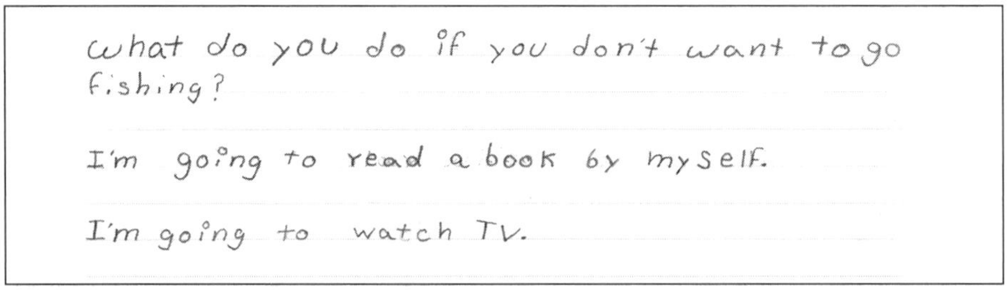

what do you do if you don't want to go fishing?

I'm going to read a book by myself.

I'm going to watch TV.

different way of protecting themselves. Show students how the author uses the different animals to answer the question that's the title of the book.

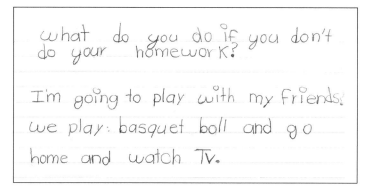

figure 6.16 *The question, "What do you do if you don't do your home-work?" encourages a student's written response.*

Active Involvement After reading through the book together, tell students that you will be making a list of questions that they might want to use as ideas for their writing. Say, "Watch me as I do it" and then list several questions on the overhead. For example, What do you do when it is time for bed? or What do you do when you want to go out-side? Invite students to add to the list you are writing by saying, "Now you give it a try." Write students' questions on the overhead.

Questions Generated by Students (with Juli's assistance)

What do you do if you don't do your homework?
What do you do if you don't want to go fishing?
What do you do when you need money?
What do you do when it is a rainy day?
What do you do when you see an animal is hurt?
What do you do when you are lost?
What do you do if you're hungry?

Off You Go Encourage students to try writing about one of the questions from the list (see Figures 6.15 and 6.16). They can use their writer's notebooks or they can try writing a draft. Allow them to work together and help each other.

3: Visualizing (Using Sensory Images)

Writers use images to explore their ideas. They constantly study mental images for direction in their pieces.

Teaching Moves

Start Up/Connection Before painting, read *The Colors of Us* with students. Talk about the different paintings in the book as you read. Have students share what they notice about the paintings.

Give Information Tell students that one of the ways writers get their ideas is through drawing and painting. Once they know what image they want, it helps them have a clear idea of what they want to write. Explain that they will be painting a watercolor portrait of themselves to help them explore their ideas. Say, "Watch me as I do it" as you get the paints, the water, and the paper

figure 6.17 *Jessica paints her portrait in the style of her favorite Japanese animated character.*

figure 6.18 *Casey also draws his inspiration from a Japanese animation.*

ready. While you do a watercolor portrait of yourself, think aloud about your ideas for the picture and the images you have.

Active Involvement Give students the opportunity to do their own portraits. Say, "Now you try it while I watch." Encourage them to talk about their ideas and images while they paint (see Figures 6.17 through 6.20).

Off You Go Continue to provide opportunities for students to explore their ideas and study their mental images with art. As students work on independent writing and other writing assignments, encourage them to draw, paint, and so on. This will assist them in organizing their thoughts.

Instructional Materials

- *The Polar Express* by Chris Van Allsburg (with tape or CD)
- White drawing paper and pencils

Lesson 4: Inferring

Writers make decisions about content inclusions/exclusions and genre/text that permit or encourage inference on the part of the reader.

Teaching Moves

Start Up/Connection Provide an opportunity for students to listen to the CD or tape for *The Polar Express* while they follow along in the book. When the tape gets to the point where it says, "I sat on Santa's knee and he asked, 'Now, what would you like for Christmas?'" have students stop listening and go no farther

figure 6.19 *Veronica's painting features her beautiful, curly hair.*

figure 6.20 *Sonia paints her portrait wearing her favorite "Baby Girl" T-shirt.*

in their books. Discuss with students how the author, Chris Van Allsburg, used the pictures and text to tell the story to this point. Have students share what they noticed about the pictures and the text with partners and then with the small group.

Give Information Tell students that writers make decisions that help readers predict what will happen in a story. Think aloud for students to model how you predict. For example, tell them, "Watch me as I do it. Look at the first page in the story. I can see that it is dark and cold and snowy, but the boy is not lying down in bed sleeping. He is awake." (As you talk, point to the appropriate places in the picture.) "I predict that he will get out of bed and look out the window." Continue giving examples of how you predict until students understand that your predictions are based on the author's text and illustrations.

Active Involvement Have students share their predictions with the group. Go through the story page by page or have them contribute their predictions at random (see Figures 6.21 and 6.22). Make sure that students indicate, by pointing or gesturing, which parts of the illustrations or text helped them predict.

Off You Go Before students listen to the end of the story, have them draw their predictions of what will happen next. They can share them with partners as they work. Encourage students to make decisions in their own stories that will help readers predict (infer).

figure 6.21 After reading part of The Polar Express *with a small group, Yoanna writes her prediction of what will come next.*

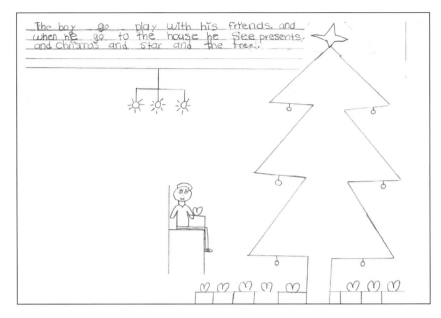

The boy go play with his friends. and when he go to the house he see presents, and chrismas and star and the tree.

figure 6.22 Cindy's prediction shows she is just moving to the early production stage of language acquisition.

A boy go home then he go living room and he see santa.

5: Monitoring Meaning and Comprehension

Writers read their work aloud to find and hear their voices.

Teaching Moves

Start Up/Connection Spend some time reading aloud with students. Discuss how important it is for writers to be able to read their writing aloud and to hear their voices. Point out different ways writers make voice heard—through dialog, powerful words, and so on. Examples of author's voice can be found in *Yo! Yes?* by Chris Raschka, *The Color of Us* by Karen Katz, and *I Hate English* by Ellen Levine.

Give Information Tell students that when an author writes, he or she has a voice, just like you have a voice when you talk. Explain to students that everyone will be reading a piece of writing to someone else. The reason for doing this is to listen to yourself as you read and to see whether you can hear your author's voice. Your partner will also let you know whether your voice can be heard.

Say to students, "Watch me as I do it." Then read a short piece of your writing for students. Stop frequently and ask, "Can you hear my voice?" If not, ask students for suggestions and model how you change your writing (add dialog, Powerful Words, etc.) to make it have more voice. Make the changes and additions to your piece of writing. Save your work for the next lesson, Fix-Up Strategies.

Juli's Writing

When I was sixteen years old, I went to take my driver's test. I wanted to get my license and I had been practicing a lot. When I got to the DMV, my father was with me. But he left me there to take my written test and then do my driving test. That meant that I had to drive the car home. But what if I didn't pass my test?

Active Involvement Encourage each student to try reading a finished piece of writing to a partner. Provide a risk-free environment by allowing students to choose their partners and where they would like to sit while they read. Provide an opportunity for the partners to give each student feedback. As they listen to the writing, ask them to think about the question, "Can you hear my voice in my writing?" Have them point out any places that are confusing.

Off You Go Encourage students to read to a partner whenever they are working on their writing. Keep a low-anxiety, risk-free environment by allowing students to choose both their own partners and where they would like to read. As students listen to each other read, ask them to give suggestions about how to change the writing (add dialog, powerful words, etc.) so that it has more voice.

6: Fix-Up Strategies

Writers revise (add, delete, and reorganize) and edit (apply correct conventions), continually seeking clarity and impact for readers. They experiment with and change overall meaning, content, wording, text organization, punctuation, and spelling.

Teaching Moves

Start Up/Connection Tell students that you are going to read them a short story that you have written. Then give them a paper with the unedited version of it at the top of the page and the edited version at the bottom. If you have already taught the Monitoring Meaning and Comprehension lesson, you can use the revised version of your writing from that lesson for this activity.

Juli's Revised Story

When I was sixteen years old—I remember that my birthday was on a Thursday—I went to take my driver's test. I wanted to get my driver's

> **Instructional Materials**
> - Copies of unedited and edited versions of teacher's story
> - Copies of unedited anonymous student's writing
> - Post-it correction tape
> - Copies of students' writing

license, and I had been practicing a lot. At the beginning, I wasn't very good. But after four months of driving with my dad on the weekends, I had improved.

I had to go to the DMV to take my test. When I got there, my father was with me. He drove me over in the car. But he left me there to take my written test and my driving test. That meant that I had to drive the car home.

I got really scared. What if I didn't pass my test?

Give Information Compare the edited and unedited versions of your story. Consider removing some of the punctuation from the unedited one to provide more of a contrast between the two versions. Show students the changes you made in the story's edited version. Ask them which version they think is easier to understand. Explain that editing is checking for capitals, punctuation, grammar and usage, and spelling. Talk to them about how writers use editing to make their writing easier for readers to understand. Show them the differences between the two versions of the story.

Active Involvement Show students a sample of writing done by an anonymous student. We use the following story. Provide them with individual copies of the unedited story and white correction tape. (See Appendix for a one-page copy of the story.)

When I Was Small

When I was small I learn to use a skateboard with my brother. He was putting me on it and I was moving but I fell on the ground but I try it over and over again. So when my bother came I was sad because I could not make it. I had bruises and didn't like it so I went to tell my brother if I could quit but said "No, no you won't". So when he showed me when I was on the skateboard so I got better and better on my skateboard. Os I saw hem doing cool tricks and I wonted to do that and he help me. So when I grow I got better and better at my skateboard and that's how I learned how to use a skateboard.

Use the first sentence to model how to edit. Read through slowly, checking for one convention. We edit for only one thing at a time, choosing capitalization, punctuation, grammar and usage, or spelling. Often the first time we edit, we check for capitalization. By editing for only one convention at a time, we can use one sample of student writing for many different editing mini-lessons. It also helps students understand that the purpose of editing is to make what's been written easier for readers to understand.

Give them a chance to try editing while you watch. Remember to have them edit for only one convention—the one that you have modeled for them. They can use the correction tape to make their changes. Have them share with partners as they work. Monitor every student to make sure they find all the necessary changes, and adjust the instructions if necessary.

Off You Go As students do their own drafts, have them work with partners to make changes that will help readers understand. Encourage them to check for just one convention at a time. By working with partners they can edit their own writing or that of their peers.

Books for Teaching Strategies to Older English Language Learners

Early Production Stage

Making Connections

Grandma and Me at the Flea by Juan Felipe Herrera
Henry's First-Moon Birthday by Lenore Look
I Hate English by Ellen Levine
Just a Minute: A Trickster Tale and Counting Book by Yuyi Morales
Work by Ann Morris

Asking Questions

Actual Size by Steve Jenkins
Amos and Boris by William Steig
DK Readers Twisters (Stage 2, Beginning to Read Alone) by Kate Hayden
Red-eyed Tree Frog by Joy Cowley
What Do You Do When Something Wants to Eat You? by Steve Jenkins
What Do You Do With a Tail Like This? by Steve Jenkins

Visualizing

The Bug in Teacher's Coffee: And Other School Poems by Kalli Dakos
The Color of Us by Karen Katz
A Movie in My Pillow by Jorge Argueta
Night of the Gargoyles by Eve Bunting

Inferring

Jumanji by Chris Van Allsburg
Just a Dream by Chris Van Allsburg
The Polar Express by Chris Van Allsburg
The Stranger by Chris Van Allsburg
The Wreck of the Zephyr by Chris Van Allsburg

figure 7.1 (top) Johnny, Bopau, and Vichneath visualize their stories by drawing before writing.

figure 7.2 (center) Drina and Patty base drawing for their writing on a mentor text.

figure 7.3 (bottom) A graphic organizer helps Gladys organize her ideas before writing.

7 SPEECH EMERGENCE

After kids have moved through the early stages of language proficiency, they enter the speech emergence stage. This happens when they can communicate more freely and are speaking in short phrases and sentences. Participating in role-plays and games motivates and encourages English Language Learners to take risks with language and feel comfortable speaking.

At this stage, there is also a noticeable increase in listening comprehension. Students can be asked to predict what will happen next, retell stories and informational text, recall a sequence of events, and summarize short selections. Describing what they are reading and restating information they have learned encourages them to use language.

They are also beginning to use English for academic purposes, facilitating participation in many of the mainstream subjects. Listening, speaking, reading, and writing expand out into content areas such as science and history.

Students define terms, categorize what they are learning, and begin to understand cause/effect and compare/contrast text structures. Lessons continue to expand students' vocabulary, and class activities are designed to encourage higher, more complex levels of language use.

Opportunities for students to interact with each other and negotiate for meaning are critical at this stage. For example, ask ELLs how and why questions that elicit short responses. Involve them in working with partners and in small-group activities. What's important is to keep kids actively involved in learning and using language.

Younger English Language Learners in Real Time

Juli makes a wonderful discovery on the shelf at a local bookstore. *Guji Guji,* written by Chih-Yuan Chen, is a three-time winner of the prestigious Hsin Yi Picture Book Award. It's the perfect book to teach writers, particularly fiction writers, how "to be aware of far more detail than they reveal in the texts they compose. This encourages readers to infer by drawing conclusions, making critical judgments, predicting, and connecting to other texts and experiences" (Keene).

On Monday she gathers the small group at a table and reads the story aloud. As they work their way through the book, she models where she makes inferences and how the writer helped her infer. Juli points out her favorite page and reads, "Mother Duck didn't notice. (She was reading.)" She talks about how the illustration helps her infer that there's going to be a surprise for Mother Duck.

After a few pages, Juli comes to another inference. "I can tell that Guji Guji is a different kind of duck," she says. To show where she makes her inference, she reads from the text: "Guji Guji always learned more quickly than the others. He was bigger and stronger, too."

Toward the end of the book, she stops on the page where three large rocks drop from the bridge and models her thinking. "Here's a place where the author uses sounds to help me infer that the crocodiles' teeth were broken. This is how the author writes it: 'The crocodiles bit down. Crack! Crack! Crack! went their pointed teeth.'"

As they finish reading the book, Juli reminds the small group that they can use some of the same techniques in their own writing to help readers infer. She encourages the kids to "give it a try" in their writer's notebooks by using sounds, pictures, and descriptive words to help readers infer.

Lessons for Younger English Language Learners

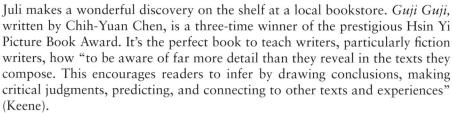

1: Making Connections

Writers think about and use what they know about genre, text structure, and conventions as they write.

Instructional Materials

- *Too Many Tamales* by Gary Soto
- Personal narratives familiar to kids

Teaching Moves

Start Up/Connection With students, talk about what they know about writing personal narratives. Discuss how they are stories about things that happen in their lives and/or things that happen in their families. As models, provide samples of personal narratives, such as the following, that they probably have already read.

> *A Birthday Basket for Tía* by Pat Mora
> *Buzz* by Janet Wong
> *Hide & Seek* by Janet Wong
> *Mice and Beans* by Pam Muñoz Ryan (fictional narrative)
> *In My Family/En mi familia* by Carmen Lomas Garza
> *One Small Girl* by Jennifer Chan
> *The Ugly Vegetables* by Grace Lin
> *The Wednesday Surprise* by Eve Bunting

Also talk with students about what they know about conventions. Help them remember that conventions include capitalization, punctuation, grammar and usage, and spelling. Remind students that the purpose of conventions is to help readers understand the writing. Have them go through the personal narratives they are familiar with and, working with partners, look for examples of different conventions.

Discuss the importance of dialog and how to punctuate it too. Provide examples from the personal narratives to serve as models for creating dialog.

Give Information Explain to students that when writers are working, they are thinking about more than one thing while they write. Writers think about how they will tell their story—what genre they will use (for example, personal narrative)—and what conventions they will use to help readers understand.

Active Involvement Read aloud *Too Many Tamales*. As you read, think aloud about how the author, Gary Soto, tells his story as a personal narrative. Encourage students to watch for dialog and point out places where he uses it to have the characters speak for themselves. They can work with partners or in a small group. Also have them share what they notice about how dialog is punctuated.

Dialog Samples from Too Many Tamales

Maria	"I'll wear the ring for just a minute," she said to herself.
Maria's mother	"Go get your father for this part," she said.
Maria	"The ring!" she screamed. Everyone stared at her.
Dolores	"What ring?" Delores asked.

Off You Go While students work on writing personal narratives, have them share how they are using dialog with partners. Once they have finished writing a draft, have them read it to partners and get feedback on how the dialog helps to tell the story. Students can use this feedback to revise their pieces.

Casey typed the following personal narrative on the computer using Microsoft Word and scanned in a photograph of his splendid new house:

When I went to my new house it was cleaner than my old house I like my new house me and my step brother we have a bed room now. We have to sleep in the living room when we were at the old house. Me and my step brother slept at my uncle house we were are playing game and drawing all day. My uncle and my other little uncle and big uncle and my step brother we were playing Resident Evil in real life my uncle was the zombie. He act like a real zombie and the master was hard to beat. My mom said lets go home to are new house. When we went to are new house I was setting my clothes so I did because so I could be clean and so I could play with my little sister. One years later in 2005 now my little sister is 9 months.

2: Asking Questions

Writers ask questions of other writers in order to confirm their choices and make revisions.

Teaching Moves

Start Up/Connection Read through *Apple Pie 4th of July* with students to remind them of the story or, if this is the first reading, to familiarize them with the content. To integrate strategy use, see the comprehension lesson for this story in *Making Sense* (2005, p. 57).

Give Information Tell students that one way writers revise and make it easier to understand their writing is to ask other writers questions. They use that information to make revisions—changes that help the reader understand the text. If you have taught the comprehension lesson in *Making Sense* previously, refer students to the Questioning Web they created for *Apple Pie 4th of July*. If not, have them work with you to make a list of questions that they think would help the writer.

Jessica and Jenny's Questions for Apple Pie 4th of July

Why did the author write, "Christmas is the only day we close"?
Why did the author use the senses to describe things like "I hear the parade" and "I smell apple pie"?
There are no quotation marks for dialog. Why didn't she use them?
Why does she repeat, "I hear the parade"?
Why does the author use the time like one o'clock, two o'clock, three o'clock, etc. to tell her story?
Why did she choose to write about the Fourth of July?

Active Involvement Have students pick a piece of writing to share with a partner. Have them read the pieces to each other and ask each other questions. Then have students make revisions to their writing. Have them make their revisions with colored pencil or ink to show what they revised. Have them share their thinking about how they revised and why with the small group.

Instructional Materials
- *Apple Pie 4th of July* by Janet Wong
- Questioning Web (*Making Sense*, 2005, p. 58)

Off You Go While students write other pieces, as a part of revising their writing, have them work with partners to ask each other questions about what they are doing. During writing conferences with you, either in a small group or individually, encourage students to share their questions and how they helped them revise their writing.

3: Visualizing (Using Sensory Images)

Writers use images to explore their ideas. They consciously study mental images for direction in their pieces.

Teaching Moves

Start Up/Connection Talk with students about their experiences before they started school. Model by thinking aloud about your own experiences before you went to school. Have them share their experiences with partners and then with the small group. To integrate strategy use, see the comprehension lesson for this story in *Making Sense* (2005, p. 58).

Give Information Explain to students that writers use their own images to explore ideas. As they write, they study mental images for direction in their pieces. Read aloud *Calling the Doves/El canto de las palomas* with the small group. Think aloud about the author's ideas and how he uses his own images to tell his story.

Share a piece of writing about your experiences before you went to school with your students. Talk to them about your images and how they helped you tell your story.

figure 7.4 *Vichneath's image of her sisters at the park, which she drew first, matches her writing.*

Juli Writes About Her Experiences

I was born in Oregon. My family moved to Arizona when I was about three years old. First we lived in Phoenix. When I was about five, we moved to Tucson.

Sometime that year I got sick. When it was time to go to first grade, I stayed home in bed—sick. My mother taught me to read and write. She'd sit on the edge of my bed listening to me read the *Little House on the Prairie* books by Laura Ingalls Wilder. Toward the end of the year, I had my tonsils out and things started to get better. When I finally got well and could go to school, everything seemed so strange.

Active Involvement Have students draw a picture of an image they have from before they went to school. Then ask them to write about the image. Have them share with partners how the image helps them write their story.

Off You Go While students are writing in their writer's notebooks and during independent writing time, encourage them to use images to tell their stories (see Figures 7.4 and 7.5). In addition, provide *The Upside Down Boy* for students to read; this is the sequel to *Calling the Doves.*

figure 7.5 *To help Bopau add more details to her story, we first encourage her to add more details to her picture.*

4: Inferring

Writers, particularly fiction and poetry writers, are aware of far more detail than they reveal in the texts they compose. This encourages readers to infer by drawing conclusions, making critical judgments, predicting, and connecting to other texts and experiences.

Teaching Moves

Start Up/Connection Discuss with students what they know about farms. Go over the different animals and their purposes. For example, cows give milk and hens lay eggs. Have students discuss what a farmer does with partners. Then have them share with the small group. To provide comprehensible input, be sure books and other materials, such as the following, about farms are available. Some others that would provide background are listed in Chapter 5, "Preproduction;" however, the ones noted here and there are not the only materials available about farms.

"Barnyard Dance" from *Rhinoceros TAP, The Book and the CD,* by Sandra Boynton
Farm Animals (DK Lift-the-Flap book)
Old MacDonald Had a Farm, illustrated by Carol Jones

> **Instructional Materials**
> ☐ *Click, Clack, Moo: Cows That Type* **by Doreen Cronin**

Rosie's Walk (big book version) by Pat Hutchins
Who Says Quack? by Jerry Smith

Give Information Tell students that writers encourage readers to infer by drawing conclusions, making critical judgments, predicting, and connecting to other texts and experiences. Read aloud the book as you model for students by pointing out the places you infer in the story and what it is that the author and illustrator did to help you infer.

Examples of Inferring in Click, Clack, Moo: Cows That Type

Showing with pictures instead of telling with words (last page)
Using typed notes, written by the cows, instead of just "telling" readers what is happening
Using sounds like "Click, clack, moo" to help readers infer that the cows are typing

Active Involvement Give copies of the book to students to use in pairs. Have them read through it again, looking for examples of how the author helps them infer. They can simply talk to each other or they can organize their inferences by categories such as drawing conclusions, making critical judgments, predicting, and connecting to other texts and experiences.

Off You Go While students write in writer's notebooks and in drafts, encourage them to think about what they can do as authors to help their readers infer. Point out that they can use the same techniques in their writing that Doreen Cronin used in *Click, Clack, Moo: Cows That Type*. They might try including notes or sounds or using pictures to help readers infer.

5: Determining Importance in Nonfiction

Writers observe their world and record what they believe is significant.

Teaching Moves

Start Up/Connection To help students build background about informational texts, share a variety of books by Gail Gibbons. With younger students, we often use *The Pumpkin Book, From Seed to Plant,* or *Sharks* to link to what they are learning about systems in living things. This includes the life cycle stages of an animal or a plant. As you read aloud for the kids, model by thinking aloud about what Gibbons does to help readers get information from her books.

Give Information Explain to students that authors like Gail Gibbons write informational texts to teach others. Show students three different layouts or formats that can be used to teach information: diagrams, fact sheets, and "how-to" pages. Look through the books with students and point out examples of each of the three ways to teach information. For example, in *The Pumpkin Book,* show students the diagrams of the parts of the pumpkin plant (for example, stamen, pollen, male flower, stigma, female flower) and the page for "How to Carve a Pumpkin." The last page of the book contains facts about pumpkins as well as directions for "How to Dry Pumpkin Seeds."

Instructional Materials

- *From Seed to Plant* by Gail Gibbons
- *The Pumpkin Book* by Gail Gibbons
- *Sharks* by Gail Gibbons
- White drawing paper and pencils

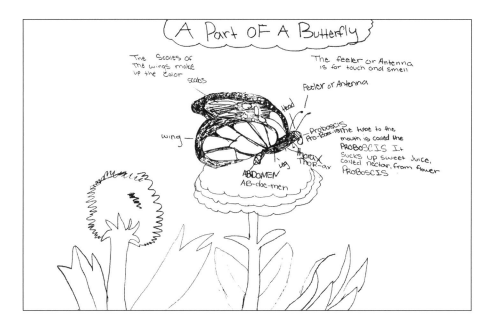

figure 7.6 *This diagram includes labels and explanations of the parts of a butterfly.*

Active Involvement Give students large sheets of white drawing paper and pencils. Have them choose one of the three layouts for teaching information and design a page. Encourage them to use a book by Gail Gibbons as a mentor text to provide models for their work. Explain that they will be sharing their pages with the others in the small group in order to confirm their choices and to use questions to help them make revisions.

We have them do just one page because it is easier for students to begin writing informational texts this way rather than to do a booklet with several pages. It helps them be more successful with writing informational text (see Figures 7.6, 7.7, and 7.8).

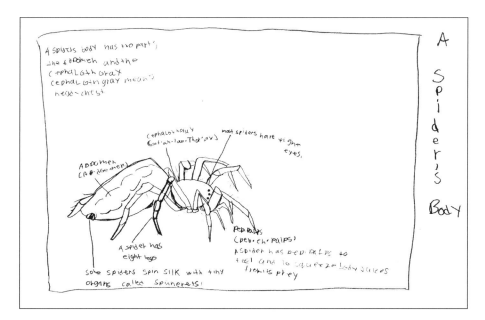

figure 7.7 *Spiders always provide motivation for writing informational text.*

figure 7.8 *This informational how-to page is designed to teach others how to plant and grow seeds.*

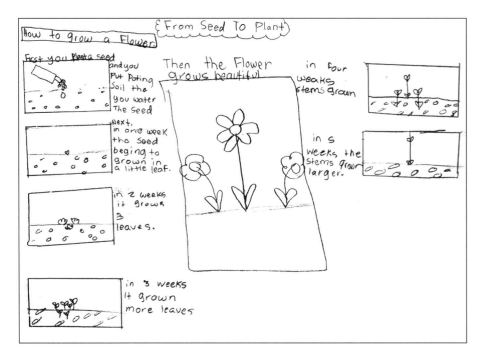

Off You Go While students finish their informational pages, have them share with partners. Encourage them to continue using diagrams, how-to pages, and lists of facts in their writer's notebooks and other informational writing.

Instructional Materials

▢ *Big Moon Tortilla* by Joy Cowley

6: Synthesizing

Writers make global and focal plans for their writing before and during the drafting process. They use their knowledge of text elements, such as character, setting, conflict, sequence of events, and resolution, to create a structure for their writing.

Teaching Moves

Start Up/Connection Talk with students about what they know about character, setting, conflict, sequence of events, and resolution (see the definitions that follow). Provide background information, if necessary, by giving kids books they are already familiar with to search for examples while they work with partners.

Suggested Books to Use

Abuela by Arthur Dorros
Apple Pie 4th of July by Janet Wong
Calling the Doves by Juan Felipe Herrera
Click, Clack, Moo: Cows That Type by Doreen Cronin
Dim Sum for Everyone by Grace Lin
The Good Luck Cat by Joy Harjo
Juan Bobo—Four Folktales from Puerto Rico Retold by Carmen
  Bernier-Grand

Mama and Papa Have a Store by Amelia Lau Carling
My Name Is Yoon by Helen Recorvitz
Too Many Tamales by Gary Soto
The Trip Back Home by Janet Wong
The Upside Down Boy by Juan Felipe Herrera

Encarta World Dictionary's Definitions of Terms

Character *Character* is "the set of qualities that make somebody or something distinctive, especially somebody's qualities of mind and feeling." These can be shown through the character's actions, speech, and appearance; also by the comments of other characters or of the author.

Setting The *setting* is "the surrounding or environment in which something exists." It includes the place and the time period in which the story takes place and may or may not be important to the story.

Conflict *Conflict* is "the opposition between or among characters or forces in a literary work that shapes or motivates the action of a plot." Sometimes it is called the problem.

Sequence of events Plot is "the story or *sequence of event*s in a narrated or presented work such as a novel, play, or movie." It includes chronological order, flashback, flash forward, and time lapse.

Resolution The *resolution* is the solution to the conflict.

Give Information Explain to students that writers make plans for their writing and use text elements—character, setting, conflict, sequence of events, and resolution—to give their writing structure. Read aloud *Big Moon Tortilla* with the small group. As you read the story, think aloud about where and how you identify the text elements.

Active Involvement After reading, go back over the story with students. Have each one work with a partner to identify the text elements in the story (see examples in the table). Have each set of partners share what they find with the small group.

Text Element Examples from Big Moon Tortilla

Characters	Marta Enos
	Grandmother
Setting	desert
	a fussing wind was blowing
	Grandmother's house
	the cookhouse
Conflict	ruined homework
	broken glasses
	grief and tears as hot as chili peppers
	"The dogs ate my homework and I can't see to do anymore!"

figure 7.9 *This student thinks a graphic organizer is helpful for writing her story, "Because you can get ideas from this."*

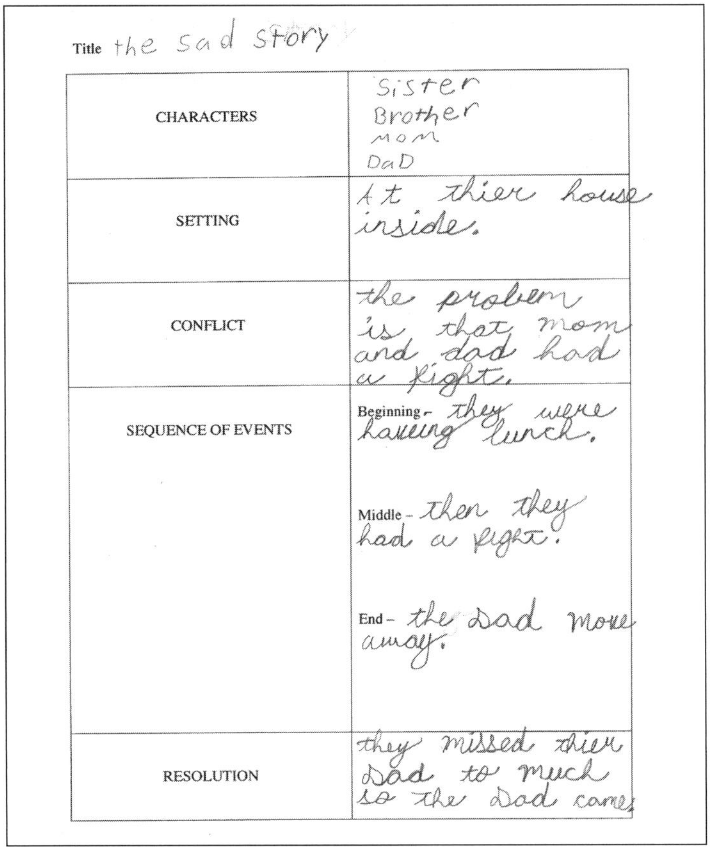

Title	the sad story
CHARACTERS	sister Brother mom DaD
SETTING	At thier house inside.
CONFLICT	the problem is that mom and dad had a fight.
SEQUENCE OF EVENTS	Beginning— they were haveing lunch. Middle— then they had a fight. End— the Dad move away.
RESOLUTION	they missed thier Dad to much so the Dad came

Sequence of events	*Beginning*—finished her homework Grandmother making tortillas thinking of tortillas
	Middle—running and knocked over the table homework papers went out the window and all over the village chased the homework papers dogs tore and chewed papers into trash broke her glasses cried
	End—Marta decided to be an eagle and danced.
Resolution	Grandmother said, "Little problems, too small for a big rainstorm." Grandmother fixed her glasses. Grandmother sang a healing song and told a story. Grandmother made a new tortilla. Marta danced.

Off You Go While students work on narrative writing, encourage them to reflect on how they can use text elements, such as character, setting, conflict, sequence of events, and resolution, to help structure their writing. Provide graphic organizers for students to use if they choose (see Figure 7.9).

7: Monitoring Meaning and Comprehension

Writers monitor their composition process to ensure that their text makes sense for their intended audience at the word, sentence, and text level.

Instructional Materials

☐ **Samples of writing from younger students**

Teaching Moves

Start Up/Connection Have students select a piece of writing. Give them an opportunity to reread it and reflect about it with a partner.

Give Information Explain to students that one of the ways writers make sure their texts make sense for their intended audience is to wait several days or weeks and reread what they have written. As they reread their work, writers think to themselves, "Does it make sense?" If they find that there are places where the text is confusing, they revise, rewrite, and rework it to get it to make sense.

Active Involvement Have students reread a piece of writing and think about the question, "Does it make sense?" Have them locate several places where they can make changes to make the meaning clearer. Have them share their papers with partners. Then encourage them to read each other's work and ask the question, "Does it make sense?"

Off You Go From time to time, encourage students to read back through their writing and ask themselves, "Does it make sense?" They can use this as a way to learn how to make sure that their texts make sense for the intended audience (see Figures 7.10 and 7.11).

figure 7.10 *(below, left) The "Insect Poem" gives students a chance to think about how a text makes sense for its intended audience.*

figure 7.11 *(below, right) This story about Pookie offers an example of how a picture helps the audience make sense of the writing.*

Insect poem

insects live anywere

its a mess insct

live anywere they want.

This is my dog, pookie. He love us when he was little, He was so cute and he like are food too. My sister was puting pookie in her hand, He was sleeping in the couch. We put him in the cage and I was sleeping like a Baby.

8: Fix-Up Strategies

Writers revise (add, delete, and reorganize) and edit (apply correct conventions), continually seeking clarity and impact for readers. They experiment with and change overall meaning, content, wording, text organization, punctuation, and spelling.

Teaching Moves

Start Up/Connection Begin by reading aloud *What Time Is It, Mr. Crocodile?* with students. Think aloud about how the crocodile is changing his thinking about the monkeys as you read. Have kids role-play the different scenes from the book, choosing roles as the monkeys or the crocodile.

Give Information Explain to students that writers constantly revise and edit their work to make it easier to understand and remember. One way they do this is to revise and edit lists that they make. Point out the crocodile's list at the beginning of the book. Talk about what's on the list and how that shows you what the crocodile is thinking.

Active Involvement Read through the book again with students. Have them look at the list at the end and work with partners to decide why the crocodile made revisions. Encourage them to share their ideas with the small group.

figure 7.12 *(below, left) A "List of Music" in a writer's notebook encourages the student to revisit, revise, and rework, looking for writing ideas.*

figure 7.13 *(below, right) Over a period of time, Veronica revised her list of foods, including the addition of junk food and veggies.*

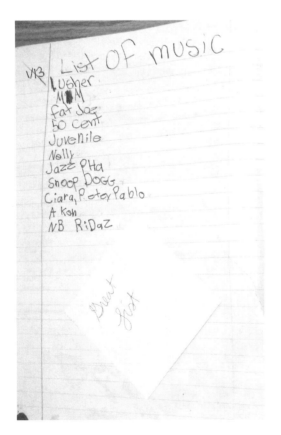

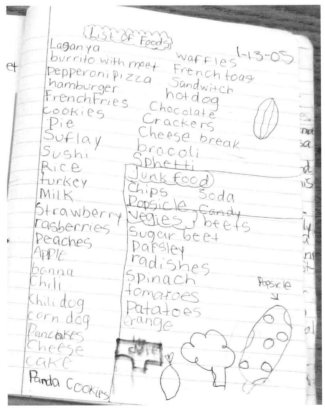

Off You Go While students work in their writer's notebooks, encourage them to keep lists of things. They can return frequently to these lists to revise and edit them as their thinking changes (see Figures 7.12 and 7.13). Lists can also serve as ideas for writing.

Books for Teaching Strategies to Younger English Language Learners

Speech Emergence Stage

Making Connections

Amelia's Road by Linda Altman
Books by Kevin Henkes (see Children's Literature in Resources)
Dim Sum for Everyone by Grace Lin
Hannah is My Name by Belle Yang
My Name Is Yoon by Helen Recorvitz
Too Many Tamales by Gary Soto
Wild About Books by Judy Sierra

Asking Questions

Apple Pie 4th of July by Janet Wong
Mama and Papa Have a Store by Amelia Lau Carling
Spiders' Secrets (DK Readers) by Richard Platt
What Lives in a Shell? by Kathleen Wiedner Zoehfeld
What Makes Day and Night? by Franklin Branley

Visualizing

Abuela by Arthur Dorros
Calling the Doves by Juan Felipe Herrera
Sky Scrape/City Scape: Poems of City Life selected by Jane Yolen
This Is the House That Jack Built by Simms Taback
The Upside Down Boy by Juan Felipe Herrera

Inferring

Click, Clack, Moo: Cows That Type by Doreen Cronin
The Good Luck Cat by Joy Harjo
Juan Bobo—Four Folktales from Puerto Rico Retold by Carmen Bernier-Grand
The Legend of the Hummingbird: A Tale from Puerto Rico by Michael Rose Ramirez
Liang and the Magic Paint Brush by Hitz Demi

Determining Importance in Nonfiction

Finding the Titanic (Hello Reader series) by Robert D. Ballard
How Mountains Are Made (Let's Read-and-Find Out About Science) by Kathleen Zoehfeld

Hungry, Hungry Sharks (Step into Reading Books) by Joanne Cole
The Moon Book by Gail Gibbons
National Geographic Kids magazine
Sharks by Gail Gibbons

Synthesizing

Big Moon Tortilla by Joy Cowley
The Great Kapok Tree by Lynne Cherry
Napí by Antonio Ramírez
Stellaluna by Janell Cannon
The Trip Back Home by Janet Wong
Fix-Up Strategies by Judy Sierra
What Time Is It, Mr. Crocodile? by Judy Sierra

Older English Language Learners in Real Time

Juli was going crazy as she searched for a way to get kids to incorporate dialog into their writing. The idea was for them to understand the importance of voice in writing and see that by using dialog they can help the reader hear their special writer's voice. After working with the whole class for several days, she began to target individual kids during writing conferences.

First, she asked them to show her examples of dialog that they had used. José's example came from his writing about learning how to skateboard. He shared what his brother said: "No, no, no! You can't do it that way!"

Casey's dialog example from his writing talked about his baby sister and how she makes only sounds, no words. "Ooh, ohh, ga-ga, whoo, whoo!"

During Steven's writing conference, he shared what his older brother said when he wouldn't go to bed: "Stop playing those stupid video games!"

But it was Viviana who needed the most help. Her writing piece, "Finding a Baby," showed that she was very confused about how to use dialog and how to punctuate it. So Juli continued one-on-one instruction with Viviana to teach her how to use dialog. During the conference time, she read other students' writing to Viviana and evaluated it for how dialog was used. In this way the student learned that there were many ways to write realistic fiction narratives.

As they worked together, Juli asked Viviana to think about the different speakers in the conversation. She told her, "Watch me as I do it" and wrote her own snippet of dialog. Then she asked Viviana to do it. "Now, you try it while I watch," she said as Vivian used highlighters to indicate the speakers, using a different colored pen for each speaker. This allowed her to see how conversations are formatted.

To improve, she also needed to produce other pieces of writing that included dialog. So Juli planned a mini-lesson that included reading aloud models of dialog using literature from a collection of realistic fiction—*Every Living Thing* by Cynthia Rylant. She wanted to immerse Viviana, and the rest of the class, in the genre. The goal was to make a connection between reading and writing by reading and using realistic fiction, such as Rylant's book, as a model for dialog.

Lessons for Older English Language Learners

1: Making Connections

Writers think about and use what they know about genre, text structure, and conventions as they write.

Instructional Materials

- *I Love Saturdays y domingos* by Alma Flor Ada

Teaching Moves

Start Up/Connection With students, talk about what they know about writing personal narratives. Discuss how they are true stories about things that happen in their lives and/or things that happen in their families.

Also talk with students about what they know about conventions. Help them remember that conventions include capitalization, punctuation, grammar and usage, and spelling. Remind students that the purpose of conventions is to help readers understand the writing. Also, discuss the importance of dialog and how to punctuate it.

Give Information Explain to students that when writers are working they are thinking about more than one thing as they write. Writers think about how they will tell their story—what genre they will use (for example, personal narrative)—and what conventions they will use to help readers understand.

Active Involvement Read aloud *I Love Saturdays y domingos*. As you read, think aloud about how the author, Alma Flor Ada, tells her story as a personal narrative. Encourage students to watch for dialog and point out places where she uses it to have the characters speak for themselves. They can share with partners or the small group. Also have them share what they notice about how dialog is punctuated.

> ### Dialog Samples *from* I Love Saturdays y domingos
>
> I say, "Hi, Grandpa! Hi, Grandma!" as I walk in.
> And they say, "Hello, sweetheart! How are you? Hello, darling!"
>
> Grandma asks me, "Do you like them sweetheart?"
> And I answer, "Oh, yes, Grandma, I love them!"

Off You Go While students work on writing personal narratives, have them share how they are using dialog with partners. Once they have finished writing a draft, have them read it to each other and get feedback on how dialog helps to tell the story. Students can use this feedback to revise their pieces.

2: Asking Questions

Writers ask questions of other writers in order to confirm their choices and make revisions.

Instructional Materials

- *The Moon Book* by Gail Gibbons
- *Stargazers* by Gail Gibbons
- White drawing paper and pencils

Teaching Moves

Start Up/Connection To help students build background about informational texts, share a variety of books by Gail Gibbons. With older students, we often use *Stargazers* and *The Moon Book* to tie in to science and their study of astronomy or *From Seed to Plant* and *Pumpkins* to link to what they are learning about systems in living things.

Give Information Explain to students that authors like Gibbons write informational texts to teach others. Show students three different layouts or formats that can be used to teach information: diagrams, fact sheets, and "how-to" pages. Look through the books with students and point out examples of each of the three ways to teach information.

For example, in *The Moon Book,* show students the diagrams of the distance between the Earth and the Moon, the page for "How to make a sun 'projector' to see a picture of a solar eclipse," and "More Moon Facts" on the last page of the book. You may also point out additional ways to teach information such as the time line used for the "Stargazing History" at the end of *Stargazers.*

To model how to ask writers questions about informational texts that will help them revise, ask, "Does this make sense?" or "What does the author want us to learn?" or "How can the author make it easier to understand?" Work with students to generate a list of questions—similar to the following—to help writers revise, then post it for students to refer to.

Questions Generated by Students to Help Writers Revise

How can I tell what this writing is about?
Where's the title?
What information do you want the reader to learn?
Why did you ＿＿＿＿＿?
Does this make sense?
How can you make it easier to understand?

figure 7.14 *Rosa and Patty confer about their informational texts.*

Active Involvement Give students large sheets of white drawing paper and pencils. Have them choose one of the three layouts for teaching information and design a page. Encourage students to use a book by Gail Gibbons as a mentor text to provide models for their work. Explain that they will be sharing their pages with the others in the small group to confirm their choices and use questions to help them make revisions.

We have students do just one page because it is easier for them to begin writing informational texts this way rather than to do a booklet with several pages. It helps them be more successful with writing informational text.

Off You Go While students finish their informational pages, have them share with partners (see Figure 7.14). Have them ask each other questions to revise their writing and to confirm their choices and make changes. Have them refer to the list of questions they generated as they work together.

Instructional Materials

■ *A Poke in the I: A Collection of Concrete Poems* selected by Paul B. Janeczko
■ White drawing paper

3: Visualizing (Using Sensory Images)

Writers use images to explore their ideas. They consciously study mental images for direction in their pieces.

Teaching Moves

Start Up/Connection Together with the small group, look through the collection of concrete poems in *A Poke in the I*. If possible, provide a copy for each student. Give students plenty of opportunity to go through the poems with partners or the small group and to share what they notice in them.

Give Information Tell students that writers use their mental images to help them write poems. Writers who do concrete poems are often referred to as visual artists.

To explain concrete poems to students, read them the blurb on the inside of the book's front cover: "The words in a concrete poem may wiggle about, curve around, or hurtle down the page but they will always startle and delight the eye." Show them examples from the book to illustrate how the words move all over the page. The "Notes from the Editor" section may also be helpful. It starts by saying, "Concrete poems are different from regular poems, in fact they're a lot more playful, as you might guess from the title of this book."

Active Involvement Provide opportunities for students to write their own concrete poems. Allow them to work in the way that suits them best. They may want to write the words first and then use their mental images to help them create a poem, or they might draw first to get mental images down on paper (see Figures 7.15 and 7.16).

figure 7.15 *José relies on his mental images to get direction for "Bear Power," his concrete poem.*

Off You Go Make many collections of poems available on an ongoing basis so that students have the opportunity to read and visualize through poetry. Encourage them to work on poems as a part of their time for writing in writer's notebooks, during independent writing, or while writing at home. A

figure 7.16 *Oscar's image of a waterfall shapes his poem.*

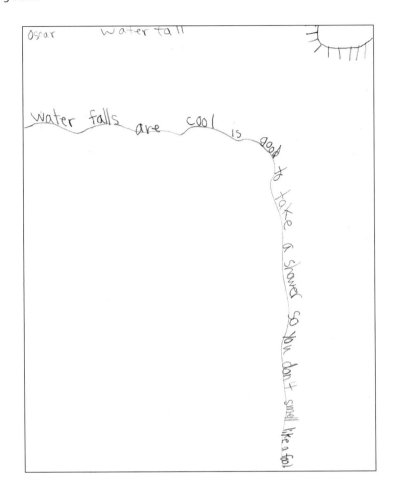

class poetry anthology for which all students choose poems they have written to include helps build motivation for writing and provides additional models for students.

4: Inferring

Writers, particularly fiction and poetry writers, are aware of far more detail than they reveal in the texts they compose. This encourages readers to infer by drawing conclusions, making critical judgments, predicting, and connecting to other texts and experiences.

Teaching Moves

Start Up/Connection Provide a variety of historical fiction picture books for students to look through and discuss with partners. For suggestions, refer to the *Notable Children's Trade Books in the Field of Social Studies* list compiled annually by the Children's Book Council in cooperation with the National Council for the Social Studies (NCSS). While they browse through the books, encourage students to share what they notice about historical fiction or any prior knowledge that they have.

Instructional Materials

- *The Firekeeper's Son* by Linda Sue Park
- Historical fiction picture books—see *Notable Children's Trade Books in the Field of Social Studies* at http://www.socialstudies.org/resources/notable/; for example, *Tenzin's Deer: A Tibetan Tale* by Barbara Soros and *Monkey for Sale* by Sanna Stanley

Give Information Tell students that in historical fiction the characters, plot, and setting are fictional, but the time period is true. Explain to students that they will be reading a historical fiction text, *The Firekeeper's Son,* and thinking about how the author helps them infer. To help their readers infer, writers do not use all the details that they know; they encourage readers to think for themselves by giving clues.

Before you read the story, turn to the end of the book and read and discuss the "Author's Note" with students to provide background information about Korea during the early 1800s. As they read along with you, they need to be aware of the importance of the time period to the story.

Active Involvement While you read, think aloud about how the author helps you infer by not giving you all the details. For example, in the text it says, "'Our part of Korea is like a dragon with many humps,' the father said.'" Explain to students that the author is helping us understand this story by using inference to describe this part of Korea.

To further explain, the father said:

"The humps are the mountains—the first hump facing the sea, the last hump facing the king's palace.

"Our mountain is the first hump.

"Our fire is the first fire."

Talk with students about the image of the mountains that the author uses to help us infer and how that helps them understand the time period of the story.

Encourage students to contribute other places in the text where the author helps them infer. Have them describe their thinking to the small group.

Where Students Inferred

"A fire on every hump of the dragon's back, all the way to the last one—the hump that could be seen from the palace walls."

"It is good to live in a time of peace."

"Something is wrong—there is no trouble from the sea, and the fire must be lit!"

"He knew the path like a friend."

"A strange noise—a groaning sound."

"One coal, glowing fiercely. Almost as if it were talking."

"Sang-hee watched the flames. He saw a great battle—soldiers, their shining swords clashing . . ."

"The gladness felt as warm as a glowing coal."

Off You Go Provide other opportunities for students to browse and read historical fiction. Encourage them to think about how authors help them to infer and to try using inference in their own writing by being aware of far more detail than they reveal.

Instructional Materials

- *Magic School Bus: Inside the Earth* by Joanna Cole
- Examples of rocks and minerals

5: Determining Importance in Informational Text

Writers observe their world and record what they believe is significant.

Teaching Moves

Start Up/Connection English Language Learners who are learning to determine importance in informational text need to be prepared to meet subject-specific terminology (for example, *igneous, metamorphic*). Every subject area has words they won't know and no one expects them to understand. This lesson identifies and highlights some of these words, ensuring that students have an understanding before heading into the text.

One resource for developing content-area vocabulary is *Words, Words, Words* by Janet Allen. It contains many examples of ways to help kids organize what they are learning when there is subject-specific terminology.

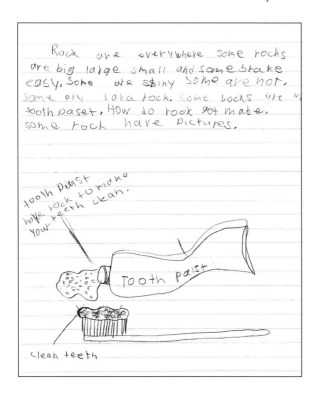

figure 7.17 *Casey records what he believes is significant about various kinds of rocks.*

To prepare kids for the earth science vocabulary in this lesson, give everyone a copy of the book and ask them to work with partners. While they browse through the text, have them look for words and concepts that they need to clarify—that they do not understand or find confusing. As they work, have them create a list of the words and include the sentences where they find them. After they have finished, go back through the sentences together and model how to use the context to understand the meaning. Also point out examples to students where the context doesn't give them enough background to understand the new words, and explain that they will need to use additional resources. To help kids with clarifying vocabulary, provide them with a dictionary, atlas, and thesaurus. In addition, encourage them to use the Internet as another resource.

To build background, provide students with concrete examples of rocks and minerals. Our students attend Outdoor Education at Camp Hi Hill in the San Gabriel Mountains. As a part of their weeklong visit, they learn about rocks and minerals. They gather rocks from around the camp and then spend time sorting, matching, and labeling them to make their own collections. The name of the rock or mineral and several of its characteristics should be included. For an example of a rock collection, see Figure 7.19. As they do this, students learn about igneous, metamorphic, and sedimentary rocks.

Information About the San Gabriel Mountains Rocks and Minerals

Igneous rocks are made from molten rock (magma or lava) that has cooled. Igneous rocks can cool slowly below the Earth's surface or quickly above the Earth's surface.

Metamorphic rocks were heated or squeezed below the surface. The heat and pressure changed them into a different rock than they once were.

Sedimentary rocks are usually made from pieces of rocks that have been stuck together. They often contain fossils. No sedimentary rocks can be found at Hi Hill.

Give Information "Now that you have gathered and organized your rock collection, think about all you learned about rocks. We're going to read *The Magic School Bus: Inside the Earth*, which has more information about earth science. After we've read and discussed it, you're going to write about what you have learned from studying rocks and reading the book." Provide a copy for each student and read through the book together. Think aloud about what you are learning about earth science as you read.

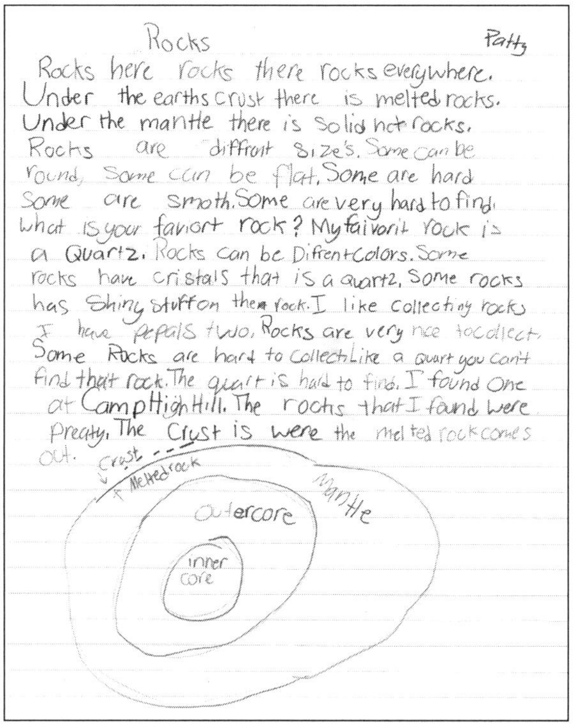

Active Involvement Before they start writing, talk with kids about leads they could use to begin their informational writing. Have them share their suggestions for leads. In addition, they can search through other information books to look for interesting ways to begin their writing.

Leads Suggested by Students

Rocks are everywhere.
I know a lot about rocks.
At Camp Hi Hill, I learned about rocks.
Do you like rocks?
Did you know there are many kinds of rocks and minerals?

Off You Go Once students have decided on a lead for their informational writing about rocks, have them work together as partners. They can share ideas with each other as they write. (See Figures 7.17 through 7.19.) This promotes academic language development and supports them as English Language Learners.

figure 7.18 *(left) To enhance her writing, Patty draws a diagram of a cross-section of the Earth.*

figure 7.19 *(below) Tomy's collection of information about rocks has lots of ideas for writing.*

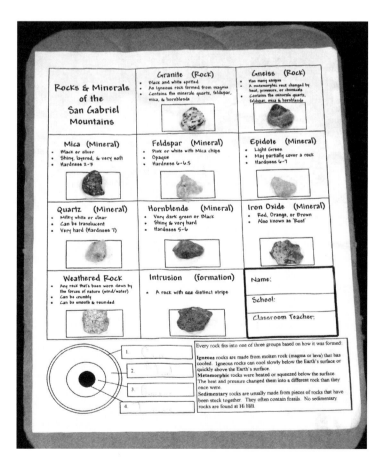

Instructional Materials

- *Tomás and the Library Lady* by Pat Mora

6: Synthesizing

Writers make global and focal plans for their writing before and during the drafting process. They use their knowledge of text elements, such as character, setting, conflict, sequence of events, and resolution, to create a structure for their writing.

Teaching Moves

Start Up/Connection Talk with students about what they know about character, setting, conflict, sequence of events, and resolution. Provide background information, if necessary. (For definitions, see Younger ELLs' Lesson 6, Synthesizing, page 102.) To integrate strategy use, see the comprehension lesson for this story in *Making Sense* (2005, p. 73).

Give Information Explain to students that writers make plans for their writing and use text elements, such as character, setting, conflict, sequence of events, and resolution, to give their writing structure. Read aloud *Tomás and the Library Lady* with the small group. As you read the story, think aloud about where and how you can identify text elements.

Active Involvement After reading, go back over the story with students. Have them work with partners to identify text elements in the story (see examples in the table). Have each set of partners share what they find with the small group.

Text Element Examples from Tomás and the Library Lady

Characters	Tomás Papá Mamá Papá Grande, his grandfather Enrique, his brother The library lady
Setting	The car Iowa The cornfields The library The town dump
Conflict	Every year Tomás went from his own house in Texas to Iowa so his family could work in the cornfields. He was hot and tired and he missed his own bed.
Sequence of events	*Beginning*—Tomás was in the old car on his way with his family from Texas to Iowa to pick corn. *Middle*—Tomás discovered the cool library downtown and met the library lady. She invited him to come in, get a drink, and read some books.

End—Tomás was back in the old car returning to Texas. He was reading a new book, a present from the library lady, to his grandfather.

Resolution

The library lady helped Tomás learn how much he loved to read and how wonderful books are. When he read, he forgot about Iowa and Texas.

Off You Go While students work on narrative writing, encourage them to reflect on how they can use text elements, such as character, setting, conflict, sequence of events, and resolution, to help structure their writing. Provide graphic organizers for students to use if they choose (see Figure 7.20).

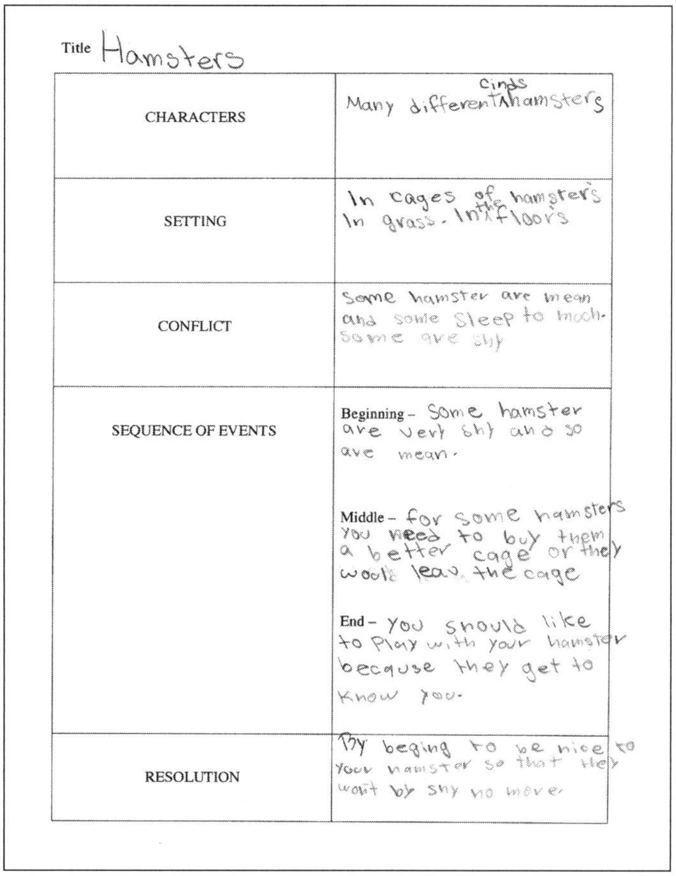

figure 7.20 *"I think that this is good because it helps us in writing and writing stories," comments Jacque about her graphic organizer for "Hamsters."*

7: Monitoring Meaning and Comprehension

Writers monitor their composition process to ensure that their text makes sense for their intended audience at the word, sentence, and text level.

Instructional Materials
- **Students' writing samples**

Teaching Moves

Start Up/Connection Have students select a piece of writing. Give them an opportunity to reread it and reflect about it.

Give Information Explain to students that one of the ways writers make sure their text makes sense for their intended audience is to wait several days or weeks and reread what they have written. While they reread their work, writers think to themselves, "Does it make sense?" If they find that there are places where it is confusing, they revise, rewrite, and rework it to get it to make sense.

Active Involvement Have students reread a piece of writing and think about the question, "Does it make sense?" Have them locate several places where they can make changes so that the meaning is clearer. Have them share their papers with partners. Then encourage them to read each other's work and ask the question, "Does it make sense?"

Off You Go From time to time, encourage students to read back through their writing and ask themselves the question, "Does it make sense?" They can use this as a way to learn how to make sure that their texts make sense for the intended audience.

8: Fix-Up Strategies

Writers revise (add, delete, and reorganize) and edit (apply correct conventions), continually seeking clarity and impact for readers. They experiment with and change overall meaning, content, wording, text organization, punctuation, and spelling.

Teaching Moves

Start Up/Connection Have students bring a piece of completed, published writing that was done a while ago, maybe several months. To begin, ask each one to reread his or her piece of writing.

Give Information Explain that one of the things proficient writers do is revise their work. Tell them that there are three things to do to help revise drafts and make them easier for readers to understand.

1. Add something that will make it easier to understand.
2. Delete something that is confusing or gets in the way of the story.
3. Reorganize something—cut and paste.

Model how to do this with a piece of your own writing.

Juli's Writing

Hummingbirds are so small. The first time I saw one I was astonished that something that tiny could actually be alive. It was hovering outside our living room window and seemed to be watching me as I looked through the glass.

   Turns out that the reason it was hanging around the window was because of the nest. It was perched precariously on a dime-sized metal connector for the outside electrical wiring.

   Over time, I watched her lay her eggs and hatch her chicks. As they grew, it looked as though the tiny thimble-sized nest would burst.

   Then one afternoon, all was quiet. The babies had fledged, and the nest was empty. I sat curled up in the big blue chair staring at the empty nest and wishing that they would come back. But they never did.

Active Involvement Have students practice revising their work.

Examples of Students Adding, Deleting, and Reorganizing

Veronica   *Added*—"delicious breakfast" to let the reader know it was yummy

                 Deleted—"lots of" because it didn't make sense

                 Reorganize—title "My Best Christmas" because it was boring

Jenny   *Added*—"One day in New York there was this lady named Carmen Rose. She dreamed about when she was in New York." I added a character to make it better.

                 Deleted—"She seen her daughter become a zombie." It don't look right.

                 Reorganize—title "The Mall with Zombies"

Jessica   *Added*—"Kitty purr at her lovely owner and she will never stop being kitty of the day." Because to make it more sense

                 Reorganize—title "My Kitty of the Day"

Off You Go Tell students that when they have finished a draft they can revise their pieces to make them better. Encourage them to also add, delete, and reorganize their writing when they use their writer's notebooks.

Books for Teaching Strategies to Older English Language Learners

Speech Emergence Stage

Making Connections

Books by Patricia Polacco (for example, *Thunder Cake, Chicken Sunday, Mrs. Katz and Tush, The Keeping Quilt, Mrs. Mack, My Rotten Redheaded Older Brother*)
I Love Saturdays y domingos by Alma Flor Ada

Asking Questions

MLB Home Run Heroes (DK Reader series) by James Buckley Jr.
The Moon Book by Gail Gibbons
The Name Jar by Yangsook Choi
The Planets in Our Solar System (Let's Read-and-Find-Out Science series) by Franklyn Branley
Stargazers by Gail Gibbons
Titanic: The Disaster That Shocked the World! (DK Readers series) by Mark Dubowski

Visualizing

beast feast: poems by Douglas Florian
Confetti: Poems for Children by Pat Mora
"Hairs"—Chapter 2 from *The House on Mango Street* by Sandra Cisneros
Hairs/Pelitos by Sandra Cisneros
lizards, frogs, and polliwogs by Douglas Florian
A Poke in the I: A Collection of Concrete Poems selected by Paul B.
   Janeczko, illustrated by Chris Raschka

Inferring

Amelia's Weave by Omar S. Castaneda
Dateline: Troy by Paul Fleischmann
The Firekeeper's Son by Linda Sue Park
The Journey of the Tunuri and the Blue Deer: A Huichol Indian Story by
   James Endredy
Nine-in-One, Grr! Grr! A Folktale from the Hmong People of Laos by
   Blia Xiong and Cathy Spagnoli

Determining Importance in Nonfiction

All About Rattlesnakes by Jim Arnosky
All About Sharks by Jim Arnosky
Magic School Bus: Inside the Earth by Joanna Cole
Magic Tree House Research Guides: Ancient Greece and the Olympics
   by Mary Pope Osborn
Surprising Sharks by Nicola Davies

Synthesizing

Fortune Cookie Fortunes by Grace Lin
How My Parents Learned to Eat by Ina R. Friedman
In the Space of the Sky by Richard Lewis
Tomás and the Library Lady by Pat Mora
Xochiti and the Flowers by Jorge Argueta

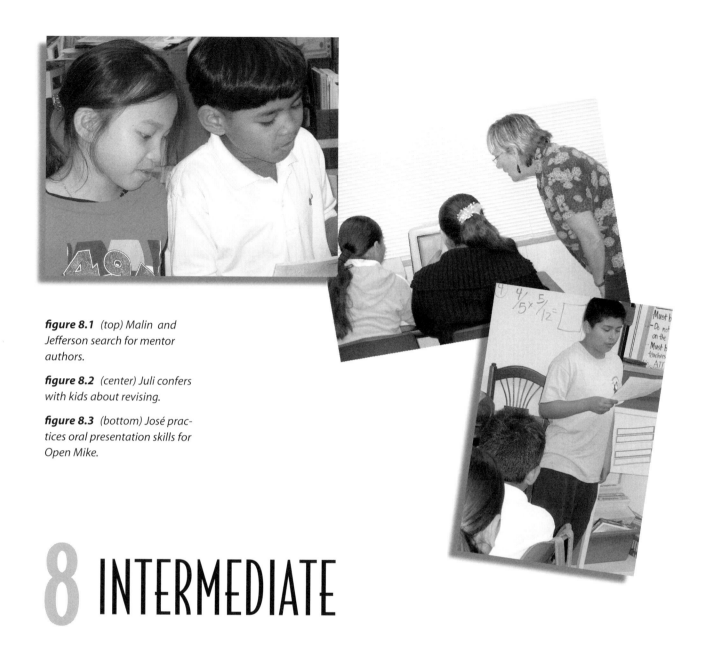

figure 8.1 *(top) Malin and Jefferson search for mentor authors.*

figure 8.2 *(center) Juli confers with kids about revising.*

figure 8.3 *(bottom) José practices oral presentation skills for Open Mike.*

8 INTERMEDIATE

As kids gain proficiency in English, they continue to face the challenges of making meaning in their writing. At the intermediate stage of language proficiency, providing background experiences—working with familiar books, learning about the world through field trips both real and virtual, and tying instruction to what is being studied in content-area subjects (for example, social science and history), as well as using their real-life experiences with families and friends—scaffolds writing for English Language Learners. When they choose mentor authors to act as their writing teachers, they take on more independence as learners and writers and move toward a lifelong love of writing.

As they express ideas comprehensibly in both oral and written communication, students are approaching native fluency. But they are still developing academic competence, especially in the areas of reading and writing. To motivate kids to take risks and to engage in conversations, use who, did what, when, why, and where questions. Also ask open-ended questions to create opportunities for more complicated responses and use of complex sentences.

While kids continue to expand their vocabularies, class activities are structured to develop higher levels of language use, incorporating reading and writing into content-area lessons. Such activities can include writing using frames, echo and choral reading, and reader's theater. Encourage students to analyze, evaluate, create, justify, defend, support, debate, examine, complete, describe in detail, compare/contrast, evaluate cause/effect, and predict.

Younger English Language Learners in Real Time

Memoir can be a difficult-to-define genre, often waffling between personal narrative, autobiographical incident, and "the stories of our lives"; however, it is an important part of who we are. According to Margaret Meek, "stories . . . create our first memories. From the stories we hear as children we inherit the way we talk about how we feel, the values [that] we hold to be important, and what we regard as the truth" (1992).

Every year Juli starts off by having kids write personal narratives. It's a great way to engage reluctant writers and help kids learn how to use prior knowledge and background information in their writing. First, she reads aloud examples from literature to immerse students in the genre. The kids enjoy *Hairs/Pelitos* by Sandra Cisneros, *Family Pictures* by Carmen Lomas Garza, *The Good Luck Cat* by Joy Harjo, *Apple Pie 4th of July* by Janet Wong, *Mama and Papa Have a Store* by Amelia Lau Carling, *The Upside Down Boy* by Juan Felipe Herrera, and/or *The Trip Back Home* by Janet Wong.

Once there has been lots of conversation about what makes a personal narrative, kids start writing. Usually everyone starts off with plenty to say, often too much. Helping them limit their stories and focus on tiny moments instead of telling an encyclopedic version is sometimes a challenge.

Juli frequently finds herself confused about the definition of memoir; of course, there's *Angela's Ashes* by Frank McCourt. But are Sandra Cisneros's books *The House on Mango Street* and *Woman Hollering Creek and Other Stories* memoir or fiction? What's the difference between personal narrative and memoir? Can a memoir be a poem or must it only be narrative writing?

So, she turns to the experts for help. Katie Wood Ray and Lester Laminack think we should try writing a genre before we start teaching it.

> I believe that to set the best tone in our writing workshops, then, our students need to see us as people who write, just as we see them in that same way. Now take heart. It is not at all necessary that they see us as great writers. It is fine for them to see us struggle as writers, to see us write things that make us (and them) say, "Oh my, that's awful!" What is so much more important than that we be great writers is that our students see us as people who think writing is a worthwhile thing to do, as people who believe in the effort it takes to write things that really matter. (2001, p. 47)

Juli gives it a try—writing memoir. She writes about the piano lessons she had growing up, the tiger skin from India that she remembers hanging on the wall in her grandparents' lower-level family room where she and her brothers slept as kids, and her wonderful cat Sandy McTavish, who was named after a character on the *Howdy Doody* TV show. In this way, Juli gains an appreciation for the challenges the kids will face.

When Juli gets stuck for ideas she turns to Judith Barrington, who advises:

> What things do you think about over and over? What stories haunt you? Which people from the past do you dream about? What makes you passionate when you think about it or talk about it? What do you argue about? (1996, p. 40)

But where does the desire to write about our lives come from? And when do we know that it's time?

In *The Art of Teaching Writing*, Lucy Calkins talks about the instinct for memoir.

> I used to think that we write memoir when our lives are done and we want to give one last, loving look back, but now I know that it is by looking back that we create our lives, our selves. The instinct for memoir is there whenever we return to a remembered place, catch a whiff of a childhood smell, feel nostalgic over a photograph. The seeds of memoir are there when we listen to stories and say, "That reminds me of when . . ." The seeds of memoir are there in notebooks, in entries that begin, "I remember . . ." or "Once, when I was little . . ." or "One time, a long time ago . . ." or "In my family, we usually . . ." (1994, p. 399–400)

As is usually the case, the kids' writing says it best (see Figure 8.4). It shows the importance of writing memoir and personal narrative as a way to understand ourselves and to relate to the world around us.

figure 8.4 *Michelle's first draft of her memoir.*

Lessons for Younger English Language Learners

1: Making Connections

Writers seek to better recognize and capitalize on their own voice for specific effects in their compositions.

Instructional Materials

- *La Mariposa* by Francisco Jimenéz
- Familiar texts—at least one for each pair of students
- Large piece of chart paper

Teaching Moves

Start Up/Connection To help kids draw on their prior knowledge about making connections, use the Think–Pair–Share strategy (Harste, Short, and Burke 1995). This strategy involves students' thinking about a topic, then working with a partner, and then sharing their discoveries and thoughts. To do this, ask kids to think about what they already know about making connections. Then provide pairs of students with familiar texts—ones they have already read and discussed. Have them work together and use the books to talk about what writers do to help them make connections to their reading. Then have them share what they learned during their discussions—either with another pair of students, a small group, or the whole class.

Give Information Talk with students about the writer's voice. Explain that voice is what helps the writer communicate with the reader and helps the reader interact and connect with the writing. Tell kids that it is their responsibility as writers to get readers engaged with the writing. They need to help them make a strong connection to the writing by giving the sense that a real person is speaking.

Read *La Mariposa* aloud to students. While you are reading, think aloud about your own connections to the story and what the writer does to help you understand his voice and how he feels about what he is writing.

Active Involvement After reading and modeling by thinking aloud for the first part of the story, allow kids to work in pairs. Continue reading, and stop every so often to allow partners to talk about what the writer is doing to make the writing come alive and to engage readers and help them connect to the story.

One of Juli's classes put together the following list about what Francisco Jimenéz does to make his writing come alive and help readers connect to the story.

Comments from Kids About How Jimenéz Writes

He uses Spanish phrases.
He writes about something we know about—going to school.
He gives examples of how he couldn't understand Spanish.
"Miss Scalpino started speaking to the class and Francisco did not understand a word she said."
"But by the end of the day, he got very tired of hearing Miss Scalapino talk because the sounds still made no sense to him."
He uses a lot of dialog.
He lets us know that his teacher did not want him to speak Spanish.
"But if Miss Scalapino heard them speaking Spanish, she would say 'NO!' with her whole body. Her head turned left and right a hundred times a second and her index finger moved from side to side as fast as a windshield wiper."

Off You Go Encourage kids to try out some of the things they noticed that Francisco Jimenéz did with his writer's voice. They can use their writer's notebooks as a place to "give it a try" by using dialog or words and phrases from a language they speak. Assist writers so that they can recognize and capitalize on their own voice for specific effects in compositions as they do other writing. Remind them that it is their responsibility as writers to find ways to help readers make connections to what they are writing.

2: Asking Questions

Writers' questions lead to revision in their own pieces and in the pieces to which they respond for other writers.

Teaching Moves

Start Up/Connection Read aloud sections from *Why? The Best Ever Question-and-Answer Book About Nature, Science and the World Around You.* Think aloud as you are reading about the different questions you have about the writing. Choose one of the selections you read (for example, we like to use "What puts the fizz in soda pop?" in Supermarket Questions) and list the questions you have on a large piece of chart paper.

Soda Pop Questions

Does the fizz come from the bubbles in the soda?
How do the bubbles get in the soda? Do they use a bubble machine?
Why does soda have fizz? Is it important?
What makes the bubbles fizz?
What makes the sound that you hear when you put your ear near the soda?
Does air move around in the bubbles?
How do they push the bubbles into the soda?
How do the bubbles disappear when you open up a soda and leave it out?
Can you put more fizz back when it has gone?

Give Information Talk with kids about how writers use questions to help them revisit, revise, and rework their writing. Discuss how writers ask questions of themselves and how they also ask others to read their pieces and ask questions about their writing to help them revise. Have them share with partners about the times they have revised and how they used questions to help.

Refer to the list of questions you generated while reading and think aloud about how the author might use the questions to revise the writing; then share a piece of student writing. We often use the following—"At the Park" by Drina. Read it with kids, thinking aloud about your own questions. Be sure to talk about how the author might use your questions to rework and revise the piece.

At the Park

Wow! When I went to the park was yesterday it was so much more fun than other parks. Why was it more fun cause you get some penuts and you just stick your hand out and squierls come to you. isn't that so cool. then once one squierl come a lot of squierls. but there is something really scary that happens. So get ready some crows come and scare the poor little squirrels just to eat the peanuts and the crows take the peanuts to there baby's just to fed them. When the crows leave i see the qquierls hiding and I give them some peanuts. they came on top of me and i take

Instructional Materials
- *Crazy Horse's Vision* by Joseph Bruchac
- *Why? The Best Ever Question-and-Answer Book About Nature, Science and the World Around You* by Catherine Ripley
- *Why I Sneeze, Shiver, Hiccup, & Yawn* (Let's Read-and-Find-Out Science 2) by Melvin and Gilda Berger
- Other books—*1,000 Questions and Answers* by Robin Kerrod and *A Boy Called Slow: The True Story of Sitting Bull* by Joseph Bruchac
- Student writing
- Chart paper

them home. My mother maria said where are you tacking the squierls. I said to the house. My mom said the dog is going to kill them. i said no they are not. she said whatever. then next thing you know the dotg looks at me. Then she jumps ontop of me. instead of killing the squierls she lickes them. she puts the squirrels in side of her house and sleeps with them. my dog thought that they were her baby's.

Some Questions About Drina's Writing

We know that you haven't edited your writing yet, but did you take the time to reread it and think about the question, "Does it make sense?" How can you come up with a way to remember to reread your writing and think about this question before you decide to stop working on your piece?

You started to make a question in the second line, "Why was it more fun" but why did you stop and not put a question mark? How can you remember to use question marks? How can you help yourself?

Did you remember to think about how a sentence always starts with a capital letter? What will help you remember?

What gave you the idea to write about the squirrels and the crows at the park?

You have some dialog when your mother, María, says, "Where are you tacking the squierls." How can you remember to use quotation marks when you write dialog? Is there something you can do to help yourself with this?

What genre of writing is this? Is it fiction or nonfiction?

Active Involvement Provide a variety of books for kids to read with a partner; for examples see this lesson's Instructional Materials. Choose books that will help kids generate questions about how writers use questions to help them revisit, revise, and rework their writing. Encourage them to share their questions and their thinking about how they could be used to revise with partners.

Off You Go Provide opportunities for kids to work with partners or a small group as they revise their writing. Have them keep a list of questions that readers ask so that they can refer to them as they work to revisit, rework, and revise.

3: Visualizing (Creating Sensory Images)

Writers create impact through the use of strong nouns and verbs whenever possible.

Teaching Moves

Start Up/Connection Allow kids to browse through poetry books such as *From the Bellybutton of the Moon and Other Summer Poems* and *Iguanas in the Snow and Other Winter Poems*. Have them talk with partners about the poems and which ones they like.

To provide kids with background information about Alarcon and the books, read the "Afterword" that he wrote on the last page of each. *From the Bellybutton of the Moon* is a collection of bilingual poems about his childhood summers in the little town of Atoyac, Mexico. *Iguanas in the Snow* is a collection of poems written to celebrate winter by the seashore, in San Francisco, and in the redwood forests of the Sierras.

Give Information Talk with kids about how poets (writers who choose to write poetry) help us visualize their poems by using strong nouns and verbs. Choose several poems from the books. We use poem 1 from "From the Bellybutton of the Moon/Del ombligo de la luna," and "Ode to Buena Vista Bilingual School." Model for the students as you read the poems and think aloud about the strong nouns and verbs Francisco Alarcon uses to help us "see" his poems. Make a list of the nouns and verbs on chart paper.

Strong Nouns and Verbs from Alarcon's Poems

Nouns	Verbs
Mexico	say
wind	feel
face	felt
window	open
trip	see
car	raised
Atoyac	spent
town	hear
mother	smell
summer vacations	write
voices	following
laughter	learn to sing
greetings	
farewells	
Grandma	
gardenias	
Spanish	
school	
English	
children	
races	
poems	
spirals	
beat	
teacher Felipe	
clave	
sing	
hearts	

Active Involvement Provide the preceding two collections of poetry as well as many others for the kids to read. Have them work with partners to make a list of the strong words they find; we call them *Powerful Words*. Provide opportunities for them to share the words they find with each other and the group.

Off You Go Since the purpose of collecting Powerful Words is to have them available to use in writing, encourage kids to keep lists of words in their writer's notebooks as a reference for their writing. During conferences with kids, have them share their words and how they are using them in their writing to help readers visualize with you.

4: Inferring

Writers carefully consider their audience in making decisions about what to describe explicitly and what to leave to the reader's interpretation.

Teaching Moves

Start Up/Connection Have kids work in pairs to write a brief retelling of the "Three Little Pigs" story (for example, see Figures 8.5 and 8.6). Then have them share their retellings with another pair of students or the group. Discuss the similarities and differences between the retellings.

Give Information Explain to kids that writers carefully consider their audience in making decisions about what to describe explicitly and what to leave to readers' interpretation. This is especially true when they are writing stories from a unique cultural point of view. Tell them that in *The Three Little Javelinas* the writer blended together Native American, Mexican, and Anglo

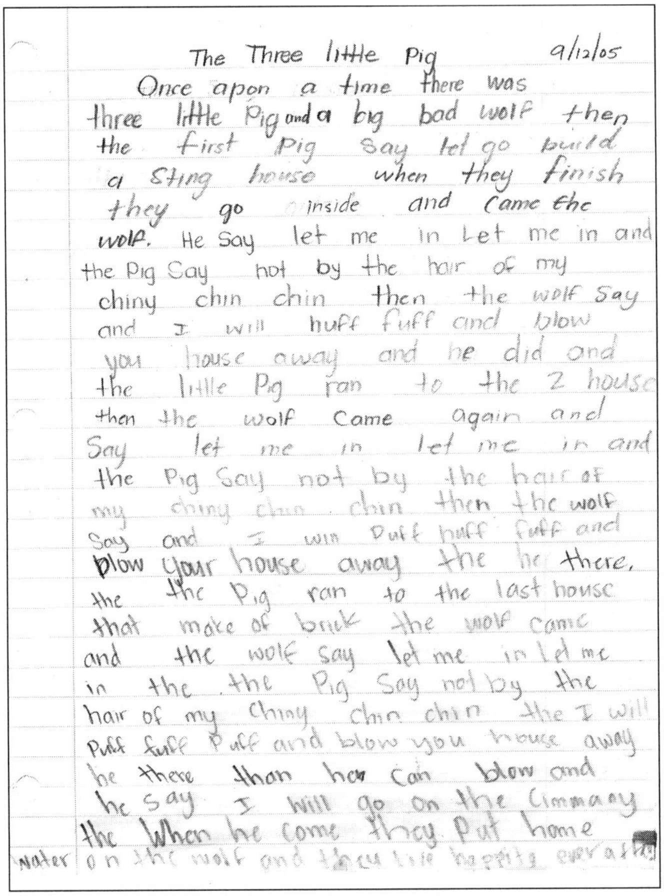

Instructional Materials

- *The Three Little Javelinas* by Susan Lowell
- *The True Story of the Three Little Pigs!* by John Scieszka
- *The Three Pigs: Nacho, Tito y Miguel/Los tres cerdos* by Bobbi Salinas

figure 8.5 *Vichneath retells the story of the "Three Little Pigs."*

figure 8.6 Vichneath's picture adds details to her retelling.

cultures to create a coyote fable. Such fables are often told by southwestern Native Americans such as the Tohono O'Odham (desert people). Read students "A Note on the Story" at the back of the book and the background information on the first page.

As you read the story, think aloud about how Susan Lowell described some things explicitly and left other things to the reader's interpretation (see the examples in the following table).

Examples of Lowell's Writing Decisions

Described Explicitly	Javelinas on the first page of the story
	Javelinas' houses
	Coyote blowing down the pigs' houses
	The sound coyote made when he went down the stovepipe
Left to Readers' Interpretation	Coyote had many magic tricks.
	He was very sneaky.
	The javelinas were suspicious of the coyote.
	He followed the javelinas' trail.

Active Involvement Provide other versions of the three little pigs story for kids to read and discuss. We use *The True Story of the Three Little Pigs!* and *The Three Pigs: Nacho, Tito y Miguel/Los tres credos*. Have kids work together to determine what the writer described explicitly and what the writer left to readers' interpretation.

Off You Go Remind kids that they can do their own versions of familiar stories and folktales. Writer's notebooks are a good place to try out this kind of writing and see how it goes. Encourage them to describe some things explicitly and to leave other things to readers' interpretation—that is, readers need to infer.

If kids want to publish their stories (take them out into the world), they can use what they have written in their writer's notebooks as seeds.

5: Determining Importance in Text

Writers make decisions about the most important ideas to include in the pieces they write. They decide which genre and structure are best to communicate their ideas.

Teaching Moves

Start Up/Connection To help kids build background, share the three nature scrapbooks by Virginia Wright-Frierson. Encourage them to discuss what they notice in the books—photographs, notes, illustrations, maps, lists, drawings, pages from other books, postcards, and so on. Talk about how the writer collected all these things into a notebook, or scrapbook, then wrote about them to give us information. Ask students to share how they collect things and whether they put them into a writer's notebook and write about them. To integrate strategy use, see the comprehension lesson for this story in *Making Sense* (2005, p. 85).

Give Information Read kids the following quote from the flyleaf of *A Desert Scrapbook:*

> What if the Sonoran Desert were your backyard? What would you see when you stepped outdoors? With paper, pencil, brush, and paints in hand, Virginia Wright-Frierson takes readers on an artist's tour of this rich and wonderful ecosystem, from the desert floor to the open sky.

Explain to the kids that as writers work on text they make decisions about the most important ideas to include in the pieces they write. Go through the book, pointing out how Virginia Wright-Frierson included information along with her personal observations.

For example, on the page about the barrel cactus, she writes: "Today, as I sketch some doves, I am startled by a roadrunner bursting from behind a nearby barrel cactus. It catches a zebra-tailed lizard and dashes off, leaving a little cloud of dust." Then as a caption for the photograph on the same page, she writes: "barrel cactus bloom—August (my favorite cactus flower)."

Also explain that writers make decisions about the best genre and structure to use to communicate their ideas. In this case, the writer chose to use a scrapbook or journal to communicate her ideas about the Sonoran Desert. So, we get to learn information as well as find out her personal observations—what she thinks.

Active Involvement Have kids work with partners and go through the books looking for how the writer includes information. Then have them check to see where and how she includes her personal observations. Provide opportunities for them to share what they find with another set of partners or the group.

Off You Go Provide kids with a variety of opportunities to use their writer's notebooks or a scrapbook to record their observations of the world and write down their personal thoughts. We often take writer's notebooks on field trips. Our kids walk around the neighborhood or go to the aquarium, the Bolsa Chica Wetlands, the El Dorado Park Nature Center, the Los Angeles Zoo, the beach, the park, or Rancho Los Alamitos. Fourth graders visit a California mission such as Mission San Gabriel.

The http://www.efieldtrips.com Web site provides opportunities for virtual field trips. On these trips kids frequently sketch and take notes to record the information they learn as well as their personal observations by adding photos and other artifacts. In this way, they use their own writing to practice determining what is important to include and what isn't.

6: Synthesizing

Writers study other writers and draw conclusions about what makes good writing. They work to replicate the style of authors they find compelling.

Possible Mentor Authors—Books Listed in Resources

Alma Flor Ada
Francisco X. Alarcon
Sandra Cisneros
Carmen Lomas Garza
Juan Felipe Herrera
Grace Lin
Lenore Look
Ken Mochizuki

Pat Mora
Naomi Shihab Nye
Patricia Polacco
Anushka Ravishankar
Gary Soto
Janet Wong
Lawrence Yep

Teaching Moves

Start Up/Connection To help kids build background, provide a variety of books for them to read aloud and have discussions about Japanese American internment during World War II. As kids read, encourage them to share what they are learning with partners. Have pairs share what they learn with other partners or with the group.

Give Information Read aloud the "Author's Note" at the beginning of the Mochizuki book where he summarizes the background of the Japanese American internment. Explain to kids that the writer, Ken Mochizuki, wrote this book as a first-person narrative. His parents were interned in Idaho at Minidoka Camp, and he used their experiences to tell how people can create a purpose for themselves while enduring injustice and humiliation.

Talk with students about how they can study other writers and draw conclusions about what makes good writing. Then they can incorporate what they learn about good writing into their pieces by writing in the style of an author they find compelling.

Point out some of the good writing that you notice in *Baseball Saved Us*. Explain that writers often choose other authors as mentors to teach them about good writing. Write examples from the story on chart paper to keep as a reference.

Instructional Materials
- *Baseball Saved Us* by Ken Mochizuki
- Books about the Japanese American internment during World War II—*The Bracelet* by Yoshiko Uchida and *The Children of Topaz: The Story of a Japanese-American Internment Camp Based on a Classroom Diary* by Michael Tunnell and George Chilcoat
- *So Far From the Sea* by Eve Bunting
- Large chart paper

Examples of Good Writing from Baseball Saved Us

We like how Ken Mochizuki includes people's thoughts and feelings.
The father's feelings—" 'Because,' he said, 'America is at war with Japan, and the government thinks that Japanese Americans can't be trusted. But it's wrong that we're in here. We're Americans too!' "
The son's feelings—"My team came up to bat and I was up next. I looked down. I thought maybe I should pretend to be sick so I wouldn't have to finish the game. But I knew that would make things even worse, because I would get picked on at school for being a chicken. And they would use the bad word, too. Then it was my turn at bat. The crowd was screaming. 'The Jap's no good!' 'Easy out!' I heard laughing."

Active Involvement Have students work with partners to find a mentor author—someone whom they find compelling, whose work they like, and from whom they can draw conclusions about what makes good writing. Provide books from many authors who write in different genres and styles. Focus on writers who write various types of books or who write in different genres.

Off You Go Once kids choose mentor authors, encourage them to try out and replicate the authors' style in their own writing. Writer's notebooks provide a risk-free environment for trying a different style of writing. When students have a style that works for them, they can try it in a piece of writing.

Instructional Materials

- Copies of student writing from a variety of genres
- Student writing anthologies from previous years
- Tape recorders and/or other audio equipment

7: Monitoring Meaning and Comprehension

Writers share their work so others can help them monitor the clarity and impact of the work.

Teaching Moves

Start Up/Connection Provide anthologies of student writing from prior years for students to browse and read (see Figure 8.7). Encourage them to share what they notice in the anthologies with partners or the group. Have them talk about their previous experiences with publishing work in a class or school anthology.

Give Information Tell kids that they will be picking something from their writing portfolios to include in an anthology. It can be for an individual classroom, a grade-level, or a schoolwide project. Our anthology projects with younger students usually focus on creating a class anthology. Explain that this is one way writers share their work so that others can help them monitor its clarity and impact and that they will be receiving feedback from readers. Establish criteria for the selection of pieces: number to choose, genre, length, necessity of editing and proofreading, and so on.

Active Involvement Have kids work with partners to go through their writing portfolios to select pieces to publish in the anthology. Encourage them to have their partners read the pieces they select and give them feedback. Forms can be provided so that each reader gives feedback about the clarity of the piece—How easy is it to understand what the writer is saying?—and its impact—Is it

figure 8.7 *Writers share their work with others through writing anthologies and audiotapes of kids reading their writing.*

memorable? Would you want to write a piece like this? (see sample feedback form in the Appendix). Once writers have selected their pieces for publication, compile them into an anthology.

In addition, provide opportunities for students to read and record their writing on tapes or another media. Audio or video equipment, or a simple tape player with a record button, can be brought in to use.

Off You Go Once the anthology is complete, provide copies for the class library for others to read. Recordings of kids reading their writing can be used for listening—just like books on tape—with individuals' personal equipment or placed at a listening post for small groups.

8: Fix-Up Strategies

Writers capitalize on their knowledge of writers' tools (that is, character, setting, conflict, theme, plot structure, leads, style, etc.) to enhance their meaning.

Teaching Moves

Start Up/Connection Working with grade-level colleagues to analyze kids' writing, it becomes clear that developing strong leads (how to begin the piece of writing) needs to be an instructional focus. To determine next steps, kids choose pieces of writing and talk with partners about leads. For example, they can discuss where they got their ideas, how they made their decisions as writers, why they thought it made a good lead for a personal narrative or memoir, and so on.

Give Information Share the information gathered by working with colleagues to assess writing with kids. Encourage them to add their observations from the conversations they have had with partners about their own writing. Explain that writers capitalize on their knowledge of writers' tools to enhance their

Instructional Materials
- Familiar books written as memoir or first-person narrative
- *Baseball Saved Us* by Ken Mochizuki
- *The Good Luck Cat* by Joy Harjo
- *Hairs/Pelitos* by Sandra Cisneros
- *La Mariposa* by Francisco Jiménez
- *Sitti's Secrets* by Naomi Shihab Nye
- Student writing (personal narratives and memoirs)

meaning; one of the tools a writer has is a lead. A strong beginning draws readers into the writing and helps them understand what the piece is about.

Go through books written as memoir and first-person narrative and discuss the ways that writers use leads to create understanding for readers. Model by thinking aloud about what you notice in some or all of the books listed in this lesson's Instructional Materials.

Active Involvement Hand out copies of personal narratives and memoirs to kids. Have them work with partners to talk about the leads and how writers created meaning for them as readers. Have kids develop leads from the examples in the books, then list them on a chart to keep as a reference.

Leads Kids Created for Personal Narratives

My grandpa (other names can be used) and I _____

When I was little _____

I went <u>walking</u>, (other actions can be substituted; based on *I Went Walking*)

One day when I _____

On <u>Monday</u>, (other days of the week can be used)

During the <u>night</u>, (other times of day can be used)

Everybody in our family has different _____ (based on *Hairs/Pelitos*)

I have a _____ (based on *The Good Luck Cat*)

Off You Go Remind kids that they can use their writer's notebooks as a place to try out writing different kinds of leads. While they work on their writing, encourage them to go back to use the list of leads they created and to search books for interesting ways to begin to build understanding for readers and to help them make meaning.

Books for Teaching Strategies to Younger English Language Learners

Intermediate Stage

Making Connections

A Is for Asia by Cynthia Chin-Lee
Dolphins by Victoria St. John
Dumpling Soup by Jama Kim Rattigan
First Day in Grapes by L. King Perez
La Mariposa by Francisco Jimenéz

Asking Questions

A Boy Called Slow: The True Story of Sitting Bull by Joseph Bruchac
Crazy Horse's Vision by Joseph Bruchac
1,000 Questions and Answers by Robin Kerrod
Why I Sneeze, Shiver, Hiccup, & Yawn (Let's Read-and-Find-Out Science 2) by Melvin Berger

Why? The Best Ever Question-and-Answer Book About Nature, Science and the World Around You by Catherine Ripley

Visualizing

From the Bellybutton of the Moon and Other Summer Poems by Francisco X. Alarcon
I'm in Charge of Celebrations by Byrd Baylor
Iguanas in the Snow and Other Winter Poems by Francisco X. Alarcon
Sagawa, The Chinese Siamese Cat by Amy Tan
Sergei Prokofiev's Peter and the Wolf (with CD), illustrated by Peter Malone and retold by Janet Schulman

Inferring

Fables by Arnold Lobel
Juan Bobo Goes to Work: A Puerto Rican Folktale by Marisa Montes
Judge Rabbit and the Spirit Tree: A Folktale from Cambodia by Cathy Spagnoli and Lina Mao Wall
Roadrunner's Dance by Rodolfo Anaya
The Stinky Cheese Man and Other Fairly Stupid Tales by John Scieszka
The Three Little Javelinas by Susan Lowell
The True Story of the Three Little Pigs! by John Scieszka

Determining Importance in Nonfiction

Cactus Hotel by Brenda Z. Guiberson
A Desert Scrapbook, Dawn to Dusk in the Sonoran Desert by Virginia Wright-Frierson
Correctamundo: Prickly Pete's Guide to Desert Facts & Cactifracts by David Lazaroff
Everglades by Jean Craighead George
An Island Scrapbook, Dawn to Dusk on a Barrier Island by Virginia Wright-Frierson
A North American Rainforest Scrapbook by Virginia Wright-Frierson

Synthesizing

Baseball Saved Us by Ken Mochizuki
The Bracelet by Yoshiko Uchida
Bread Song by Frederick Lipp
Chato's Kitchen by Gary Soto

Older English Language Learners in Real Time

The fifteen kids in Juli's pullout class are working in small groups "doing" centers, also called literacy workstations. (For an explanation of literacy workstations, see *Literacy Work Stations*, 2003, and *Practice with Purpose*, 2005, by Debbie Diller.)

There are three centers in Juli's classroom. In one center, kids work on computers to read and write, using the strategies they are learning to enhance understanding and make meaning. Another center encourages kids to listen to books on tape for independent reading. At the third center, Juli teaches small group reading and writing mini-lessons. When a small timer rings after twenty minutes, kids move from one center to the next, completing a rotation of all three in about an hour. The composition of the groups ranges from random, with kids choosing where to work, to structured, with Juli assigning kids to a group based on their instructional needs.

Juli decides it's time to immerse kids in poetry. She chooses *A Writing Kind of Day* by Ralph Fletcher to match the needs of her eleven- and twelve-year-old students. She hands out copies of the book to the small group working in the teacher-directed center and asks kids to read through and find a poem they like. As they look through, everyone is enthralled with the way Fletcher writes about everyday occurrences—things that really happen in kids' lives.

Jenny likes the last poem, "It's a Writing Kind of Night." She reads it for the group and comments, "I like the way the words sound. It's like rhyming but it's not."

Jessica likes the "Squished Squirrel Poem." "It's funny writing about a squished squirrel," she says with a twinkle in her eye. "Sometimes I see squirrels at the park playing around. They're big."

José likes "My Little Brother" because it describes "an evil little brother" just like his.

Sonia likes "She Wrote Me a Love Poem." "This is terrible," she says. "The writer is really sad—well, maybe he's angry."

The group likes these poems because of the topics that Ralph Fletcher chose to write about. As Nestor says, referring to "She Wrote Me a Love Poem," "I hate love poems but this one is cool!"

The bell rings to signal the end of the small-group discussion and send kids on to their next literacy station. Before they leave, Juli tells them, "So remember. When you're writing in your writer's notebooks, try writing some poems about the things in your life that are important to you, just like Fletcher does in *A Writing Kind of Day*. I'll check in with you during writing conferences to see how it's going."

Lessons for Older English Language Learners

Instructional Materials

- *My Name Was Hussein* by Hristo Kyuchukov
- Familiar texts—at least one for each pair of students
- Overhead transparency sheet

1: Making Connections

Writers seek to better recognize and capitalize on their own voice for specific effects in their compositions.

Teaching Moves

Start Up/Connection To help kids draw on their prior knowledge about making connections, use the Think–Pair–Share strategy. To do this, ask them to think about what they already know about making connections. Then provide pairs of students with familiar texts. Have them work together and use the texts to talk about what writers do to help them make connections to their reading.

Then have kids share what they learned in their discussions, either with another pair of students, a small group, or the whole class.

Give Information Talk with students about writer's voice. Explain that voice is what helps the writer communicate with readers and that it helps readers interact and connect with the writing. Tell kids that it is their responsibility as writers to get readers engaged with the writing. They need to help them make a strong connection to the writing by giving readers the sense that a real person is speaking.

Read aloud the story, *My Name Is Hussein*, to students. While you are reading, think aloud about your own connections to the story and what the writer does to help you understand his voice and how he feels about what he is writing.

Active Involvement After reading and modeling by thinking aloud for the first part of the story, allow kids to work in pairs. Continue reading, and stop every so often to allow them to talk about what the writer is doing to make the writing come alive, to engage readers, and to help them connect to the story. One of Juli's classes created the following list on an overhead sheet about what Hristo Kyuchukov does to make his writing come alive and help readers connect to his story.

Comments About How Kyuchukov Connects to Readers

He talks about how his family is Muslim and he tells us how they do
  things.

"In our family, we are Muslims.
  That is our religion.
  We celebrate many holidays.
  For every holiday, my mother cooks
  beautiful foods for us to eat.
  Our house smells delicious.
  I love the smells."

He writes about something we all have in common and that is important
  to us—our names and our grandparents.

He gives examples of how his family observes Ramadan.

"We observe Ramadan.
  For a month, my parents do not
  eat during the day.
  During this time, they pray
  extra prayers.
  At night, we eat a special meal called *iftar*."

He uses dialog for the soldier to let us know that the soldier wants his
  family to change their names.

"You must change your names," he said.
  "You must choose Christian names.
  Come back with new names
  And you will get new identity cards."

Off You Go Encourage kids to try out some of the things they noticed that Kyuchukov did with his writer's voice. They can use their writer's notebooks as a place to "give it a try." Help writers to better recognize and capitalize on their own voices for specific effects in their compositions as they do other writing. Remind them that it is their responsibility as writers to help readers make connections to what they are writing.

2: Asking Questions

Writers' questions lead to revisions in their own pieces and in the pieces to which they respond for other writers.

Teaching Moves

Start Up/Connection Read aloud sections from *Through My Eyes* by Ruby Bridges. Think aloud as you are reading about the different questions you have about the writing. Choose one of the selections you read. We like to use "What a Passerby Wrote" on pages 24 and 25. It includes a section written by Bridges, a selection written by John Steinbeck from *Travels With Charley*, and Norman Rockwell's famous painting—*The Problem We All Live With*. List the questions you have on an overhead transparency.

Give Information Talk with kids about how writers use questions to help them revisit, revise, and rework their writing. Discuss how writers ask questions of themselves and how they also ask others to read their pieces and ask questions about their writing to help them revise. Have them share with partners about the times they have revised and how they used questions to help.

Refer to the list of questions you generated while reading "What a Passerby Wrote," and think aloud about how the author might use the questions to revise the writing. Then, share a piece of student writing (for

figure 8.8 *Jessica organizes her thoughts for writing by drawing a picture first.*

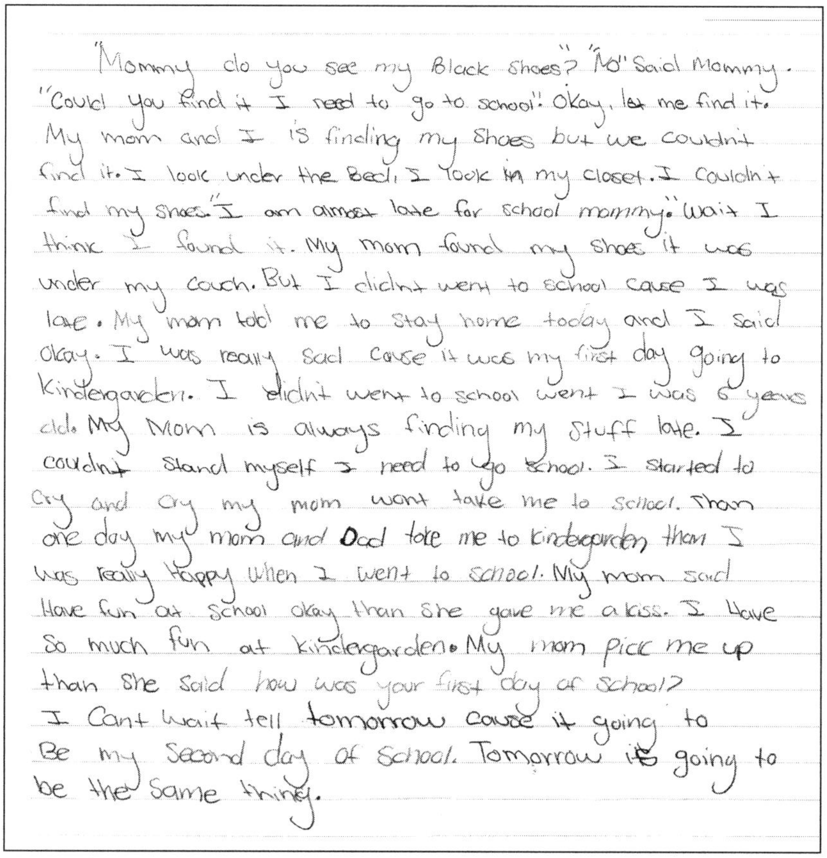

figure 8.9 *Encouraging Jessica to ask questions about her writing will help her to revise.*

example, see Figures 8.8 and 8.9). Read it with the kids, thinking aloud about your own questions. Be sure to talk about how the author might use your questions to rework and revise his or her piece.

Questions About Jessica's Writing

We noticed that Jessica uses a lot of dialog. How can she remember that you need to indent when you change speakers?

We also noticed that Jessica has only one paragraph in the whole piece. How can she divide it up into more paragraphs? Will dialog help her do that? How?

We wonder whether Jessica read this piece aloud to herself, listening to her writing and thinking about the question, "Does it make sense?" How can she use a partner to help her revise her piece?

We like the way that Jessica drew a picture before she started writing. Why did she do this? How did this help her write her story?

Active Involvement Provide a variety of books for kids to read with partners. For examples see the additional books listed in this lesson's Instructional Materials. Choose books that will help kids generate questions about how the writers used questions to help them revisit, revise, and rework their writing.

Encourage them to share their questions and their thinking about how they could be used to revise with their partners.

Off You Go Provide opportunities for kids to work with partners or a small group as they revise their own writing. Have them keep a list of questions that readers ask about their writing so that they can refer to them as they work to revisit, rework, and revise.

Instructional Materials

- *Angels Ride Bikes and Other Fall Poems* by Francisco X. Alarcon
- *Laughing Tomatoes and Other Spring Poems* by Francisco X. Alarcon
- Overhead transparency sheet
- Writer's notebooks

3: Visualizing

Writers create impact through the use of strong nouns and verbs whenever possible.

Teaching Moves

Start Up/Connection Allow kids to browse through the Alarcon poetry books. Have them talk with partners about the poems and which ones they like. To provide kids with background information about Francisco Alarcon and the books, read the "Afterword" that he wrote on the last pages of each of the books.

Angels Ride Bikes . . . is a collection of bilingual poems about fall in Los Angeles—the City of the Angels. *Laughing Tomatoes* . . . is a collection of poems that were written to share Alarcon's dream of a world filled with gardens.

Here's what Alarcon's "Afterword" says about writing poetry: "I started writing down poems by jotting down the songs my grandma used to sing to us. I would write at the kitchen table, surrounded by our pets, smelling my grandma's delicious cooking. For me, poetry is about life, family, community" (1999).

Give Information Talk with kids about how poets (writers who choose to write poetry) help readers visualize their poems by using strong nouns and verbs. Choose several poems from the books; we use "My Grandma's Songs" and "Day of the Dead." Model for students as you read the poems and think aloud about the strong nouns and verbs Francisco Alarcon uses to help us "see" his poems. Make a list of the nouns and verbs on an overhead sheet.

Strong Nouns and Verbs from Alarcon's Poems

Nouns	Verbs
beat	follow
washing machine	turning
kitchen	consoling
dance floor	delighting
chairs	putting to sleep
family portraits	giving flavor
walls	used to sing
sheet	could make
clothesline	come out
flavor	could turn

boiling pot of beans	going back
songs	laugh and cry
grandma	brings
stars	take
young girl	dedicate
river	share
water	want to recall
joy	imagine
dead	place
people	comes to visit
flowers	
tombs	
home	
altar	
family dinner	
stories	
offerings	
bread	
music	
photo	

Active Involvement Provide two Alarcon collections of poetry as well as many others for the kids to read. Have them work with partners to make a list of the strong words; we call them *Powerful Words*. Provide opportunities for them to share the words they find with each other and the group.

Off You Go Since the purpose of collecting Powerful Words is to have them available to use, encourage kids to keep lists of words in their writer's notebooks as a reference for their writing. During conferences with kids, have them share their words with you and have them tell you how they are using them in their writing to help readers visualize.

4: Inferring

Writers, particularly fiction and poetry writers, are aware of far more detail than they reveal in the texts they compose. This encourages readers to infer by drawing conclusions, making critical judgments, predicting, and connecting to other texts and experiences.

Instructional Materials
- *Chato and the Party Animals* by Gary Soto
- Student writing

Teaching Moves

Start Up/Connection Have kids share information with each other about their friends and the things they do together. Encourage them to talk about where they live and the parties and other events that happen in the neighborhood. Have them focus on birthday parties. Kids can share their thoughts with partners or in a small group.

Give Information Explain that *Chato and the Party Animals* is fiction. It was written by Gary Soto, who has experience and knowledge of life in *el barrio*. He created this story as an imaginary way to write about friends and friendship. Tell students that writers are aware of far more detail than they reveal in the texts they compose. This is often referred to as "showing not telling"; it encourages readers to infer by drawing conclusions, making critical judgments, predicting, and connecting to other texts and experiences.

Active Involvement As you read the story to them, think aloud about places where the writer helps you infer by drawing conclusions, making critical judgments, predicting, and connecting to other texts and experiences. While you're reading, encourage kids to also share what they find with partners or the group. For reference, keep a list—similar to the one in the table—of what you and they discover during the reading.

Places in Chato and the Party Animals *Where Soto Helps Readers Infer*

Drawing Conclusions

"I don't know when I was born. I never knew my *mami*. I never even had a birthday party, or nothing."
Birthdays are really important to Novio Boy because he was abandoned and has never celebrated his birthday with his family or anyone else.

Making Critical Judgments

"'*Pobrecito*. Everybody needs a birthday party,' Chato said to himself when he got home. 'I'm going to give my *carnal* a party.'"
We can tell that Chato is a good friend. He really wants to do something for Novio Boy and he knows that birthdays are important to him. We wonder what will happen with the party. How will he organize it?

Predicting

"Novio Boy hung his head and said, 'No, thanks. I don't feel hungry.' His eyelashes were shining with tears."
We predict that Novio Boy is really unhappy about something because he is crying.

Connecting to Other Texts and Experiences

The glossary at the front of the book reminds us of other books we read that use words from Spanish or other languages. They often have a glossary to help readers understand unfamiliar words.
This book reminds us of another book about Chato and Novio Boy that was written by Gary Soto, *Chato's Kitchen*. They are really good friends.

Off You Go Encourage kids to try out helping readers infer by "showing not telling" in their writing. They can do this in writer's notebooks or pieces of writing. Provide opportunities for them to share their writing with partners. Have them watch for places where writers encourage readers to infer by drawing conclusions, making critical judgments, predicting, and connecting to other texts and experiences.

5: Determining Importance in Text

Writers make decisions about the most important ideas to include in the pieces they write. They decide which genre and structure are best to communicate their ideas.

Instructional Materials
- *Exploding Ants: Amazing Facts About How Animals Adapt* by Joanne Settel
- Additional informational texts

Teaching Moves

Start Up/Connection To help kids build background, provide lots of informational books for them to look through. As they browse through the books, encourage them to share what they notice with partners or the group. Things to notice include the table of contents, glossary, index, photographs, captions, illustrations, maps, lists, drawings, and so on, and how the writer makes the information they want readers to learn interesting.

Give Information Read kids the following quote from the flyleaf of *Exploding Ants*.

> A wasp lays its eggs under a caterpillar's skin so that its young can eat the caterpillar's guts as they grow. A young head louse makes its home on a human hair and feasts on human blood. Frogs use their eyeballs to help swallow their food.
>
> From small worms that live in a dog's nose mucus to exploding ants to regurgitating mother gulls, this book tells of the unusual ways animals find food, shelter, and safety in the natural world.

Explain to them that as writers work on text they make decisions about the most important ideas to include in the pieces they write.

Go through the book, pointing out how Joanne Settel uses titles such as "invasion of the body snatchers," "swelling, expanding, and exploding bodies," and "murderous nest mates" to get us interested, to draw us into her book, and to make us want to learn some of these amazing facts about how animals adapt. For example on page 10, about "murderous nest mates," Settel writes:

> Sharing a nest with a newly hatched cuckoo bird can be a deadly proposition. Cuckoo young aren't big on sharing. In fact, they make certain that they won't have to share food or space by throwing their nest mates out of the nest.

Then as a caption for the photograph on the next page, she writes: "A warbler feeds a large cuckoo chick. The young cuckoo has pushed all of the warbler's own eggs and chicks out of the nest."

Also explain that writers make decisions about the best genre and structure to communicate their ideas. In this case, the writer chose to organize the text by using some of the features of informational text, such as a table of contents, glossary, index, photographs, captions, titles, and so on.

Active Involvement Have kids work with partners and go through informational books looking for how writers make them interesting. Have them think about the decisions the writer made to determine what was important for the book. Then have students check to see where and how writers organize their information using a table of contents, glossary, index, photographs, captions, titles, and so on. Provide opportunities for them to share what they find with another set of partners or the group.

Off You Go Provide kids with a variety of opportunities to use their writer's notebooks to record information they learn or facts about things that interest them. Encourage them to write informational texts using a table of contents, glossary, index, photographs, captions, titles, illustrations, maps, lists, drawings, and so on. In this way, they practice determining what is important to include and what isn't and which genre they want to use and how to structure their writing.

6: Synthesizing

Writers study other writers and draw conclusions about what makes good writing. They work to replicate the style of authors they find compelling.

Teaching Moves

Start Up/Connection To help kids build background, have them talk with partners about special times they have had with their grandparents, times they remember from growing up, or stories they have been told. Have partners share their experiences with other partners or with the group. To integrate strategy use, see the comprehension lesson for this story in *Making Sense* (2005, p. 97).

Give Information Read aloud the "Author's Note" at the beginning of the book. Explain to kids that the writer, Lenore Look, wrote it as a first-person narrative. Growing up in Seattle, she spent many Saturdays in her grandmother's kitchen. Like the girl in the story, as the flyleaf notes, she "loves to eat crab, especially when it's cooked the Chinese way with lots of ginger and *daosee* (black bean paste)."

Talk with them about how, as writers, they can study other writers and draw conclusions about what makes good writing. Then they can incorporate what they learn into their writing by using the style of authors they find compelling.

Point out some of the good writing that you notice in *Love as Strong as Ginger*. Explain that writers often choose other authors as mentors to teach them about good writing. Write examples from the story on an overhead transparency sheet.

Good Writing Examples from Love as Strong as Ginger

We like how Lenore Look uses Chinese words to help us understand the story, for example:

"*'Chiubungbung,'* she replied, meaning stinky-stinky in Taishanese, our Chinese dialect."
"She taught me how to make *doong*, sticky rice dumplings wrapped in bamboo leaves."

Instructional Materials
- *Love as Strong as Ginger* by Lenore Look
- Overhead transparency sheet
- Possible mentor authors' books (see list on page 117)

We like how she writes advice into her story, for example:

"'Sure,' she said. 'Katie, in America, you can become whatever you dream.'"

"'You're strong enough to do other things . . . to become whatever you dream.'"

Active Involvement Have students work with a partner to find a mentor author—someone they find compelling, whose work they like, and from whom they can draw conclusions about what makes good writing. Provide books from many authors who write in different genres and styles. Focus on writers who write various types of books or who write in different genres.

Kids Choose Mentor Authors

As kids choose their mentor authors, it's slow at first. They are hesitant and watchful, but it's such an adventure.

Sokunteer chooses Sandra Cisneros, the author of *Hairs/Pelitos*. She likes how the text is in English on the top of the page and Spanish on the bottom. She thinks she will try to write a story with English at the top and Khmer (Cambodian) on the bottom.

Gary Soto is a very popular mentor author with our writers. Guadalupe, Francisco, Jorge, and Ericka want to use *Too Many Tamales* as a mentor text. They love his description of the kitchen: "They made twenty-four tamales as the windows grew white with delicious-smelling curls of steam."

Jane Yolen is popular with Fernando and Sokun. In *Owl Moon*, they like the way she describes the owl's call: "The owl's call came closer, from high up in the trees on the edge of the meadow. Nothing in the meadow moved."

Off You Go Once kids choose mentor authors, encourage them to try out and replicate the authors' style in their own writing. Writer's notebooks provide a risk-free environment for trying a different style of writing. Once they find a style that works for them, they can try it in a piece of writing.

7: Monitoring Meaning and Comprehension

Writers share their work so that others can help them monitor the clarity and impact of the pieces.

Teaching Moves

Start Up/Connection The concept of Open Mike at our school was developed by teachers Wendy Wahlen and Saroeung Yoeun. Working with struggling fifth-grade students at risk of retention, they looked for ways to motivate them to share their writing and get feedback. They have shown us how something as simple as bringing an imaginary microphone into a classroom can help create a community of writers.

Provide photos and digital recordings of previous Open Mike performances for students. Share with them about how excited kids are to share their writing and get feedback from others when they read their pieces out loud (see Figure 8.10). Encourage kids to share their previous experiences when reading

Instructional Materials

- Copies of student writing from a variety of genres (writing portfolios)
- Student writing anthologies from previous years
- Microphones (real or imagined)

figure 8.10 *Four girls collaborate by writing and reading together.*

their writing to a class or group. Talk about what makes it exciting and fun.

Give Information Tell kids that they will be picking pieces from their writing portfolios to read for Open Mike. Explain that this is one way writers share their work so that others can help them monitor the clarity and impact of the pieces and that they will be receiving feedback from listeners.

Establish criteria for selection of pieces: number to choose, genre, length, necessity of editing and proofreading, and so on.

Active Involvement Have kids work with partners to go through their writing portfolios to select pieces to publish in the anthology. Encourage them to have their partners read the pieces they select and to give them feedback. Forms can be provided so that each reader gives feedback about the clarity of the piece—How easy is it to understand what the writer is saying?—and the impact of the work—Is it memorable? Would you want to write a piece like this?

Once writers have selected their pieces for reading at Open Mike, have kids write invitations (see Figures 8.11 and 8.12) and then explain the procedures in the following table to them.

Directions for Open Mike

1. You'll need a microphone (real or imaginary). We started with an imaginary one that was introduced by a very dramatic and believable teacher. She would step up to "the mike" at the front of the class, pretend to be adjusting it, and then go through a litany of "Testing, testing. Can you hear me?" The kids ate this up. They loved it!
2. Kids need to have work that is ready to publish and "go public." The first year we introduced Open Mike we did it at the end of our first

figure 8.11 *Students design the covers of invitations to Open Mike.*

unit of study. From then on, it was the kids who were always asking, "When is the next Open Mike?" They were using that expectation to plan and organize their writing work.

3. Everyone needs to be open to the spontaneity that arises from such an event as Open Mike.

4. It needs to be simple. All you need is an imaginary or real microphone, student writing, and an eager audience.

5. Open Mike needs to be scheduled regularly and frequently to have the best chance of motivating writers to be ready to publish their work.

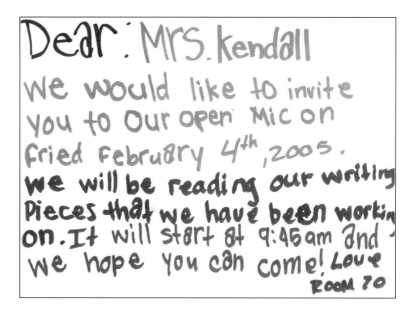

figure 8.12 *The letterlike format personalizes the Open Mike invitation.*

Off You Go Once the Open Mike performance is finished (we try to schedule one every four or five weeks because it is so motivating), provide photos and digital recordings of the performances for kids to view and reflect about their writing and their performances; comments about what some students learned about their writing by reading for Open Mike follow. It is difficult to describe the impact Open Mike has had for our writers. It changes them from reluctant and struggling into eager and prepared. We wouldn't teach writing without it.

Students' Comments About Open Mike

Sonia, "When Ms. Wahlen Lost Her Keys"—"I'd make it shorter because I felt like it took a long time to read."

Jacquie, "My Pet Hamster"—"To make it longer because it only had a little bit of details. When I read the story, I realized I needed more details."

Veronica, "Rosita, A Mexican Cinderella Story"—"I need more pictures in my story. I need more powerful words."

Jenny, "My Trip to the Zoo"—"I need more dialog because it was boring. It didn't make sense when I was reading it without the dialog."

Nestor and José, "The Haunted Bathrooms"—"The beginning was good because it sounded right. In the middle, it didn't sound right. We need to make it more scary by using, '. . . and then when the ceiling fell on him, his spirit stayed in the girl's bathroom.'"

Mary, "Me Turn Cuckoo"—"I thought it was funny to me and it made the audience laugh. It would be better if I could tell what my little sister did to me to make me laugh."

Casey, "Doom III"—"Give more information. Tell them what is the Cheat Codes and how you get invisible."

Joseph, "The Muddy Day"—"I liked when I used the powerful words *cardiac arrest.* I would add more powerful words to make it better."

Gladys, "Going to L.A."—"I wrote a book. You shouldn't read the whole book because it would take you forever to read. They probably get bored."

Drina, "My Two Best Teachers"—"I need details because I only had a little bit of details about the teachers. I'll ask them what things they have in common."

Oscar and Steven, "The Grudge and the Ring"—"Put powerful words, scary words. Words like *frightened, bloody face.* If it's a scary story, use your lead to scare people and give them more scary details."

8: Fix-Up Strategies

Instructional Materials

▢ *National Geographic Kids* magazine at http://www.national-geographic.com/ngkids/

▢ *Time for Kids* magazine at http://www.timeforkids.com

Writers capitalize on their knowledge of writers' tools (that is, character, setting, conflict, theme, plot structure, leads, style, etc.) to enhance their meaning.

Teaching Moves

Start Up/Connection Working with grade-level colleagues to analyze kids' writing, it becomes clear that developing strong leads (how to begin the piece of writing) needs to be an instructional focus. To determine next steps, kids choose a piece of writing and talk with partners about leads. For example, they can discuss where they got their ideas, how they made their decisions as writers, why they thought it made a good lead for a personal narrative or memoir, and so on.

Give Information Share the information gathered by working with colleagues to assess kids' writing. Encourage them to add their observations from the conversations they had with partners about their writing. Explain that writers capitalize on their knowledge of writers' tools to enhance their meaning. One of the tools writers have is a lead. A strong beginning draws readers into the writing and helps them understand what the piece is about. The *National Geographic Kids* and *Time for Kids* magazines both make successful efforts to have strong writing and great leads. They are wonderful resources for teaching writing to English Language Learners because they feature short, quality text that is highly motivating to kids and that can be used as models for student writing.

For example, go through magazines, such as *National Geographic Kids,* and discuss the ways that the writers use leads to create understanding for readers. Model by thinking aloud about what you notice.

Active Involvement Next, we work together to do "try-its"; this time the focus is on leads. Have kids work with partners or in small-group conferences to do this. Remind yourself that the setting should be "safe, even playful." Before kids write things down, talk with them and encourage them to try out different ways to say things.

We took the following first sentences from four articles in the December 2002 *National Geographic Kids* as mentors for some kids' resulting "try-its."

Examples of Student Try-its

Lead from "Time Travel"

"Time travel isn't something only for the future."

Try-it #1: *Kangaroo Jack* isn't a movie only for little kids.

Try-it #2: *Dragonball Z* isn't a cartoon show just for little kids. It's for teens, too.

Try-it #3: Cheetahs aren't just mammals, they are members of the cat family.

Try-It #4: The hound dog isn't just a dog. It's also an Elvis Presley song.

Lead from "Survivor"

"The arctic fox relies on three tricks to get by—stealing, storing, and snuggling."

Try-it #1: The polar bear relies on being very strong to catch his food.

Try-it #2: *The Addams Family* movie relies on scaring people away from their house.

Try-it #3: Deion Sanders relies on three skills to get by—backpedaling, jumping, and catching.

Lead from "Smart Toys"

"Your new toy may be smarter than a Dexter's laboratory invention."

Try-it #1: The Siberian Husky may be smarter than the wolf.

Try-it #2: College football may be more fun than high school football.

Lead from "The Wild Thornberry's Movie"

"Admit it: helping a rhino who has told you poachers were after him can be pretty cool."

Try-it #1: Admit it: helping a snow fox to find food if a polar bear was after him could be pretty scary.

Try-it #2: Admit it: watching people walk up the wall and do back flips can be pretty cool. (*The Matrix*)

Try-it #3: Admit it: snow dogs are much better than regular dogs. They work harder.

Off You Go Remind kids that they can use their writer's notebooks as a place to try out writing different kinds of leads. As they work on writing, encourage them to go back to the list of leads chart and other magazines and books to search for interesting ways to begin their writing so that they can build understanding for readers.

Books for Teaching Strategies to Older English Language Learners

Intermediate Stage

Making Connections

Look to the North, A Wolf Pup Diary by Jean Craighead George
My Name Was Hussein by Hristo Kyuichukov
My Very Own Room by Amada Irma Perez
Smoky Night by Eve Bunting
"Wolf to Woof, Evolution of Dogs" from *National Geographic Magazine*, January 2002
Wolves by Gail Gibbons

Asking Questions

Aunt Harriet's Underground Railroad in the Sky by Faith Ringgold
Follow the Drinking Gourd by Janette Winter
If You Traveled on the Underground Railroad by Ellen Levine
Martin's Big Words by Doreen Rappaport
Sweet Clara and the Freedom Quilt by Deborah Hopkinson
Through My Eyes by Ruby Bridges

Visualizing

Angels Ride Bikes and Other Fall Poems by Francisco X. Alarcon
Into the Sea by Brenda Z. Guiberson
Laughing Tomatoes and Other Spring Poems by Francisco X. Alarcon
Saint Saens' Carnival of the Animals (with CD) by John Lithgow
Wings by Christopher Myers

Inferring

Chato and the Party Animals by Gary Soto
The Green Frogs: A Korean Folktale by Yumi Heo
La Llorona, The Weeping Woman by Joe Hayes
The Old Man and His Door by Gary Soto
Prietita and the Ghost Woman by Gloria Anzaldua

Determining Importance in Nonfiction

Animal Defenses: How Animals Protect Themselves by Etta Kaner
Animals Nobody Loves by Seymour Simon
Do Tarantulas Have Teeth? Questions and Answers About Poisonous Creatures by Melvin Berger
Exploding Ants: Amazing Facts About How Animals Adapt by Joanne Settel
Wings, Stings, and Wriggly Things, Insects/Minibeasts by Martin Jenkins

Synthesizing

Angel Child, Dragon Child by Michele Surat
Love as Strong as Ginger by Lenore Look
The Table Where Rich People Sit by Byrd Baylor

figure 9.1 (top) These boys enjoy using computers for their first drafts.

figure 9.2 (center) Henry, Nestor, and Mary work on their writing using mentor texts.

figure 9.3 (bottom) Newspapers act as mentor texts for writing informational pieces.

9 ADVANCED

At the advanced stage of language proficiency, students demonstrate nativelike oral fluency. They are comfortable speaking with friends and in class. The vocabularies of English Language Learners are growing and they often enjoy opportunities to work collaboratively with a small group and make oral presentations.

But these same students face literacy challenges (reading and writing). They may struggle with reading for content areas and need extensive vocabulary development, including words and concepts for various subjects—science, math, history and social science, physical education, music, and fine arts. It is important to concentrate on extensive, contextualized academic vocabulary development. Strategies for learning should include accessing prior knowledge; building background through hands-on, concrete experiences; and a multitude of opportunities to use new words and concepts.

To master grade-level content, kids need to learn specific words and concepts that match the standards they are mastering. This helps to make textbooks accessible to them. Include grade-level text and other materials for content-area reading when selecting what to use for strategy instruction. To make it easier for kids to read textbooks and other resources, teach them how to use the features of informational text (that is, the table of contents, chapter headings, photographs, illustrations, captions, charts, graphs, glossary, and index). Then provide them with lots of experiences reading and writing a variety of informational texts.

Frequent, ongoing writing opportunities encourage kids to write in many genres and to develop their own approach to the craft. Persuasive essays and reports about information offer them ways to use what they are learning to inform others.

Younger English Language Learners in Real Time

"Do we have Journalism today?" the kids call out as Juli crosses the playground from her bungalow classroom to the office.

"Of course!" she responds. "We're going to celebrate publishing our third edition of *Whittier Times*." She knows that the cookies are on the table and the juice boxes are chilled, but she needs a few more copies of the latest issue of the newspaper so that everyone will have their own.

As they pile into the classroom, chairs are spread out in a wide circle to accommodate all the journalists. It's a group of kids whose reading and writing levels were a year and a half below grade level, and it's working as a way to bring them to grade level and beyond.

So now the room is bulging with life, and everyone's eager to share their articles. Juli begins by handing everyone a copy of the newspaper and a juice box with a napkin full of cookies. As kids jump into reading, slurping and crunching fill the air.

Joel is always the first one to want to share. He reads his article as everyone listens and then asks for responses and questions from the kids. They want to know how he got so lucky as to have his photo with the principal published, and he smiles and says, "'Cause I'm handsome!" Everyone laughs, and the next brave volunteer starts to read. The group continues on for forty-five minutes until everyone has taken a turn reading and responding. But it doesn't all happen in just one week.

Over time a rhythm for publishing the newspaper established itself. The first week was devoted to reading, sharing, and commenting on the most current issue. Next came a week of brainstorming, picking topics, and forming groups to write articles. Then, two weeks were spent interviewing, photographing, surveying, writing, and revising. Finally, a week was devoted to meeting a deadline and getting it all ready to publish.

In all, it took five weeks for a newspaper to go out into the world. Not a bad way to motivate reluctant writers to get their work up to grade-level standards!

Lessons for Younger English Language Learners

1: Making Connections

Writers use knowledge of their audience to decide what to include and exclude.

Teaching Moves

Start Up/Connection Talk with kids about what they know about writing for an *audience*—the people who will be reading a piece of writing. Encourage them to share how they determine an audience for their writing. Have them share some of their writing with partners and talk about the audience for the pieces.

Give Information Explain to kids that writers use knowledge of their audience to decide what to include and exclude. *You Have to Write* is written for an audience of kids—kids who have to write but have nothing to write about. As you read the book, think aloud about how the writer includes things based on her knowledge of the audience. On chart paper, list examples of what Janet Wong includes in her writing because she knows the audience—kids who don't have anything to write.

> *Examples of What's Included in* **You Have to Write**
>
> What can you do when you don't have anything to write about?
>
> Stop and think.
>
> No one else can tell your stories.
> No one else can tell what it was like when bad things happened to you.
> But what if you don't like what you write?
> There are all sorts of ways to change it, to make it better.
> Keep on playing with your words, putting them together in different ways.

Instructional Materials

- ☐ *You Have to Write* by Janet Wong
- ☐ Student writing
- ☐ Chart paper

figure 9.4 Sergio's letter to Mrs. Kendall shows his knowledge of his audience.

Dear Mrs. Kendal 10-20-04

I am sorry for not listening to you and for hitting dalvin and next time I go with you I will behave myself and keep my hands and feet to myself and listen to you. I realize that you are helping me to go to middle school; I will try harder next time.

From: sergio Ayala

Active Involvement Have kids go through some of their writing and think about the audience for their pieces (for example, see Figure 9.4). Have them ask themselves such things as the following:

> Who am I writing this for?
> How do I know that they will understand what I am saying?
> What else should I include in this piece of writing for this audience?
> Is there anything I should take out or exclude?

Have them share what they learn about their writing with a partner.

Off You Go While kids work on writing in different content areas and genres, encourage them to pay attention to the audience for their pieces. Have them think about what they should include and what they should take out to help the audience make sense of their writing.

2: Asking Questions

Writers' questions lead to revision in their pieces and in the pieces to which they respond for other writers.

Teaching Moves

Start Up/Connection Hand out a variety of newspapers for kids to browse and read. Ask them to pay close attention to the photographs and how they add to the articles. Encourage them to share what they notice in the newspapers with partners or a small group.

Give Information Explain to kids that they are going to learn how journalists use questions—who, what, when, where, why, and how—to help them write. Such questions will lead to revisions in their own pieces and in the pieces to which they respond for other writers/journalists.

Share the "News Snapshot" Web site with kids. Print out a copy of the student handout for each class member. Also print the teacher's page, which includes answers to the questions and a link to the related article.

Active Involvement Hand out the student's page. Have kids work with partners to use their knowledge of current events, the picture, and the quotation as clues to answer the questions on the page. Review kids' answers by having them share with the group. Talk about how they found the answers to the questions (who, what, when, where, why, and how) and how they can use the answers to these questions to write their own articles.

Off You Go Provide opportunities for kids to try out writing news articles using the who, what, where, when, why, and how questions to revise their writing (see Figure 9.5). The "News Shapshot" Web site suggests the following:

> Have each student create his or her own News Snapshot by choosing an interesting photograph from the newspaper, reading the related article, and creating a series of questions and answers based on the photograph. Students can also find Web sites related to the snapshots chosen.

Instructional Materials

- *New York Times Learning Network,* Grades 3–12, at http://www.nytimes.com/learning/
- "News Snapshot," a Current Events Activity for Grades 3–5, at http://www.nytimes.com/learning/teachers/snapshot/index.html
- Printouts of student handout and teacher's page
- Copies of newspapers

figure 9.5 *Sam and Ryan revise using who, what, where, when, why, and how questions.*

3: Visualizing (Using Sensory Images)

Writers learn from the images created in their minds as they read. They study other authors' use of images as a way to improve their own.

Teaching Moves

Start Up/Connection Tell kids you want to find out what they already know about visualizing and creating images in their minds. Give them a minute or two to think, and then ask them to discuss their thoughts with partners. Have each set of partners share with the group. As kids share, list what they already know about visualizing on a piece of chart paper.

Give Information Explain to kids that writers spend a lot of time reading to learn from the images created in their minds as they read. Studying other authors' use of images helps writers improve their own. Read aloud several poems in English from *My Name Is Jorge*. To model for kids, as shown in the following, think aloud about the poems you read and how they create images in your mind.

> *Examples of Images Created by Medina's Poems*
>
> *Poem*—"My Name Is Jorge"
>
>   "George!
>   What an ugly sound!
>   Like a sneeze!"
>
> *Image*—I see someone sneezing every time he says his name.

Instructional Materials

- *My Name Is Jorge: On Both Sides of the River, Poems in English and Spanish* by Jane Medina
- Chart paper

Poem—"Why Am I Dumb?"

"In my country
I was smart
Only tens!
Never even an eight!"

Image—I see this kid looking at his spelling paper, scratching his head, and shaking it back and forth in disbelief.

Poem—"The Busy Street"

"At least,
we crossed
the river
only once.

We have to cross
this street
every day."

Image—I see a little boy who is afraid to cross a busy street like one near our school. He's standing at the crosswalk holding his mother's hand and waiting until it's safe to cross.

figure 9.6 *The first page of José's poem shows how words can be moved around to help readers visualize.*

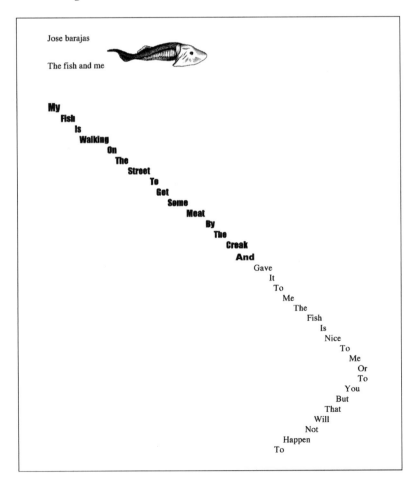

Active Involvement Hand out copies of *My Name Is Jorge* and ask kids to browse through the poems. Encourage them to choose poems to read and to discuss the images they create in their minds with partners.

Off You Go While kids are writing poems, provide lots of poetry, including student poems, for them to read. As they read, tell them to pay attention to how the writers' poems create images in their minds. Remind them that they can also help readers create images in the poems they write by helping them to visualize (see Figure 9.6).

4: Inferring

Writers, particularly fiction and poetry writers, are aware of far more detail than they reveal in the texts they compose. This encourages readers to infer by drawing conclusions, making critical judgments, predicting, and connecting to other texts and experiences.

Instructional Materials
- *Sitti's Secrets* by Naomi Shihab Nye
- Student writing

Teaching Moves

Start Up/Connection Have kids share something about their grandparents with each other. Encourage them to talk about where they live or lived, the languages they speak, and what they have learned about and from their grandparents. Kids can share their thoughts with partners or in a small group.

Give Information Explain that the story *Sitti's Secrets* is fiction. It was written by Naomi Shihab Nye, who has a grandmother living in Palestine. She created this story to tell about a special relationship between a grandchild and a grandparent. Tell students that writers are aware of far more detail than they reveal in the texts they compose. This is often referred to as "showing not telling"; it encourages readers to infer by drawing conclusions, making critical judgments, predicting, and connecting to other texts and experiences.

Active Involvement While you read the story, think aloud about places where the writer helps you infer by drawing conclusions, making critical judgments, predicting, and connecting to other texts and experiences. As you're reading, encourage kids to also share what they find with partners or the group. For reference, keep a list—similar to the following table—of what you and the kids discover during the reading.

Inferences Chart for Sitti's Secrets

Drawing Conclusions

"My grandmother lives on the other side of the earth."
Her grandmother lives very far away.

Making Critical Judgments

"Between us are fish and cities and buses and fields and presidents and clotheslines and stop signs and signs that say DO NOT ENTER . . ."
It sounds like there may be some problems. Maybe people don't get along or like each other.

Predicting

"My grandmother and I do not speak the same language."
The little girl and her grandmother are going to find a way to talk to each other even if they don't know the same languages.

Connecting to Other Texts and Experiences

"We thanked the cow, with whistles and clicks, for the fresh milk that we carried home in Sitti's little teapot."
This reminds us of when we are in other countries and to get the milk you have to bring your own bottle or container.

"Some days we stuffed little zucchini squash with rice for dinner . . . We cracked almonds and ate apricots, called *mish-mish*, while we worked."
This reminds us of the books, Bread Song *and* Love as Strong as Ginger, *in which the grandchild and the grandparent have a special relationship and it involves food like crab or bread.*

Off You Go Encourage kids to try out "showing not telling" in their writing. They can do this in writer's notebooks or pieces of writing. Provide opportunities for them to share their writing with partners. Have readers watch for places where writers encourage them to infer by drawing conclusions, making critical judgments, predicting, and connecting to other texts and experiences.

Instructional Materials

- *Cesar Chavez: A Hero for Everyone* by Gary Soto
- *Cesar Chavez: A Struggle for Justice/Cesar Chavez: La lucha por la justicia* by Richard Griswold del Castillo
- *First Day in Grapes* by L. King Perez
- *Harvesting Hope, The Story of Cesar Chavez* by Kathleen Krull
- *Lives of the Writers: Comedies, Tragedies (and What the Neighbors Thought)* by Kathleen Krull
- *Wilma Unlimited: How Wilma Rudolph Became the World's Fastest Woman* by Kathleen Krull

5: Determining Importance in Text

Writers reveal their biases by emphasizing some elements.

Teaching Moves

Start Up/Connection Help kids draw on their prior knowledge about the farmworkers and Cesar Chavez by using the Think–Pair–Share strategy (Harste, Short, and Burke 1995). This strategy involves students thinking about a topic, then working with partners, then sharing their discoveries and thoughts. To do this, ask kids to think about what they already know about the farmworkers and Cesar Chavez. In California, some school districts have a holiday that celebrates his birthday, and kids study his life and his role in the farmworkers' movement.

Over several days, read aloud *Cesar Chavez: A Struggle for Justice/Cesar Chavez: La lucha por la justicia, Cesar Chavez: A Hero for Everyone*, and *First Day in Grapes*. Think aloud as you read about the farmworkers and the role of Cesar Chavez. Encourage kids to share what they are learning as you read.

After reading all three books, give pairs of students the opportunity to discuss what they learned about farmworkers and Cesar Chavez. Then have them share—either with another pair of students, a small group, or the whole class—what they learned during their reading and their discussions.

Give Information Explain to kids that they will be learning about how writers reveal their biases (point of view) by emphasizing some elements when they write biographies. Because they often provide students with people who can serve as role models, biographies are an important genre.

Before reading aloud *Harvesting Hope*, read kids the "Author's Note" at the back of the book. In it Kathleen Krull describes the different points of view about her topic—Cesar Chavez.

> Chavez was—and is—controversial. Especially among those resistant to change, he had many enemies and received constant death threats. Even today, some argue about him and his goals, and others have forgotten him or never heard of him. But many continue to see him as a hero—for his utter sincerity, his belief that peaceful dedication to a cause is more effective than force, and his self-sacrifice in the face of overwhelming odds.

As you read the book, think aloud about where the writer shows bias and how she does it. For example, when she describes what it was like for the young Cesar to work in the fields, she shows her bias (point of view) by writing: "Farm chores on someone else's farm instead of on his own felt like a form of slavery."

Active Involvement Have kids go back through Griswold del Castillo, Krull, and Soto to look for how the writers use their writing to show their bias (point of view). Encourage them to share what they find with each other.

Off You Go Provide other biographies for kids to read and browse for the writers' bias and how they show it. Kathleen Krull has written a series of short biographies that has many volumes. We often use *Lives of the Writers: Comedies, Tragedies (and What the Neighbors Thought)* from that series. She also wrote *Wilma Unlimited: How Wilma Rudolph Became the World's Fastest Woman*, which we also use.

6: Synthesizing

Writers reveal themes in a way that suggests their importance. Readers can create a cogent synthesis from well-written material.

Teaching Moves

Start Up/Connection Talk with kids about what they already know about synthesizing. If necessary, remind them that *synthesizing* is realizing and understanding how our thinking changes as we read well-written material. Encourage them to share stories, essays, and other forms of text that lead to changes in their thinking as they read. Have them discuss how they can write so that their readers will also be able to synthesize.

Give Information Explain to kids that writers reveal themes in a way that suggest their importance to readers. Because of this, readers can create a cogent synthesis from well-written material. To model how to do this, tell kids that you will be using the following Synthesizing Frame (Kendall and Khuon 2005) to create a synthesis from *Tea Leaves*. We use this frame to scaffold use of the

Instructional Materials
- *Tea Leaves* by Frederick Lipp
- Student writing

synthesizing strategy and to help students understand how thinking changes as we read well-written material.

Synthesizing Frame

I first thought this . . .

But then I learned . . .

Next I learned . . .

But this changed everything because . . .

This is way different from what I thought at the beginning. My thinking changed because . . .

As you read aloud *Tea Leaves*, use the Synthesizing Frame to model how you can create a cogent synthesis from well-written material. While you work, think aloud about how the writer reveals the themes of (1) love of family, (2) wanting to see more of the world, and (3) learning from your experiences. Kids may be able to generate other themes the writer uses in the story.

Juli's Synthesizing Frame for Tea Leaves

I first thought this was going to be a story about Shanti going to school because it says in the story: "Five minutes into her walk to school . . ."

But then I learned that none of the children in Shanti's class had ever seen the sea even though they live on the island of Sri Lanka.

Next I learned that Shanti's mother, Ammma, picks tea leaves and that "the tea leaves are sent in ships across the sea to England and other places."

But this changed everything because I learned that her uncle, Nochi, takes the tea leaves on a train to the Indian Ocean. He thinks Shanti should go on his diesel engine to a town by the sea so she can see it for herself.

This is way different from what I thought at the beginning. My thinking changed because first I thought the story was about Shanti and where she lived and now I realize that it's about having a dream, like seeing the sea. In the story Shanti learns from the sea using her senses—seeing, hearing, smelling, tasting, and feeling. When she goes home, she shares what she learned with her mother.

Active Involvement Have kids choose a piece of their writing to share with partners. Have each partner read the other's writing and use the Synthesizing Frame to develop a synthesis. Encourage them to work together to revise, rewrite, or rework writing that is difficult to synthesize and to pay attention to how the writer reveals themes.

Encourage kids to incorporate the language of the Synthesizing Frame into their discussions of the writing. Here's an example of how Patti worked with Jacqueline to use the Synthesizing Frame to help her revise, rewrite, and rework her hamster story.

My Pet Hamster

I have a pet hamster her name is Paula she is nice but she sleep to much the first time she hade babies when she hade 7 of them. The last time she hade babies she hade 12 of them. I sold the babies so that they won't fit. One of them hade ran off. Then the one that was big was the one that is made at all of them. Then they don't get with the other ones too. Now she has left but if I find her I will be happy. I will buy a biter cage for her to live in. the cage it was cool.

What Patti Said About Jacqueline's Story

OK, I first thought this that you were writing about your hamster that lives with you because you said "is." That made me think you have her now. If you used "was" that means you used to have her.

But then I learned that your hamster had 12 babies and I wondered how she took care of them all. Maybe you could give us more information about how she took care of them like how she feeds them and cleans them and gets them to go to sleep.

Next I learned that one of the babies ran away. I think you should change "One of them hade ran off" to "One of them ran away." You also need to check how you spell "had" because you have an "e" on the end.

But this changed everything because I realized you really need to revise some of the things you are saying because it doesn't make sense. Like this one, "I sold the babies so that they won't fit." I think you mean "so they won't fight."

This is way different from what I thought at the beginning. My thinking changed because at the end of the story, I learned that your hamster is gone and it seems like you miss her. Maybe you could add some more to the end of the story so we will know why you will be happy if you find her.

Off You Go Provide other opportunities for kids to read each other's writing and use the Synthesizing Frame to develop a synthesis. Sharing with each other encourages writers to revise and alerts them to where their writing doesn't make sense to readers.

7: Monitoring Meaning and Comprehension

Writers share their work so that others can help them monitor the clarity and impact of the pieces.

Teaching Moves

Start Up/Connection This lesson is designed for both younger (kindergarten, first-, and second-grade) and older (fourth- and fifth-grade) students. The purpose of the lesson is for fourth and fifth graders to write stories that they can

Instructional Materials
- Variety of simple picture books
- Student-created picture books

share with kindergarten, first-, or second-grade kids to monitor the clarity and impact of their work.

Provide a wide variety of simple picture books that are appropriate for kindergarten, first-, and/or second-grade English Language Learners for the fourth and fifth graders to read and browse. We use the picture books for younger students listed in Chapter 6, "Preproduction," and Chapter 7, "Early Production." Examples of student-published children's stories help students visualize how to do this project. An example story (written and picture book versions)—Veronica's "My First Communion in Mexico"—can be found in the Appendix. It includes her original text version of the story and an adaptation for her children's book.

Have the fourth and fifth graders work with partners to decide what kind of book they think the kindergarten, first, or second graders would enjoy and why. Have partners share their conclusions with the group. Encourage kids to explore many aspects of writing simple picture books, including the following:

- Where do writers get their ideas?
- How do they use illustrations to help tell the story?
- How do they make their stories clear and easy to understand?
- How do they create the impact (the strong effect) that the story has?

Give Information Explain to kids that writers share their work so that others can help them monitor the clarity and impact of the pieces. Tell them that they will be working in pairs and writing simple picture books to share with kindergarten, first-, or second-grade children. Our school goes from kindergarten through fifth grade, so this is easily managed by coordinating among intermediate and primary teachers.

Active Involvement Provide time over several weeks for kids to work with their partners to write a simple picture book. We use this simple process:

- Brainstorm ideas.
- Write a draft (include illustrations).
- Share the story with others to get help for revising, reworking, and rewriting.
- Edit using the Five Finger Rule for Editing and also have a peer editor review the story.
- Confer with the teacher.
- Publish the story.

Off You Go Have kids read their stories to younger kids. Often we put everyone in pairs—two older students reading and two younger students listening and responding. They can visit each other's classrooms or meet someplace cozy, perhaps in the school library or at a media center.

8: Fix-Up Strategies

Writers capitalize on their knowledge of writers' tools (that is, character, setting, conflict, theme, plot structure, leads, style, etc.) to enhance their meaning.

Teaching Moves

Start Up/Connection Provide articles that include information from surveys for kids to read. Use a variety of sources such as newspapers and magazines. Be sure to include surveys written by kids (see the following example). Have them work with partners to see how the survey is structured around a question or series of questions. Have pairs share what they notice with the group.

Instructional Materials
- Copies of surveys written by students
- Copies of articles about surveys
- Analyzing Surveys with Kids (ASK), Listening to Student Voices, at http://www. nwrel. org/scpd/scc/ studentvoices/ask.shtml

A Student Survey by Melissa and Gabi

What Do You Think Would Make Whittier More Beautiful?

Do you want to make school better?

We interviewed students and teachers of Whittier so they could give us ideas to make Whittier more beautiful. We asked a lot of students, "What do you want?"

Grade 1: Maria—flowers, Melanie—trees, Miss Henderson—more colors

Grade 2: Mrs. Landis—decorated trash cans, José—more basketballs, Jasmine—more tetherballs

Grade 3: Sofia—more games, Ms. Williams—a mural on the ball shed, Jocelyn—monkey bars

Grade 4: William—more books to read, Amanda—decorations, Malcolm—more plants and more trees, Ruth—"I want more balls. We need more grass."

Grade 5: Miriam—change the school blue, Heydi—have a soccer field, Alma—swings and slides, Victor—good lunches

Give Information Tell kids that writers capitalize on their knowledge of writers' tools (that is, character, setting, conflict, theme, plot structure, leads, style, etc.) to enhance their meaning. Surveys are one style that writers use for informational articles. Hand out copies of "A Student Survey" by Melissa and Gaby.

While you read through the survey with kids, think aloud about how the surveyor used questions to gather information about school. Talk about how surveyors usually identify the issue they want to investigate and prepare their questions before they start surveying *or* asking questions.

Active Involvement Have kids work together in pairs to create a survey. First, they need to identify a question or concern they want to investigate. Then they can create questions to ask. Have each pair of kids give their survey to at least one other pair. To collect more data, they can survey more kids. After collecting the data, have each pair present its survey's results to the group. Encourage kids to give feedback about the survey and how they think it could be revised to provide more or better information.

Off You Go Provide additional reasons for kids to do surveys. We have a school newspaper, which motivates kids to identify issues to survey, create questions, do surveys, and then write articles about the information they collected. After revision and editing, the articles are published in the newspaper.

Books for Teaching Strategies to Younger English Language Learners

Advanced Stage

Making Connections

Dia's Story Cloth: The Hmong People's Journey of Freedom by Dia Cha
Every Living Thing by Cynthia Rylant
Jingle Dancer by Cynthia Leitich Smith
Silent Lotus by Jeanne E. Lee
Snapshots from the Wedding by Gary Soto
You Have to Write by Janet Wong

Asking Questions

. . . If You Grew Up With George Washington by Ruth Belov Gross
New York Times Learning Network, Grades 3–12, at
  http://www.nytimes.com/learning/
The New Way Things Work by David McCauley
Something Permanent by Cynthia Rylant and Walker Evans
*What Makes an Ocean Wave? Questions and Answers About Oceans
  and Ocean Life* by Melvin and Gilda Berger

Visualizing

Come With Me: Poems for a Journey by Naomi Shihab Nye
Joyful Noise: Poems for Two Voices by Paul Fleischmann
*My Name Is Jorge: On Both Sides of the River, Poems in English and
  Spanish* by Jane Medina
Panther, Shadow of the Swamp by Jonathon London
Tyrannosaurus Time (Just for a Day book) by Joanne Ryder
Wings by Christopher Myers

Inferring

Annie and the Old One by Miska Miles
The Frog Prince Continued by John Scieszka
Grandma Fina and Her Wonderful Umbrellas by Benjamin Alire Saenz
My Freedom Trip: A Child's Escape from North Korea by Frances and
  Ginger Park
Sitti's Secrets by Naomi Shihab Nye

Determining Importance in Text

Harvesting Hope: The Story of Cesar Chavez by Kathleen Krull
Kids Discover magazine at http://www.kidsdiscover.com
National Geographic Explorer magazine at http://magma.national
  geographic.com/ngexplorer/
National Geographic Kids magazine at http://www.nationalgeographic.
  com/ngkids/
Sports Illustrated for Kids magazine at http://www.sikids.com/
Time for Kids magazine at http://www.timeforkids.com

Synthesizing

The Circuit: Stories from the Life of a Migrant Child by Francisco
  Jimenéz
My Diary From Here to There by Amanda Irma Perez
Hiroshima by Lawrence Yep
The Pot That Juan Built by Nancy Andrews Goebel
Ruby Lu, Brave and True by Lenore Look
Tea Leaves by Frederick Lipp

Older English Language Learners in Real Time

After many years of trying, Juli finally found a way to get kids really excited about publishing their writing—participate in an online collaborative project. It turns out it was a poetry slam!

So how did this all start? During spring, as usual, the conversation on a reading/writing listserv turned to poetry. Musing about online communities and students writing poetry, one of the teachers had a brainstorm. He suggested they try to pull together an online poetry slam and said he would be glad to coordinate. Teachers could volunteer to be involved and have their students post poems on a Web site dedicated to the project, and then students could read each other's poems and post appropriate comments. It sounded like fun, so several folks signed up.

As fall came around, the teacher queried the listserv again to ask whether there were any others who would like to join, and more people signed up. The group agreed to have the project go from mid-November to mid-December. Enter the online technology coordinator for the project. He set up a Web site, actually a blog site, so each teacher had a blog where they could have students post their poems. He arranged it so that all comments posted by students would need to be approved by a teacher before they appeared on the site—a great added feature.

Before Thanksgiving, to get kids motivated, Juli handed out a stack of poetry books and everyone spent several weeks reading published poems and talking about the qualities of a good poem. After reading lots and lots of poems, everyone agreed that a poem needed to be written so that readers could visualize what the writer was saying. Kids decided to focus on details.

Poems were posted on the Web site during the first week in December and the fun began. Almost as soon as the poems were up, comments started flooding in. Of all of them—well over 250—there were only one or two comments about students' poems that needed to be deleted. They weren't actually "bad," just a little insensitive. And such great constructive criticism the kids got on their writing. The surprise was how well they took suggestions from others. It was a huge growth experience for all of them!

When teachers needed help, the online technology coordinator posted the following suggestions.

Banging on a garbage
  can,
Bam bam bam.
Mattie says it's time
For a poetry slam.

  —FROM *HEY YOU!
  C'MERE: A
  POETRY SLAM*
  BY ELIZABETH
  SWADOS

We're starting to get poems posted and students are starting to enter comments. Here are some tips.

- *Comments' Quality:* Rather than the quick student response of "I like it" or "Good job!" we would like for students to enter a bit more to show some thinking about the poem.

- Suggestions for things to comment on:

  1. What connections did you make with this poem (for example, thoughts, feelings, other writing, or other things you were reminded of)?
  2. What words, phrases, images, or poetic techniques did you find particularly effective?
  3. Do you have any questions or suggestions for the poet?

- You could post these three questions by computers so that students can refer to them.

Our school wasn't the only one involved. There were fourteen others in the poetry slam, and all of them posted poems and received comments. What a great way to get kids to publish their work and get responses to their writing from a far-flung audience.

Lessons for Older English Language Learners

Instructional Materials

- *A Bird About to Sing* by Laura Nyman Montenegro
- Student writing
- Overhead transparency sheet

1: Making Connections

Writers use knowledge of their audience to decide what to include and exclude.

Teaching Moves

Start Up/Connection Talk with kids about what they know about writing for an *audience*—the people who will be reading a piece of writing. Encourage them to share how they determine the audience for their writing. Have them share some of their writing with partners and talk about the audience for the pieces. *Give Information* Explain to kids that writers use knowledge of their audience to decide what to include and exclude. *A Bird About to Sing* is written for an audience of kids—kids who think writing poetry is fun but that reciting poetry out loud is not. While you read the book, think aloud about how the writer includes things based on her knowledge of the audience. On an overhead transparency, list examples—similar to the following—of what Laura Nyman Montenegro puts in her writing because she knows the audience—kids who don't want to read their poetry out loud.

Content Examples from A Bird About to Sing

Laura Nyman Montenegro includes poetry written by Natalie, the poet in the story. This lets the audience see exactly what her poetry is like.

Monica, her poetry teacher, wants her to read her poem out loud. She says, "Nope. No way. Never!" This lets the audience know she is shy and nervous, and ready to fly away.

Monica takes Natalie to a poetry reading so that she can see others read their poems.

Her title, *A Bird About to Sing*, tells the audience that something is about to happen.

Active Involvement Have kids go through some of their writing and think about the audience for their pieces. Have them ask themselves:

- Who am I writing this for?
- How do I know that they will understand what I am saying?
- What else should I include in this piece of writing for this audience?
- Is there anything I should take out—exclude?

Have them share what they learn about their writing with partners.

Off You Go While kids work on writing in different content areas and genres, encourage them to pay attention to the audience for their pieces. Have them think about what they should include and what they should take out to help the audience make sense of their writing.

2: Asking Questions

Writers' questions lead to revisions in their pieces and in the pieces to which they respond for other writers.

Teaching Moves

Start Up/Connection Hand out a variety of informational articles for kids to browse and read. Ask them to pay close attention to the photographs, illustrations, graphs, maps, and so on and how they add to the articles. Encourage them to share what they notice in the articles with partners or a small group.

Give Information Explain to kids that they are going to learn how writers use who, what, when, where, why, and how questions to help them write informational articles. Such questions will lead to revisions in their own pieces and in the pieces to which they respond for other writers.

Share information from the "How Stuff Works" Web site questions with kids.

Active Involvement Have kids work with partners to browse the site and locate an online article to read. They can read it onscreen or print it out to read away from the computer. As they read their articles, have them discuss how writers answer the who, what, when, where, why, and how questions. Review the kids' answers by having them share with the group. Talk about how they found the answers to the questions and how they can use the questions' answers to write their own articles.

Instructional Materials

- "How Stuff Works," Web site for asking questions, at http://www.howstuffworks.com/
- *The New How Things Work* by David Macaulay

Off You Go Provide opportunities for kids to try out writing informational articles using the questions—who, what, where, when, why, and how—to revise their writing. For example, they can select their own topics for "how stuff works" articles and then work together to answer the questions as they write and revise. When their pieces are ready to be published, they can be included in a class anthology and placed in the classroom library for kids to read.

Instructional Materials

■ *Cool Salsa: Bilingual Poems on Growing Up Latino in the United States* **edited by Lori M. Carlson**
■ **Overhead transparency sheet**

3: Visualizing (Using Sensory Images)

Writers learn from the images created in their minds as they read. They study other authors' use of images as a way to improve their own.

Teaching Moves

Start Up/Connection Tell kids you want to find out what they already know about visualizing and creating images in their minds. Give them a minute or two to think, and then ask them to discuss their thoughts with partners. Have each set of partners share with the group. As kids share, list what they already know about visualizing on an overhead transparency. To integrate strategy use, see the comprehension lesson for this story in *Making Sense* (2005, p. 122).

Give Information Explain to kids that writers spend a lot of time reading to learn from the images created in their minds as they read. They study other authors' use of images as a way to improve their own. Read aloud several poems in English from *Cool Salsa*. To model for kids, as in the following examples, think aloud about the poems you read and how they create images in your mind.

> *Images Created by Poems in* Cool Salsa
>
> Nestor's image from "Abuelita Who" by Sandra Cisneros
> *"When I read the poem, I see an old man curled up underneath the bed and very, very confused. He's talking to himself."*
>
> Oscar's image from "Brown Girl, Blonde Okie" by Gary Soto
> *"When I'm reading the poem, I see two boys sitting outside after dinner and talking about girls they want to marry. They're trying to figure out why anyone would love them."*

Active Involvement Hand out copies of *Cool Salsa* and ask kids to browse through the poems. Encourage them to choose poems to read and to discuss the images they create in their minds with partners. Have them talk about what they as writers do to help readers create images in their minds as they read the poems they write.

Off You Go While kids are writing poems, provide lots of books of poetry, including student poems, for them to read. As they read poems, tell them to pay attention to how writers create images in their minds. Remind them that they can also help their readers create images in the poems they write by helping them to visualize.

4: Inferring

Writers carefully consider their audience in making decisions about what to describe explicitly and what to leave to readers' interpretation.

Teaching Moves

Start Up/Connection Have kids work independently to do a *Quick Write*—five minutes to write everything they know about a topic—(Elbow 1973, 1981) about Iraq (see the following example). They are to stop after five minutes even if they haven't finished. Have them share their Quick Writes with partners. Discuss the similarities and differences between what each pair writes with the group.

Quick Writes About Iraq

Amie writes: The thing I know about Iraq is they fight with our people. They try to win for their people. In the news people are seeing Iraq people or what ever you call them Army people are walking in or around the state. One question is to myself. Why is the Iraq people or army traveling in one state? Are they looking for somebody? My answer to number 1 question is . . .

Teacher's notes—Amie demonstrates a clear understanding about the conflict in Iraq. I need to encourage her to go back to this writing and add to her writing. She had to stop because of the five-minute time limit. During conferences, I'll check in to see whether she continues to write on this topic.

Emmanuel writes: Iraq is a place where the water got on and many people died because cacidilies (crocodiles) and any sort of animal in the sea that were dangerous. A herican (hurricane) got Iraq and now only to be safe is you can get on the roof

Teacher notes—Wow! I'm so glad I had the kids do a Quick Write on this topic. It gave me a quick assessment of their understanding. I can see that Emmanuel has confused the conflict in Iraq with the recent hurricanes in the southern United States. To help sort this out, I need to give kids more info about Iraq. Maybe we can watch some TV newsclips about Iraq, and then have conversations in small groups about what we understand. This might help him clarify his confusion between the two events.

Give Information Explain to kids that writers carefully consider their audience in making decisions about what to describe explicitly and what to leave to readers' interpretation. This is especially true when they are writing stories from a unique cultural point of view. Tell them that in *The Librarian of Basra,* the writer used a story from the *New York Times* about Alia Muhammad Baker, chief librarian of Basra's Central Library, as the basis for her writing.

Read students "A Note from the Author" at the back of the book and the quote at the beginning of the book: "In the *Koran,* the first thing God said to Muhammad was 'Read'" (Alia Muhammad Baker, *New York Times,* July 27,

2003). As you read the story, think aloud about how Jeanette Winter described (see the following table) some things explicitly and left other things to readers' interpretation.

Examples of Winter's Writing Decisions

Described Explicitly:

The job Alia Muhammad Baker has
That she is worried the war will destroy the library books
Soldiers waiting with guns on the roof of the library
Everyone abandoning the library

Left to Readers' Interpretation

Discussing "matters of the world and of the spirit" at the library
"She takes matters into her own hands."
". . . rumors become reality."
"At last, the beast of war moves on."

Active Involvement Provide other books with themes about war for kids to read. We often use *Baseball Saved Us, The Butterfly,* and *Rose Blanche. Faithful Elephants* is also a possibility, but its message may be too powerful for some students. Have kids work together to determine what the writers described explicitly and what the writers left to readers' interpretation.

Off You Go Remind kids that they can do their own writing about war. Writer's notebooks are a good place to try out this kind of writing to see how it goes. Encourage them to describe some things explicitly and to leave other things to readers' interpretation—inference. If kids want to publish their stories (take them out into the world), they can use what they have written in their writer's notebooks as seeds.

5: Determining Importance in Text

Writers reveal their biases by emphasizing some elements.

Teaching Moves

Start Up/Connection Help kids draw on their prior knowledge about Celia Cruz and salsa music by using the Think–Pair–Share strategy (Harste, Short, and Burke 1995). This strategy involves students thinking about a topic, then working with partners, and then sharing their discoveries and thoughts. In the "Author's Note" at the back of the book, Veronica Chambers writes about the importance of Celia Cruz:

> In her life, Celia Cruz recorded more than seventy albums, many of which went gold or platinum. She won five Grammy Awards and appeared in ten movies, including the critically acclaimed *Mambo Kings.* In Africa, she performed at the sold-out concert that was the prelude to the famous "Rumble in the Jungle" boxing match between Muhammad Ali and Joe Frazier.

Instructional Materials

- *Celia Cruz, Queen of Salsa* by Veronica Chambers
- *My Name Is Celia: The Life of Celia Cruz/Me llamo Celia: La vida de Celia Cruz* by Monica Brown
- *Celia Cruz and Friends: A Night of Salsa* (CD) by Celia Cruz
- *Hits Mix* (CD) by Celia Cruz
- *Lives of the Writers: Comedies, Tragedies (and What the Neighbors Thought)* by Kathleen Krull

Over several days, play Celia Cruz's music and read aloud *My Name Is Celia: The Life of Celia Cruz*. Share your thinking about the importance of Celia Cruz and her music with kids. Have them work in pairs to talk about her music. Then have kids share—either with another pair of students, a small group, or the whole class—what they learned about Celia Cruz and her music.

Give Information Explain to kids that they will be learning about how writers reveal their biases (point of view) by emphasizing some elements when they write biographies. Because they often provide students with people who can serve as role models, biographies are an important genre.

Before reading aloud *Celia Cruz, Queen of Salsa*, read kids the "Author's Note" at the back of the book. In it Chambers describes different points of view about her topic—Celia Cruz:

> I was born in Panama, and as my mother likes to say, she gave me the milk, but the music of Celia Cruz sweetened it. When I grew up, Celia Cruz became a role model for me because she was *Latinegra*. She taught me that despite the common media images, Latinas come in all colors.

As you read the book, think aloud about where the writer shows bias and how she does it. For example, when she describes how Celia could not return to Cuba after she left, she shows her bias (point of view) by writing:

> But once she left Cuba, politics dictated that she could never return. She would never again hear the cries of the *pregón* that were the bass and treble of Cuban street life. It was a heartache she carried her whole life through.

Active Involvement Give kids copies of *Celia Cruz, Queen of Salsa* to read and browse through to look for how Veronica Chambers uses her writing to show her bias (point of view). Encourage them to share what they find with each other.

Off You Go Provide other biographies for kids to read and browse for the writer's bias and how they show it. Kathleen Krull has written a series of short biographies that has many volumes. We often use *Lives of the Writers: Comedies, Tragedies (and What the Neighbors Thought)* from that series.

6: Synthesizing

Writers reveal themes in a way that suggests their importance to readers. Readers can create a cogent synthesis from well-written material.

Teaching Moves

Start Up/Connection This lesson integrates strategy instruction with a lesson in *Making Sense* (2005, p. 126).

Talk with kids about what they already know about synthesizing. If necessary, remind them that synthesizing is realizing and understanding how our thinking changes as we read well-written material. Encourage them to share stories, essays, and other forms of text that helped change their thinking as

Instructional Materials

- *Anne Frank: The Diary of a Young Girl* by Anne Frank
- *The Diary of Ma Yan: The Struggles and Hopes of a Chinese Schoolgirl* by Ma Yan
- *Zlata's Diary* by Zlata Filipovic
- Optional: *The Freedom Writers Diary: How a Teacher and 150 Teens Used Writing to Change Themselves and the World Around Them* by The Freedom Writers with Erin Gruwell
- Student writing

they read. Have them discuss how they can write so that their readers will also be able to synthesize.

Give Information Explain to kids that writers reveal themes in a way that suggest their importance to readers. Because of this, readers can create a cogent synthesis from well-written material. To model how to do this, tell kids that you will be using the following Synthesizing Frame (Kendall and Khuon 2005) to create a synthesis from a diary entry in *Zlata's Diary*. We use this frame to scaffold use of the synthesizing strategy and to help us understand how our thinking changes as we read well-written material.

Synthesizing Frame

I first thought this . . .

But then I learned . . .

Next I learned . . .

But this changed everything because . . .

This is way different from what I thought at the beginning. My thinking changed because . . .

As you read aloud a diary entry from *Zlata's Diary*, use the Synthesizing Frame to model how you can create a cogent synthesis from well-written material. While you work, think aloud about how Zlata reveals the themes of (1) loving her family, (2) a peaceful life, and (3) the horrors of war. Kids may be able to generate other themes she uses in the diary entry. The following is based on the entry from Thursday, October 14, 1993 (p. 198).

Juli's Synthesizing Frame for Zlata's Diary

I first thought this was going to be a story about crazy people who live up in the hills around Sarjevo because Zlata wrote, "Those lunatics up in the hills."

But then I learned that she was really talking about the people in the hills who keep shooting things. They must have rockets because she wrote, "Shells fell all around the market place."

Next I learned that Zlata is writing to Mimmy to tell her she thinks the people who are fighting and shooting have stolen a peaceful life from everyone—young and old.

But this changed everything because I learned that her diaries are going to be published abroad. She wrote, "I allowed it, so you could tell the world what I wrote to you. I wrote to you about the war, about myself and Sarajevo in the war, and the world wants to know about it."

This is way different from what I thought at the beginning. My thinking changed because first I thought the entry was about shooting and danger but then I realized that Zlata wrote about herself and how she felt about her family, her friends, Sarajevo, and the war.

Active Involvement Have kids choose a piece of their writing to share with partners. They could also choose something from their writer's notebook or a diary entry. Have each partner read the other's writing and use the

Synthesizing Frame to develop a synthesis. Encourage them to work together to revise, rewrite, or rework writing that is difficult to synthesize and to pay attention to how the writer reveals themes.

Off You Go Provide other opportunities for kids to read diary entries and use the Synthesizing Frame to develop a synthesis. Some additional diaries to use include *The Diary of Ma Yan: The Struggles and Hopes of a Chinese Schoolgirl* and *Anne Frank: The Diary of a Young Girl*. Sharing with each other encourages writers to revise and alerts them to where their writing doesn't make sense to readers.

A note about the optional text—*The Freedom Writers Diary*: Use this book with discretion. Although it has been edited for publication, it contains profanity and words considered unacceptable by some. There are, however, some older at-risk English Language Learners, especially boys, who make strong connections to the writing and find this book motivating for their own writing. It is possible to go through the entries and select ones that would be appropriate for use by students in your class.

7: Monitoring Meaning and Comprehension

Writers share their work so that others can help them monitor the clarity and impact of the pieces.

Teaching Moves

Start Up/Connection A note about this lesson: It can be difficult to motivate older kids to write. Very jaded older English Language Learners have responded positively to this lesson about an endangered species. The fact that it dealt with a mystery about the possible extinction of the ivory-billed woodpecker encouraged lots of writing, sharing, and growth on the part of the writers.

Begin by having kids view the Web site's QuickTime movie. After watching it on the Internet, allow time for kids to talk about what they noticed and ask questions.

Provide a wide variety of texts about the ivory-billed woodpecker for kids to read and browse; we include Web sites since they are highly motivating to kids. Have them work with partners to discover how writers handle informational text. Have partners share their conclusions with the group.

Encourage them to explore many aspects of informational writing as they work together. They can discuss various questions, including these:

- Where do writers get their ideas for informational writing?
- How do writers use illustrations, graphics, charts, and photos to help tell the story?
- How do writers make their informational writing clear and easy to understand?
- How do writers create an impact (a strong effect) with their informational writing?

Give Information Explain to kids that writers share their work so that others can help them monitor the clarity and impact of the pieces. Tell them that they

Instructional Materials

- *The Race to Save the Lord God Bird* by Phillip Hoose
- "Researchers Find the Avian Elvis," *Wildbird* magazine (July–August 2005, p. 6)
- *In Search of the Ivory-Billed Woodpecker* by Jerome A. Jackson
- "Updates from Arkansas," page 6, *Wildbird* magazine (September–October 2005, p. 6)
- Other information:
  - Big Woods Conservation Partnership at http://www.ivorybill.org
  - QuickTime movie of the rediscovery of the ivory-billed woodpecker at http://www.ivorybill.org/video.html
- Posterboard or chart paper

will be working in pairs and writing an informational text about the ivory-billed woodpecker. Then they will share their text with the group by reading aloud. After the presentations, the listeners will discuss the clarity and impact of the work with the writers.

Begin by modeling how you would go about writing an informational text about the ivory-billed woodpecker. You can use posterboard and/or chart paper to make your text more interesting and easier to share with a group. When you have finished, ask students to discuss the clarity and impact of your work.

Active Involvement Provide time over several weeks for kids to work with their partners to write an informational text about the ivory-billed woodpecker. We use the following simple process:

- Brainstorm ideas.
- Write a draft (include illustrations, charts, photos, graphics, etc.).
- Share the text with others to get help for revising, reworking, and rewriting.
- Edit using the Five Finger Rule for Editing and also have a peer editor review the text.
- Confer with the teacher.
- Share with others so that they can monitor the clarity and impact of the informational text.

Off You Go The purpose of this lesson is to provide students with the background information they need to do their own informational writing.

For example, one class responded to an incident of vandalism at the local aquarium by creating informational pieces about sharks. They researched individual topics and prepared their presentations on posterboard. They planned an evening event for parents and other guests at which they presented their joint projects and raised money to sponsor a shark at the aquarium.

Instructional Materials
- Copies of interviews written by students
- Copies of newspaper and magazine interviews
- Interview with Gary Soto (see http://www.garysoto.com/faq.html)

8: Fix-Up Strategies

Writers capitalize on their knowledge of writers' tools (that is, character, setting, conflict, theme, plot structure, leads, style, etc.) to enhance their meaning.

Teaching Moves

Start Up/Connection Provide written interviews from a variety of sources such as newspapers and magazines for kids to read. Be sure to include interviews written by kids. Have them work with partners to see how the interviewers structure the interview around a series of questions. Have them share what they notice with the group about the style of interviews.

Abigail and Sinai's Interview with the Lunch Ladies

We interviewed the lunch ladies about their jobs. Their names are Francisca, Mayra, Tho, and Cyd.

Question #1—Do you have fun working in the cafeteria?
Answer—It's very fun working in the cafeteria.

Question #2—How do you feel when kids drop their food and ask for more?
Answer—It's all right.

Question #3—How do you feel when kids don't want to get your food?
Answer—It's OK!

Question #4—How do you feel when kids insult your food?
Answer—We hope that kids use good manners and are polite, but we don't let it bother us.

Question #5—Do you like it when kids treat you nice?
Answer—WE LOVE IT SO MUCH!

Question #6—How long does it take to cook the food?
Answer—It depends what we're serving and how long it takes to cook, maybe an hour or two.

Give Information Tell kids that writers capitalize on their knowledge of writers' tools (that is, character, setting, conflict, theme, plot structure, leads, style, etc.) to enhance their meaning. Interviews are one style that writers use for informational articles. Hand out copies of the Soto interview. While you read through the interview with kids, think aloud about how the interviewer used questions to gather information about Gary Soto. Talk about how interviewers usually prepare their questions before they start interviewing.

Active Involvement Have kids work together in pairs to interview each other. First, they need to create a list of questions they want the interviewee to answer and then they do the interviews. After each kid has been interviewed, have the pairs of students share the interview responses with another pair of students (see the following example). Encourage them to give feedback about the questions and how they think they could be revised to provide more interest or to get better information. The second example that follows is a different "take" on interviews.

Alex and Manuel's Interview with the Counselor

Question: What is your job all about?
Answer: To help kids, to talk to them.

Question: Do you love your job?
Answer: I love it!

Question: What is a counselor?
Answer: A counselor is someone who helps kids and listens.

Question: How long have you been a counselor?
Answer: I have been working for two years.

Question: Have you ever had another job?
Answer: Yes. I worked for a big company and gave money away.

Question: What is the most important thing in your new job?
Answer: To help kids believe in themselves.

Daniel B., Pablo, Joel, Daniel O., and Mauricio Interview a Mystery Teacher

Do you want to know about the Mystery Teacher? Here are the answers to some questions.
I have dark brown hair.
My favorite singer is Chayanne. My favorite TV show is *Oprah*. My favorite movie is *Sweet Home Alabama*. My favorite clothes to wear are pants. My favorite book is *Charlotte's Web*.
My eyes are brown. My favorite food is posole.
I have been to Nevada, Atlanta, Arizona, Utah, Colorado, and California. Who am I?

Off You Go Provide additional opportunities for kids to find authentic opportunities to do interviews. We have a school newspaper, so this provides motivation for kids to create interview questions, do interviews, and then write an article to be published in the newspaper. By doing interviews, they learn that interviews are one style that writers use for informational articles.

Books for Teaching Strategies to Older English Language Learners

Advanced Stage

Making Connections

A Bird About to Sing by Laura Montenegro
Caged Birds of Phnom Phen by Frederick Lipp
Kite Fighters by Linda Sue Park
Ruby's Wish by Shirin Yim Bridges
A Summer Life by Gary Soto
Woman Hollering Creek and Other Stories by Sandra Cisneros

Asking Questions

Ben Franklin's Almanac, Being a True Account of the True Gentleman's Life by Candace Fleming
How Would You Survive as an Ancient Roman? by Anita Ganeri
So You Want to Be President? by Judith George
"How Stuff Works," Web site for asking questions, at http://www. howstuffworks.com/

Visualizing

Cool Salsa: Poems on Growing Up Latino in the United States edited by Lori M. Carlson
Laughing Out Loud, I Fly (poems) by Juan Felipe Herrera
Salting the Ocean: 100 Poems by Young Poets edited by Naomi Shihab Nye

A Suitcase of Seaweed and Other Poems by Janet Wong
Wáchale: Poetry and Prose About Growing Up Latino in America edited
  by Ilan Stevens

Inferring

Between Earth and Sky: Legends of Native American Sacred Places by
  Joseph Bruchac
A Gift from Papá Diego by Benjamin Alire Saenz
The Librarian of Basra: A True Story from Iraq by Jeanette Winter
The Man Who Walked Between the Towers by Mordecai Gerstein
The Moon Lady by Amy Tan

Determining Importance in Text

Celia Cruz, Queen of Salsa by Veronica Chambers
A History of Us (10-book set) by Joy Hakim
Kids Discover magazine at http://www.kidsdiscover.com
National Geographic Explorer magazine at http://magma.national
  geographic.com/ngexplorer/
National Geographic Kids magazine at
  http://www.nationalgeographic.com/ngkids/
Sports Illustrated for Kids magazine at http://www.sikids.com/
Time for Kids magazine at http://www.timeforkids.com

Synthesizing

Anne Frank: The Diary of a Young Girl by Anne Frank
Coolies by Yin
Freedom Writers Diary by The Freedom Writers with Erin Gruwell
Salsa Stories by Lulu Delacre
Zlata's Diary by Zlata Filipovic

Monitoring Meaning and Comprehension

The Race to Save the Lord God Bird by Phillip Hoose
In Search of the Ivory-Billed Woodpecker by Jerome A. Jackson
"Researchers Find the Avian Elvis," *Wildbird* magazine (July–August
  2005, p. 6)
"Updates from Arkansas," *Wildbird* magazine (September–October
  2005, p. 6)

Resources and References

Writers Talk About Writing

Gita Wolf—"A Good Book Is a Door to Another World"
http://southasia.oneworld.net/article/view/93858/1/1801

Gary Soto
http://www.garysoto.com/faq.html

Amy Tan—Salon.com Interview
http://www.salon.com/12nov1995/feature/tan.html

Janet Wong—"Getting Behind the Wheel, A Chat with Poet Janet Wong" by Sylvia Wong, *Asian Week* 21(20), Thursday, January 13, 2000.
http://www.asianweek.com/2000_01_13/ae_behindthewheel.html

Sandra Cisneros—Brainy Quote Web site
http://www.brainyquote.com

Yuyi Morales—"Interview with Yuyi Morales," Mariuccia Iaconi Book Imports
http://www.mibibook.com/auth_ill/forauth_ill_fall2003.html

Alma Flor Ada and Isabel Campoy—"One Page at a Time, Co-authoring Books for Children"
http://www.mibibook.com/auth_ill/words.html

Ken Mochizuki—"Artist Profiles"
http://www.heritagesource.com/profiles.htm#MochizukiKen

Pat Mora— "Pat Mora: Child's Play" by Scott Nicholson
http://www.hauntedcomputer.com/ghostwr29.htm

Carmen Lomas Garza—"Answers and Comments" by Carmen Lomas Garza
http://www.carmenlomasgarza.com/questionsanswers.html

Juan Felipe Herrera—"Learning to Not Write: An Interview with Juan Felipe Herrera" by Michael Luis Medrano
http://english.cla.umn.edu/creativewriting/dislocate/fall04/Herrera_interview.html

Francisco X. Alarcon—"Francisco Alarcon Is a Poet—First, Last and Always" by Elisabeth Sherwin
http://www.dcn.davis.ca.us/go/gizmo/1997/alarcon.html

Naomi Shihab Nye—"Interview with Naomi Shihab Nye" by Rachel Barenblat
http://www.pifmagazine.com/SID/240/

Web Sites

Analyzing Surveys with Kids (ASK), Listening to Student Voices
http://www.nwrel.org/scpd/scc/studentvoices/ask.shtml

Big Woods Conservation Partnership
http://www.ivorybill.org

Chickenscope 1.5, Explore Embryology
http://chickscope.itg.uiuc.edu/explore/embryology/

eFieldtrips Web site
http://www.efieldtrips.org

"How Stuff Works," Web site for asking questions
http://www.howstuffworks.com/

New York Times Learning Network, Grades 3–12
http://www.nytimes.com/learning/

"News Snapshot," a Current Events Activity for Grades 3–5
http://www.nytimes.com/learning/teachers/snapshot/index.html

Notable Children's Trade Books in the Field of Social Studies
http://www.socialstudies.org/resources/notable/

QuickTime movie of the rediscovery of the ivory-billed woodpecker
http://www.ivorybill.org/video.html

CDs

Cruz, Celia. 2000. *Celia Cruz and Friends: A Night of Salsa*. Rmm Records.

———. 2002. *Hits Mix*. Sony International.

Video

Brown, Mick and Bob. 1975. VHS. *Chick, Chick, Chick*. Chicago: Illinois Society for Visual Education.

Magazine Articles

"Researchers Find the Avian Elvis." *Wildbird* (July–August 2005). Irvine, CA: BowTie Magazines.

"Updates from Arkansas." *Wildbird* (September–October 2005). Irvine, CA: BowTie Magazines.

Student Magazines

Kids Discover
  http://www.kidsdiscover.com

National Geographic Kids
  http://www.nationalgeographic.com/ngkids/

National Geographic Explorer
  http://magma.nationalgeographic.com/ngexplorer/

Sports Illustrated for Kids
  http://www.sikids.com/

Time for Kids
  http://www.timeforkids.com

Professional Literature

Allen, Janet. 1999. *Words, Words, Words: Teaching Vocabulary in Grades 4–12*. Portland, ME: Stenhouse.

Anderson, Carl. 2000. *How's It Going? A Practical Guide to Conferring with Student Writers*. Portsmouth, NH: Heinemann.

Barrington, Judith. 1996. *Writing the Memoir: From Truth to Art*. Portland, OR: Eighth Mountain Press.

Bomer, Randy, and Katherine Bomer. 2001. *For a Better World: Reading and Writing for Social Action*. Portsmouth, NH: Heinemann.

Calkins, Lucy. 1994. *The Art of Teaching Writing*. Portsmouth, NH: Heinemann.

Carasquillo, A. L., and V. Rodriguez. 2002. *Language Minority Students in the Mainstream Classroom* (2nd ed.). Philadelphia: Multilingual Matters.

CREDE. 2005. "The Five Standards of Effective Pedagogy." Santa Cruz, CA: Center for Research on Education, Diversity and Excellence (http://www.crede.org/standards/standards.html).

Cummins, Jim. 1981. "The Role of Primary Language Development in Promoting Educational Success for Language Minority Students." In *Schooling and Language Minority Students: A Theoretical Framework* (pp. 3–49). Los Angeles: California State University, Evaluation, Dissemination, and Assessment Center.

———. 2000. *Language, Power, and Pedagogy: Bilingual Children in the Crossfire*. Clevedon, UK: Multilingual Matters.

Diller, Debbie. 2003. *Literacy Work Stations*. Portland, ME: Stenhouse.

———. 2005. *Practice with Purpose: Literacy Work Stations for Grades 3–6*. Portland, ME: Stenhouse.

Elbow, Peter. 1973. *Writing Without Teachers*. New York: Oxford University Press.

———. 1981. *Writing With Power: Techniques for Mastering the Writing Process*. New York: Oxford University Press.

Fletcher, Ralph. 1996. *A Writer's Notebook: Unlocking the Writer Within You*. New York: HarperTrophy.

Fletcher, Ralph, and Joann Portalupi. 1998. *Craft Lessons: Teaching Writing K–8*. York, ME: Stenhouse.

Fountas, Irene C., and Gay Sue Pinnell. 2001. *Guiding Readers and Writers (Grades 3–6): Teaching Comprehension, Genre, and Content Literacy*. Portsmouth, NH: Heinemann.

Freeman, Yvonne, and David Freeman. 2004. "Connecting Students to Culturally Relevant Texts." *Talking Points* 15 (2). NCTE, April/May 2004, pp. 7–11.

Graves, Donald. 2003. *Writing: Teachers and Children at Work, 20th Anniversary Edition*. Portsmouth, NH: Heinemann.

Harste, Jerome, Kathy Short, and Carolyn Burke. 1995. *Creating Classrooms for Authors and Inquirers*. Portsmouth, NH: Heinemann.

Keene, Ellin. 2002. *Cornerstone Literacy Newsletter*. New York: Cornerstone Literacy (http://www.cornerstoneliteracy.org/NEWSLET-TER/052902/ellin.html).

Keene, Ellin, and Susan Zimmermann. 1997. *Mosaic of Thought: Teaching Comprehension in a Reader's Workshop*. Portsmouth, NH: Heinemann.

Kendall, Juli. 2001–2005. "Juli Kendall's Reading/Writing Workshop Journals." Little Switzerland, NC: MiddleWeb (http://www.middleweb.com/mw/workshop/R_W_Project.html).

Kendall, Juli, and Outey Khuon. 2005. *Making Sense: Small-Group Comprehension Lessons for English Language Learners*. Portland, ME: Stenhouse.

Krashen, Stephen. 1981. *Second Language Acquisition and Second Language Learning*. New York: Pergamon Press.

Krashen, S. D., and Terrell, T. D. 1983. *The Natural Approach: Language Acquisition in the Classroom*. Englewood Cliffs, NJ: Prentice Hall.

Lamott, Anne. 1994. *Bird by Bird: Some Instructions on Writing and Life*. New York: Anchor Books.

McCarrier, Andrea, Irene Fontas, and Gay Sue Pinnell. 1999. *Interactive Writing: How Language and Literacy Come Together, K–2*. Portsmouth, NH: Heinemann.

Meek, Margaret. 1992. *On Being Literate*. Portsmouth, NH: Heinemann.

Morgan, Bruce with Deb Odom. 2005. *Writing Through the Tween Years: Supporting Writers, Grades 3–6*. Portland, ME: Stenhouse.

Portalupi, Joann and Ralph Fletcher. 2001. *Nonfiction Craft Lessons: Teaching Information Writing K–8*. Portland, ME: Stenhouse.

Ray, Katie Wood. 1999. *Wondrous Words: Writers and Writing in the Elementary Classroom.* Urbana, IL: NCTE.

———. 2002. *What You Know by Heart: How to Develop Curriculum for Your Writing Workshop.* Portsmouth, NH: Heinemann.

Ray, Katie Wood, and Lester L. Laminack. 2001. *The Writing Workshop: Working Through the Hard Parts (And They're All Hard Parts).* Urbana, IL: NCTE.

Thomas, W. P., and Collier, V. 1997. *School Effectiveness for Language Minority Students* (NCBE Resource Collection Series, No. 9). Washington, DC: National Clearinghouse for Bilingual Education.

———. 2002. *A National Study of School Effectiveness for Language Minority Students' Long-Term Academic Achievement.* Santa Cruz, CA: Center for Research on Education, Diversity and Excellence. Retrieved February 21, 2003, from http://www.crede.ucsc.edu/research/llaa/1.1_final.html.

Tovani, Cris. 2000. *I Read It, But I Don't Get It: Comprehension Strategies for Adolescent Readers.* Portland, ME: Stenhouse.

Children's Literature

2003. *Farm Animals* (DK Lift-the-Flap Series). New York: DK Publishing.

Ada, Alma Flor. 1994. *The Gold Coin.* New York: Aladdin.

———. 1997. *Gathering the Sun: An Alphabet in English and Spanish.* New York: Rayo.

———. 2002. *I Love Saturdays y domingos.* New York: Atheneum.

Alarcon, Francisco X. 1997. *Laughing Tomatoes and Other Spring Poems.* San Francisco: Children's Book Press.

———. 1998. *From the Bellybutton of the Moon and Other Summer Poems.* San Francisco: Children's Book Press.

———. 1999. *Angels Ride Bikes: And Other Fall Poems.* San Francisco: Children's Book Press.

———. 2001. *Iguanas in the Snow and Other Winter Poems.* San Francisco: Children's Book Press.

Altman, Linda. 1995. *Amelia's Road.* New York: Lee & Low Books.

Anaya, Rudolfo. 2000. *Roadrunner's Dance.* New York: Hyperion.

Anno, Mitsumasa. 1986. *Anno's Counting Book.* New York: HarperTrophy.

Anzaldua, Gloria. 2001. *Prietita and the Ghost Woman.* San Francisco: Children's Book Press.

Argueta, Jorge. 2001. *A Movie in My Pillow.* San Francisco: Children's Book Press.

———. 2003. *Xochiti and the Flowers*. San Francisco: Children's Book Press.

Arnosky, Jim. 2002. *All About Rattlesnakes*. New York: Scholastic.

———. 2003. *All About Sharks*. New York: Scholastic.

Baker, Jeannie. 2004. *Home*. New York: Greenwillow Books.

Ballard, Robert D. 1993. *Finding the Titanic* (Hello Reader series). New York: Scholastic.

Banyai, Istvan. 1998. *Zoom*. New York: Puffin Books.

———. 1998. *Re-Zoom*. New York: Puffin Books.

Barrett, Judi. 2001. *Which Witch Is Which?* New York: Atheneum Books for Young Readers.

Baylor, Byrd. 1998. *I'm in Charge of Celebrations*. New York: Aladdin.

———. 1998. *The Table Where Rich People Sit*. New York: Aladdin Picture Books.

Berger, Melvin, and Gilda Berger. 2001. *What Makes an Ocean Wave? Questions and Answers About Oceans and Ocean Life*. New York: Scholastic.

———. 2000. *Do Tarantulas Have Teeth? Questions and Answers About Poisonous Creatures*. New York: Scholastic.

———. 2000. *Why I Sneeze, Shiver, Hiccup, & Yawn*. New York: HarperTrophy.

Bernier-Grand, Carmen. 1995. *Juan Bobo—Four Folktales from Puerto Rico*. New York: HarperTrophy.

Blount, Roy Jr. 2000. *I am puppy, hear me yap: The ages of dog*. New York: HarperCollins Publishers Inc.

Boynton, Sandra. 1993. *Barnyard Dance*. New York: Workman Publishing.

———. 2004. *Rhinocerous TAP, The Book and the CD*. New York: Workman Publishing.

Branley, Franklyn. 1986. *What Makes Day and Night?* New York: HarperTrophy.

———. 1998. *The Planets in Our Solar System* (Let's Read-and-Find-Out Science). New York: HarperTrophy.

Bridges, Ruby. 1999. *Through My Eyes*. New York: Scholastic.

Bridges, Shirin Yim. 2002. *Ruby's Wish*. San Francisco: Chronicle Books.

Brown, Michelle. 2004. *My Name Is Celia: The Life of Celia Cruz/Me llamo Celia: La vida de Celia Cruz*. Flagstaff, AZ: Rising Moon Books.

Bruchac, Joseph. 1998. *A Boy Called Slow: The True Story of Sitting Bull*. New York: Putnam Publishing Group.

———. 1999. *Between Earth and Sky: Legends of Native American Sacred Places*. New York: Voyager Books.

———. 2000. *Crazy Horse's Vision*. New York: Lee & Low Books.

Buckley, James Jr. 2001. *MLB Home Run Heroes* (DK Readers Series). New York: DK Publishing.

Bunting, Eve. 1989. *The Wednesday Surprise*. Boston: Clarion Books.

———. 1990. *How Many Days to America?* Boston: Clarion Books.

———. 1998. *So Far From the Sea*. Boston: Clarion Books.

———. 1999. *Night of the Gargoyles*. Boston: Clarion Books.

———. 1999. *Smoky Night*. New York: Voyager Books.

Cannon, Janell. 1993. *Stellaluna*. San Diego: Harcourt Children's Books.

Carle, Eric. 1980. *Where's Spot?* New York: Putnam Juvenile.

Carling, Amelia Lau. 1998. *Mama and Papa Have a Store*. New York: Dial Books.

Carlson, Lori M., ed. 1995. *Cool Salsa: Poems on Growing Up Latino in the United States*. New York: Fawcett.

Castaneda, Omar S. 1995. *Abuela's Weave*. New York: Lee & Low Books.

Cha, Dia. 1996. *Dia's Story Cloth: The Hmong People's Journey of Freedom*. Denver: Museum of Natural History.

Chambers, Veronica. 2005. *Celia Cruz, Queen of Salsa*. New York: Dial Books for Young Readers.

Chan, Jennifer. 1993. *One Small Girl*. Chicago: Polychrome Publishing.

Chen, Chin-Yuan. 2004. *Guji Guji*. La Jolla, CA: Kane/Miller Book Publishers.

Cherry, Lynne. 2000. *The Great Kapok Tree: A Tale of the Amazon Rain Forest*. New York: Voyager Books.

Chin-Lee, Cynthia. 1999. A *Is for Asia*. New York: Orchard Books.

Choi, Yangsook. 2003. *The Name Jar*. New York: Dragonfly Books.

Cisneros, Sandra. 1991. "Hairs." In *The House on Mango Street*. New York: Vintage.

———. 1992. *Woman Hollering Creek and Other Stories*. New York: Vintage Books.

———. 1997. *Hairs/Pelitos*. New York: Dragonfly Books.

Cole, Joanna. 1989. *Hungry, Hungry Sharks*. New York: Random House.

———. 1989. *Magic School Bus: Inside the Earth*. New York: Scholastic.

Cowley, Joy. 1999. *Red-Eyed Tree Frog*. New York: Scholastic.

———. 2002. *Big Moon Tortilla*. Honesdale, PA: Boyds Mills Press.

Cronin, Doreen. 2000. *Click, Clack, Moo: Cows That Type*. New York: Simon & Schuster.

Dakos, Kalli. 2002. *The Bug in Teacher's Coffee: And Other School Poems*. New York: HarperTrophy.

Davies, Nicola. 2003. *Surprising Sharks*. Cambridge, MA: Candlewick Press.

Day, Alexandra. 2002. *Puppy Trouble* (pop-up version). New York: Farrar, Straus and Giroux.

dePaola, Tomie. 1990. *Pancakes for Breakfast*. New York: Voyager Books.

Delacre, Lulu. 2000. *Salsa Stories*. New York: Scholastic.

Demi, Hitz. 1982. *Liang and the Magic Paint Brush*. New York: Henry Holt & Co.

Dorros, Arthur. 1997. *Abuela*. New York: Puffin Books.

Dubowski, Mark. 1998. *Titanic: The Disaster That Shocked the World!* (DK Readers Series). New York: DK Publishing.

Endredy, James. 2003. *The Journey of the Tunuri and the Blue Deer: A Huichol Indian Story*. Rochester, VT: Bear Cub Books.

Filipovic, Zlata. 1995. *Zlata's Diary: A Child's Life in Sarajevo*. New York: Penguin Books.

Fleischmann, Paul. 1992. *Joyful Noise: Poems for Two Voices*. New York: HarperTrophy.

———. 1996. *Dateline: Troy*. Cambridge, MA: Candlewick Press.

Fleming, Candace. 2003. *Ben Franklin's Almanac, Being a True Account of the True Gentleman's Life*. New York: Atheneum.

Fletcher, Ralph. 2005. *A Writing Kind of Day: Poems for Young Poets*. Honesdale, PA: Boyds Mills Press.

Florian, Douglas. 1998. *beast feast: poems*. New York: Voyager Books.

———. 2001. *lizards, frogs, and polliwogs: poems and paintings*. San Diego: Harcourt Children's Books.

Frank, Anne. 1993. *Anne Frank: The Diary of a Young Girl*. New York: Bantam.

Freedom Writers with Erin Gruwell. 1999. *Freedom Writers Diary: How a Teacher and 150 Teens Used Writing to Change Themselves and the World Around Them*. New York: Main Street Books (Doubleday).

Friedman, Ina R. 1984. *How My Parents Learned to Eat*. Boston: Houghton Mifflin.

Ganeri, Anita. 1996. *How Would You Survive as an Ancient Roman?* New York: Franklin Watts/Grolier.

Garza, Carmen Lomas. 1990. *Family Pictures/Cuadros de familia*. San Francisco: Children's Book Press.

———. 2000. *In My Family/En mi familia*. San Francisco: Children's Book Press.

George, Jean Craighead. 1997. *Everglades*. New York: HarperTrophy.

George, Judith. 2000. *So You Want to Be President?* New York: Philomel Books.

Gerstein, Mordecai. 2003. *The Man Who Walked Between the Towers*. Brookfield, CT: Roaring Brook.

Gibbons, Gail. 1993. *From Seed to Plant*. New York: Holiday House.

———. 1993. *Sharks*. New York: Holiday House.

———. 1994. *The Planets*. New York: Holiday House.

———. 1998. *The Moon Book*. New York: Holiday House.

———. 1999. *Stargazers*. New York: Holiday House.

———. 2000. *The Pumpkin Book*. New York: Holiday House.

Goebel, Nancy Andrews. 2002. *The Pot That Juan Built*. New York: Lee & Low Books.

Griswold del Castillo, Richard. 2002. *Cesar Chavez: A Struggle for Justice/Cesar Chavez: La lucha por la justicia*. Houston: Piñata Books.

Gross, Ruth Belov. 1993. *. . . If You Grew Up With George Washington*. New York: Scholastic.

Guiberson, Brenda Z. 1993. *Cactus Hotel*. New York: Henry Holt & Co.

———. 2000. *Into the Sea*. New York: Henry Holt & Co.

Hakim, Joy. 2003. *A History of Us: War, Terrible War, Book Six*. Oxford, UK: Oxford University Press.

Harjo, Joy. 2000. *The Good Luck Cat*. New York: Harcourt Children's Books.

Hayden, Kate. 2000. *Twisters* (DK Readers Series). New York: DK Publishing.

Hayes, Joe. 1987. *La Llorona, The Weeping Woman*. El Paso: Cinco Puntos Press.

Heard, Georgia. 1992. *Creatures of the Earth, Sea, and Sky: Poems*. Honesdale, PA: Boyds Mills Press.

Henkes, Kevin. 1988. *Chester's Way*. New York: Greenwillow Books.

———. 1990. *Julius, the Baby of the World*. New York: Greenwillow Books.

———. 1991. *Chrysanthemum*. New York: Greenwillow Books.

———. 1993. *Owen*. New York: Greenwillow Books.

———. 2000. *Wemberly Worried*. New York: Greenwillow Books.

Heo, Yumi. 1996. *The Green Frogs: A Korean Folktale*. Boston: Houghton Mifflin.

Herrera, Juan Felipe. 1998. *Laughing Out Loud, I Fly.* New York: Joanna Cotler (Harper Children's).

———. 2000. *The Upside Down Boy.* San Francisco: Children's Book Press.

———. 2001. *Calling the Doves.* San Francisco: Children's Book Press.

———. 2002. *Grandma and Me at the Flea.* San Francisco: Children's Book Press.

Hill, Eric. 1980. *Where's Spot?* (Lift-the-Flap Series). New York: Putnam Books.

Ho, Minfong. 1996. *Hush! A Thai Lullaby.* New York: Orchard Books.

———. 2004. *Peek! A Thai Hide-and-Seek.* Cambridge, MA: Candlewick Press.

Hoban, Tana. 1987. *Is It Red? Is It Yellow? Is It Blue?* New York: HarperTrophy.

Hodgson, Mona. 2004. *Bedtime in the Southwest.* Flagstaff, AZ: Rising Moon.

Hopkinson, Deborah. 1995. *Sweet Clara and the Freedom Quilt.* New York: Dragonfly Books.

Hoose, Phillip. 2004. *The Race to Save the Lord God Bird.* New York: Farrar, Straus and Giroux.

Hutchins, Pat. 1992. *Rosie's Walk* (big book version). New York: Scholastic.

Innocenti, Roberto. 2003. *Rose Blanche.* New York: Random House Children's Books.

Jackson, Jerome A. 2004. *In Search of the Ivory-Billed Woodpecker.* Washington, DC: Smithsonian Books.

Janeczko, Paul B. (selected by). 2001. *A Poke in the I: A Collection of Concrete Poems.* Cambridge, MA: Candlewick Press.

Jenkins, Martin. 1996. *Wings, Stings, and Wriggly Things, Insects/Minibeasts.* Cambridge, MA: Candlewick Press.

Jenkins, Steve. 2001. *What Do You Do When Something Wants to Eat You?* Boston: Houghton Mifflin.

———. 2003. *What Do You Do With a Tail Like This?* Boston: Houghton Mifflin.

———. 2004. *Actual Size.* Boston: Houghton Mifflin.

Jiménez, Francisco. 1997. *The Circuit: Stories from the Life of a Migrant Child.* Albuquerque: University of New Mexico Press.

———. 2000. *La Mariposa.* Boston: Houghton Mifflin.

Jones, Carol. 1998. *Old MacDonald Had a Farm.* Boston: Houghton Mifflin.

Kaner, Etta. 1999. *Animal Defenses: How Animals Protect Themselves.* Tonawanda, NY: Kids Can Press.

Katz, Karen. 1999. *The Color of Us*. New York: Henry Holt & Co.

Kerrod, Robin. 2002. *1,000 Questions and Answers*. Boston: Kingfisher.

Krull, Kathleen. 1994. *Lives of the Writers: Comedies, Tragedies (and What the Neighbors Thought)*. New York: Harcourt Children's Books.

———. 2000. *Wilma Unlimited: How Wilma Rudolph Became the World's Fastest Woman*. New York: Voyager Books.

———. 2003. *Harvesting Hope: The Story of Cesar Chavez*. San Diego: Harcourt.

Kyuchukov, Hristo. 2004. *My Name Was Hussein*. Honesdale, PA: Boyds Mills Books.

Lazaroff, David. 2001. *Correctamundo: Prickly Pete's Guide to Desert Facts & Cactifracts*. Tucson: Arizona–Sonoran Desert Museum Press.

Lee, Jeanne E. 1994. *Silent Lotus*. New York: Farrar, Straus and Giroux.

Lehman, Barbara. 2004. *The Red Book*. Boston: Houghton Mifflin.

Levine, Ellen. 1993. *. . . If You Traveled on the Underground Railroad*. New York: Scholastic.

———. 1995. *I Hate English*. New York: Cartwheel Books.

Lewis, Richard. 2002. *In the Space of the Sky*. San Diego: Harcourt Children's Books.

Lin, Grace. 2001. *Dim Sum for Everyone*. New York: Knopf Books.

———. 2001. *The Ugly Vegetables*. Watertown, MA: Charlesbridge Publishing.

———. 2004. *Fortune Cookie Fortunes*. New York: Knopf Books.

Lipp, Frederick. 2000. *The Caged Birds of Phnom Penh*. New York: Holiday House.

———. 2003. *Tea Leaves*. New York: Mondo.

———. 2004. *Bread Song*. New York: Mondo.

Lithgow, John. 2004. *Saint Saens's Carnival of the Animals* (with CD). New York: Simon & Schuster Books for Young Readers.

Liu, Jae Soo. 2002. *Yellow Umbrella*. La Jolla, CA: Kane/Miller Book Publishers.

Lobel, Arnold. 1983. *Fables*. New York: HarperTrophy.

London, Jonathon. 2000. *Panther, Shadow of the Swamp*. Cambridge, MA: Candlewick Press.

Look, Lenore. 1999. *Love as Strong as Ginger*. New York: Atheneum.

———. 2001. *Henry's First-Moon Birthday*. New York: Atheneum.

———. 2004. *Ruby Lu, Brave and True*. New York: Atheneum.

Lowell, Susan. 1992. *The Three Little Javelinas*. Flagstaff, AZ: Rising Moon Books.

Malone, Peter, and Janet Schulman. 2004. *Sergei Prokofiev's Peter and the Wolf* (with CD). New York: Knopf.

Marshall, James. 1974. *George and Martha Back in Town*. Boston: Houghton Mifflin.

———. 1977. *George and Martha Encore*. Boston: Houghton Mifflin.

———. 1986. *George and Martha Tons of Fun*. Boston: Houghton Mifflin.

———. 1991. *George and Martha Round and Round*. Boston: Houghton Mifflin.

———. 1997. *George and Martha: The Complete Stories of Two Best Friends*. Boston: Houghton Mifflin.

Martin, Bill, Jr., and Eric Carle. 1996. *Brown Bear, Brown Bear, What Do You See?* New York: Henry Holt & Co.

McCauley, David. 1998. *The New Way Things Work*. Boston: Houghton Mifflin.

McCourt, Frank. 1999. *Angela's Ashes*. New York: Touchstone.

McCully, Emily Arnold. 2001. *Four Hungry Kittens*. New York: Dial Books for Young Readers.

Medina, Jane. 1999. *My Name Is Jorge: On Both Sides of the River, Poems in English and Spanish*. Honesdale, PA: Boyds Mills Press.

Miles, Miska. 1985. *Annie and the Old One*. New York: Little, Brown.

Mochizuki, Ken. 1995. *Baseball Saved Us*. New York: Lee & Low Books.

———. 1997. *Heroes*. New York: Lee & Low Books.

———. 1997. *Passage to Freedom: The Sugihara Story*. New York: Lee & Low Books.

Montenegro, Laura Nyman. 2004. *A Bird About to Sing*. New York: Houghton Mifflin.

Montes, Marisa. 2000. *Juan Bobo Goes to Work: A Puerto Rican Folktale*. New York: HarperCollins.

Mora, Pat. 1994. *Pablo's Tree*. New York: Simon & Schuster.

———. 1997. *A Birthday Basket for Tía*. New York: Aladdin Picture Books.

———. 1999. *Confetti: Poems for Children*. New York: Lee & Low Books.

———. 2000. *Tomás and the Library Lady*. New York: Dragonfly Books.

Morales, Yuyi. 2003. *Just a Minute: A Trickster Tale and Counting Book*. San Francisco: Chronicle Books.

Morris, Ann. 1993. *Hats, Hats, Hats*. New York: HarperTrophy.

———. 1994. *On the Go*. New York: HarperTrophy.

———. 1998. *Shoes, Shoes, Shoes*. New York: HarperTrophy.

———. 1998. *Tools*. New York: HarperTrophy.

———. 1998. *Work*. New York: HarperCollins.

———. 2000. *Families*. New York: HarperCollins.

Most, Bernard. 2003. *The Cow That Went Oink*. New York: Voyager Books.

Myers, Christopher. 2000. *Wings*. New York: Scholastic.

———. 2001. *Fly*. New York: Jump at the Sun.

Nye, Naomi Shihab. 1997. *Sitti's Secrets*. New York: Aladdin Picture Books.

———. 2000. *Come With Me: Poems for a Journey*. New York: Greenwillow Books.

Nye, Naomi Shihab, ed. 2000. *Salting the Ocean: 100 Poems by Young Poets*. New York: Greenwillow Books.

Osborne, Mary Pope. 2004. *Magic Tree House Research Guides: Ancient Greece and the Olympics*. New York: Random House Books for Young Readers.

Park, Frances, and Ginger Park. 1998. *My Freedom Trip: A Child's Escape from North Korea*. Honesdale, PA: Boyds Mills Press.

———. 2000. *The Royal Bee*. Honesdale, PA: Boyds Mills Press.

Park, Linda Sue. 2000. *Kite Fighters*. Boston: Clarion Books.

———. 2004. *The Firekeeper's Son*. Boston: Clarion Books.

Perez, Amada Irma. 2000. *My Very Own Room*. San Francisco: Children's Book Press.

———. 2002. *My Diary From Here to There*. San Francisco: Children's Book Press.

Perez, L. King. 2002. *First Day in Grapes*. New York: Lee & Low Books.

Perkins, Lynn Rae. 2003. *Snow Music*. New York: Greenwillow.

Platt, Richard. 2002. *Spiders' Secrets* (DK Readers Series). New York: DK Publishing.

Polacco, Patricia. 1994. *Firetalking (Meet the Author)*. Katonah, NY: R. C. Owen.

———. 1995. *Babushka's Doll*. New York: Aladdin.

———. 1995. *Babushka's Mother Goose*. New York: Philomel.

———. 1996. *Meteor!* New York: Putnam Juvenile.

———. 1996. *Rechenka's Eggs*. New York: Putnam.

———. 1997. *In Enzo's Splendid Garden*. New York: Philomel.

———. 1997. *Thunder Cake*. New York: PaperStar Books.

———. 1998. *Chicken Sunday*. New York: PaperStar Books.

———. 1998. *My Rotten, Redheaded Older Brother*. New York: Aladdin.

———. 2000. *The Butterfly*. New York: Philomel.

———. 2001. *Mrs. Katz and Tush*. New York: Dragonfly Books.

———. 2001. *Mrs. Mack*. New York: Putnam.

———. 2001. *Thank You, Mr. Falker*. New York: Philomel.

———. 2001. *The Keeping Quilt*. New York: Aladdin.

———. 2002. *When Lightning Comes in a Jar*. New York: Philomel.

Ramírez, Antonio. 2004. *Napí*. Toronto: Douglas & McIntyre.

Ramirez, Michael Rose. 1998. *The Legend of the Hummingbird: A Tale from Puerto Rico*. New York: Mondo.

Rappaport, Doreen. 2001. *Martin's Big Words*. New York: Scholastic.

Raschka, Chris. 1998. *Yo! Yes?* New York: Orchard Books.

Rattigan, Jama Kim. 1998. *Dumpling Soup*. New York: Megan Tingley.

Ravishankar, Anushka. 2002. *Anything But a Grabooberry*. Chennai, India: Tara Publishing.

———. 2003. *Alphabets Are Amazing Animals*. Chennai, India: Tara Publishing.

———. 2003. *Today Is My Day*. Chennai, India: Tara Publishing.

———. 2003. *Wish You Were Here*. Chennai, India: Tara Publishing.

———. 2004. *Tiger on a Tree*. New York: Farrar, Straus and Giroux.

Ravishankar, Anushka, and Anita Leutwiler. 2003. *Excuse Me, Is This India?* Chennai, India: Tara Publishing.

Ravishankar, Anushka, and Sirish Rao. 2003. *One, Two, Three!* Chennai, India: Tara Publishing.

Recorvitz, Helen. 2003. *My Name Is Yoon*. New York: Farrar, Straus and Giroux.

Ringgold, Faith. 1995. *Aunt Harriet's Underground Railroad in the Sky*. New York: Dragonfly Books.

Ripley, Catherine. 2001. *Why?: The Best Ever Question-and-Answer Book About Nature, Science and the World Around You*. Toronto: Maple Tree Press.

Rohmann, Eric. 1997. *Time Flies*. New York: Dragonfly Books.

———. 2002. *My Friend Rabbit*. New York: Scholastic.

Ryan, Pam Muñoz. 2001. *Mice and Beans*. New York: Scholastic.

Ryder, Joanne. 1999. *Tyrannosaurus Time* (Just for a Day Book). New York: Morrow Junior Books.

Rylant, Cynthia. 1988. *Every Living Thing*. New York: Aladdin Paperbacks.

Rylant, Cynthia, and Walker Evans. 1994. *Something Permanent*. San Diego: Harcourt, Brace & Co.

Saenz, Benjamin Alire. 1998. *A Gift from Papá Diego.* El Paso: Cinco Puntos Press.

————. 2001. *Grandma Fina and Her Wonderful Umbrellas.* El Paso: Cinco Puntos Press.

Salinas, Bobbi. 1998. *The Three Pigs: Nacho, Tito y Miguel/Los tres cerdos.* Houston: Piñata Books.

Scieszka, John. 1989. *The True Story of the Three Little Pigs!* New York: Putnam.

————. 1992. *The Stinky Cheese Man and Other Fairly Stupid Tales.* New York: Viking.

————. 1994. *The Frog Prince Continued.* New York: Puffin.

Selsam, Milllicent Ellis, and Barbara Wolff. 1987. *Egg to Chick.* New York: HarperTrophy.

Settel, Joanne. 1999. *Exploding Ants: Amazing Facts About How Animals Adapt.* New York: Atheneum.

Shea, Peggy Deitz. 1996. *The Whispering Cloth: A Refugee's Story.* Honesdale, PA: Boyds Mills Press.

Sierra, Judy. 2004. *What Time Is It, Mr. Crocodile?* San Diego: Gulliver Books (Harcourt).

————. 2004. *Wild About Books.* New York: Knopf Books for Young Readers.

————. 2002. *Animals Nobody Loves.* New York: SeaStar Books.

Sis, Peter. 2000. *An Ocean World.* New York: HarperTrophy.

Smith, Cynthia Leitich. 2000. *Jingle Dancer.* New York: Morrow Junior Books.

Smith, Jerry. 1991. *Who Says Quack?* New York: Grosset & Dunlap.

Snowball, Diane. 1995. *Chickens.* Greenvale, NY: Mondo.

Soros, Barbara. 2004. *Tenzin's Deer: A Tibetan Tale.* Eastbourne, England: Gardeners Books.

Soto, Gary. 1991. *A Summer Life.* New York: Laurel Leaf (Random House).

————. 1994. *Neighborhood Odes.* New York: Scholastic.

————. 1996. *Too Many Tamales.* New York: Putnam Publishing Group.

————. 1997. *Chato's Kitchen.* New York: PaperStar Books (Putnam Publishing Group).

————. 1998. *Snapshots from the Wedding.* New York: Putnam Publishing Group.

————. 1998. *The Old Man and His Door.* New York: Putnam Publishing Group.

————. 2000. *Chato and the Party Animals.* New York: Putnam Publishing Group.

———. 2003. *Cesar Chavez: A Hero for Everyone.* 2003. New York: Aladdin.

Spagnoli, Cathy, and Lina Mao Wall. 1992. *Judge Rabbit and the Tree Spirit: A Folktale from Cambodia.* San Francisco: Children's Book Press.

St. John, Victoria. 2001. *Dolphins.* Bothell, WA: Wright Group/McGraw-Hill.

Stanley, Sanna. 2002. *Monkey for Sale.* New York: Farrar, Straus and Giroux.

Stavans, Ilan, ed. 2001. *Wáchale: Poetry and Prose About Growing Up Latino in America.* Chicago: Cricket Books (Carus Publishing).

Steig, William. 1992. *Amos and Boris.* New York: Farrar, Straus and Giroux.

———. 1993. *Shrek!* New York: Farrar, Straus and Giroux.

Surat, Michele. 1989. *Angel Child, Dragon Child.* New York: Scholastic.

Swados, Elizabeth. 2002. *Hey You! C'mere: A Poetry Slam.* New York: Arthur A. Levine Books.

Taback, Simms. 1997. *There Was an Old Lady Who Swallowed a Fly.* New York: Viking.

———. 1999. *Joseph Had a Little Overcoat.* New York: Viking Children's Books.

———. 2002. *This Is the House That Jack Built.* New York: G. P. Putnam Sons.

Tafuri, Nancy. 1991. *Have You Seen My Duckling?* New York: HarperTrophy.

Tan, Amy. 1995. *The Moon Lady.* New York: Aladdin Picture Books.

———. 2001. *Sagawa, The Chinese Siamese Cat.* New York: Aladdin.

Thong, Roseanne. 2000. *Round Is a Mooncake: A Book of Shapes.* San Francisco: Chronicle Books.

———. 2001. *Red Is a Dragon: A Book of Colors.* San Francisco: Chronicle Books.

———. 2004. *One Is a Drummer: A Book of Numbers.* New York: Chronicle Books.

Tsuchiya, Yukio. 1997. *Faithful Elephants: A True Story of Animals, People, and War.* Boston: Houghton Mifflin.

Tunnell, Michael, and George Chilcoat. 1996. *The Children of Topaz: The Story of a Japanese-American Internment Camp Based on a Classroom Diary.* New York: Holiday House.

Uchida, Yoshiko. 1996. *The Bracelet.* New York: Putnam Publishing Group.

Van Allsburg, Chris. 1981. *Jumanji.* Boston: Houghton Mifflin.

———. 1983. *The Wreck of the Zephyr.* Boston: Houghton Mifflin.

———. 1984. *The Mysteries of Harris Burdick*. Boston: Houghton Mifflin.

———. 1985. *The Polar Express*. Boston: Houghton Mifflin.

———. 1986. *The Stranger*. Boston: Houghton Mifflin.

———. 1990. *Just a Dream*. Boston: Houghton Mifflin.

Vincent, Gabrielle. 2000. *A Day, A Dog*. Honesdale, PA: Front Street.

Wallace, Karen. 2001. *Diving Dolphins* (DK Readers Series). New York: DK Publishing.

———. 2001. *Rockets and Spaceships* (DK Readers Series). New York: DK Publishing.

Weisner, David. 1991. *Free Fall*. Boston: Clarion Books.

———. 1995. *June 29, 1999*. Boston: Clarion Books.

———. 1997. *Tuesday*. Boston: Clarion Books.

———. 1999. *Sector 7*. Boston: Clarion Books.

Wells, Rosemary. 2001. *Yoko's Paper Cranes*. New York: Hyperion Books for Children.

Wick, Walter. 1999. *I Spy Treasure Hunt: A Book of Picture Riddles* (*I Spy* books). New York: Scholastic.

———. 2002. *Can You See What I See?* (*I Spy* books). New York: Scholastic.

Willems, Mo. 2003. *Don't Let the Pigeon Ride the Bus!* New York: Hyperion.

Wilson, Karma. 2003. *Bear Wants More*. New York: Margaret K. McElderry.

Winter, Jeanette. 1992. *Follow the Drinking Gourd*. New York: Dragonfly Books.

———. 2005. *The Librarian of Basra: A True Story from Iraq*. New York: Harcourt.

Wolf, Gita, and Anushka Ravishankar. 2002. *Puppets Unlimited, With Everyday Materials*. Chennai, India: Tara Publishing.

———. 2002. *Trash! On Ragpicker Children and Recycling*. Chennai, India: Tara Publishing.

Wong, Janet. 1996. *A Suitcase of Seaweed and Other Poems*. New York: Margaret K. McElderry.

———. 2000. *The Trip Back Home*. San Diego: Harcourt Children's Books.

———. 2002. *Apple Pie 4th of July*. San Diego: Harcourt Children's Books.

———. 2002. *Buzz*. New York: Voyager.

———. 2002. *You Have to Write*. New York: Margaret McElderry.

———. 2005. *Hide & Seek*. San Diego: Harcourt Children's Books.

Wood, Don, and Audrey Wood. 1984. *The Little Mouse, the Red, Ripe Strawberry, and the Big Hungry Bear.* Wiltshire, UK: Child's Play (International) Ltd.

Worth, Valerie. 1996. *all the small poems and fourteen more.* New York: Farrar, Straus and Giroux.

Wright-Frierson, Virginia. 1996. *A Desert Scrapbook: Dawn to Dusk in the Sonoran Desert.* New York: Simon & Schuster.

———. 1998. *An Island Scrapbook: Dawn to Dusk on a Barrier Island.* New York: Simon & Schuster.

———. 2003. *A North American Rain Forest Scrapbook.* New York: Walker & Company.

Xiong, Blia, and Cathy Spagnoli. 1989. *Nine-in-One, Grr! Grr! A Folktale from the Hmong People of Laos.* San Francisco: Children's Book Press.

Yan, Ma. 2005. *The Diary of Ma Yan: The Struggles and Hopes of a Chinese Schoolgirl.* New York: HarperCollins.

Yang, Belle. 2004. *Hannah Is My Name.* Cambridge, MA: Candlewick Press.

Yep, Lawrence. 1992. *The Rainbow People.* New York: HarperTrophy.

———. 1996. *Hiroshima.* New York: Scholastic.

———. 1996. *The Lost Garden.* New York: HarperTrophy.

———. 2002. *The Khan's Daughter: A Mongolian Folktale.* New York: Scholastic.

Yin. 2001. *Coolies.* New York: Puffin Books.

Yolen, Jane. 1996. *Sky Scrape/City Scape, Poems of City Life.* Honesdale, PA: Boyds Mills Press.

———. 2003. *How Do Dinosaurs Get Well Soon?* New York: Blue Sky Press.

Zelinsky, Paul. 1990. *The Wheels on the Bus.* New York: Dutton Children's Books.

Zoehfeld, Kathleen Weidner. 1994. *What Lives in a Shell?* New York: HarperTrophy.

———. 1995. *How Mountains Are Made.* New York: HarperTrophy.

Appendix

Integrating Strategy Instruction

Several of the lessons in this book can be used with lessons in *Making Sense* (Kendall and Khuon 2005) to integrate strategy instruction. They match the same text or related texts for teaching strategies in reading and writing.

For example, when we work with younger English Language Learners at the early production stage of language acquisition, we use *Mice and Beans* by Pam Muñoz Ryan to teach kids about making connections in both reading and writing. It's a story about a grandmother's preparations for her granddaughter's birthday party.

The comprehension strategy lesson for making connections using *Mice and Beans* is on page 40 of *Making Sense*. Kids build background by using realia and making the recipe for rice and beans on the back cover of the book. Next, as the teacher reads the text aloud, she models how to make text-to-self connections by thinking aloud and keeping track of her own connections on sticky notes. Then, as kids read through the book again with the teacher, they share their own connections, write them on sticky notes, and place them on a chart. Finally, a collection of predictable books provides additional opportunities for kids to make their own text-to-self connections.

The writing strategy lesson for making connections using *Mice and Beans* appears on page 75 of this book. Using the prior knowledge they gained from doing the previous lesson, kids switch gears to reading as writers. They are encouraged to share pictures of their own families participating in activities like birthday parties. Next, the teacher and students look at each picture carefully, pointing to and labeling items and characters and talking about the relationship between Rosa Maria, the grandmother, and the importance of her youngest grandchild's birthday. Together they talk about how a writer's content comes from and builds on his or her experiences. Then, kids use what they know from their own experiences with their families to get ideas for writing. They begin by drawing a picture of a family birthday party, sharing their pictures with partners or the group, and then writing a story. They are encouraged to use their writer's notebooks to get their ideas down.

197

When we work with older English Language Learners at the advanced stage of language acquisition, we use *Cool Salsa: Bilingual Poems on Growing Up Latino in the United States* edited by Lori M. Carlson to teach kids about visualizing in both reading and writing. It includes poems by Pat Mora, Sandra Cisneros, Gary Soto, and many others.

The comprehension strategy lesson for visualizing and creating mental images using *Cool Salsa* is on page 122 of *Making Sense*. Kids build background by talking about their experiences and prior knowledge about growing up in the United States. Next, as they read two poems, "Good Hot Dog" by Sandra Cisneros and "Mango Juice" by Pat Mora, the teacher models by thinking aloud about her own mental images about the poems. Then, as kids read through the poems again with the teacher they share their own visualizations and how the poets help them create mental images. Finally, they draw and illustrate their mental images for the poems.

The writing strategy lesson for visualizing and using sensory images for *Cool Salsa* appears on page 168 of this book. Using the prior knowledge gained from doing the previous lesson, kids switch gears to reading as writers. They work together to make a list of what they already know about visualizing. This draws on their prior knowledge about creating mental images.

Next, the teacher and kids together read two poems from the collection— "Abuelito Who" by Sandra Cisneros and "Brown Girl, Blonde Okie" by Gary Soto. While reading, the teacher models what she is visualizing. They talk about how writers spend a lot of time reading to learn from the images created in their minds as they read and how writers study other authors' use of images as a way to improve their own visualizing.

After that, using individual copies of *Cool Salsa*, kids read poems with a partner and share their visualizations. Finally, kids continue to read lots and lots of poems from different sources and use what they learn from the poets to help them as they write their own poems.

Texts and Lessons for Integrating Strategy Instruction

Preproduction Stage

Older English Language Learners

Asking Questions

How Many Days to America? by Eve Bunting
Comprehension lesson—*Making Sense* (2005, p. 32)
Writing lesson—*Writing Sense*, page 68

Early Production Stage

Younger English Language Learners

Making Connections

Mice and Beans by Pam Muñoz Ryan
Comprehension lesson—*Making Sense* (2005, p. 40)
Writing lesson—*Writing Sense*, page 75

Older English Language Learners

Asking Questions

What Do You Do When Something Wants to Eat You? by Steve Jenkins
What Do You Do With a Tail Like This? by Steve Jenkins
Comprehension lesson—*Making Sense* (2005, p. 46)
Writing lesson—*Writing Sense,* page 86

Speech Emergence Stage

Younger English Language Learners

Asking Questions

Apple Pie 4th of July by Janet Wong
Comprehension lesson—*Making Sense* (2005, p. 57)
Writing lesson—*Writing Sense,* page 97

Visualizing

Calling the Doves by Juan Felipe Herrera
The Upside Down Boy by Juan Felipe Herrera
Comprehension lesson—*Making Sense,* (2005, p. 58)
Writing lesson—*Writing Sense,* page 98

Older English Language Learners

Synthesizing

Tomás and the Library Lady by Pat Mora
Comprehension lesson—*Making Sense* (2005, p. 73)
Writing lesson—*Writing Sense,* page 116

Intermediate Stage

Younger English Language Learners

Determining Importance in Text

A Desert Scrapbook, Dawn to Dusk in the Sonoran Desert by Virginia
  Wright-Frierson
Comprehension lesson—*Making Sense* (2005, p. 85)
Writing lesson—*Writing Sense,* page 130

Older English Language Learners

Synthesizing

Love as Strong as Ginger by Lenore Look
Comprehension lesson—*Making Sense* (2005, p. 97)
Writing lesson—*Writing Sense,* page 144

Advanced Stage

Older English Language Learners

Visualizing

Cool Salsa: Poems on Growing Up Latino in the United States edited by
  Lori M. Carlson
Comprehension lesson—*Making Sense* (2005, p. 122)
Writing lesson—*Writing Sense,* page 168

Synthesizing

Zlata's Diary by Zlata Filipovic
Comprehension lesson—*Making Sense* (2005, p. 126)
Writing lesson—*Writing Sense,* page 171

Revision Checklist

_____ I reread my writing aloud, listening to what I wrote.

_____ I asked myself, "Does it make sense?"

_____ I made changes that make it easier to understand my writing.

_____ I had my partner read my writing aloud to me.

_____ I asked my partner, "Does it make sense?"

_____ My partner helped me make changes that make it easier to understand my writing.

Editing Checklist

_____ I checked my capitalization.

    _____ At the beginning of sentences

    _____ Proper names

    _____ Titles

    _____ Dialog

_____ I checked my punctuation.

    _____ Sentences and periods

    _____ Question marks

    _____ Exclamation points

    _____ Paragraphs (indents)

    _____ Dialog (quotation marks, capitals, commas, paragraphs)

    _____ Underlining

_____ I checked my grammar.

    _____ I reread the writing and asked myself, "Does it sound right?"

    _____ I made changes to make it sound better.

_____ I checked my sentence structure.

    _____ I reread to see whether I used a variety of sentence structures (simple and compound).

    _____ I reread to see whether I used different kinds of sentences (declarative, interrogative, imperative, exclamatory).

_____ I checked my spelling.

    _____ I used the spell-checker.

    _____ I used the dictionary.

    _____ I asked a friend.

    _____ I asked the teacher.

_____ I had a partner reread and edit my writing with me.

_____ I used the Five Finger Rule for Editing.

Writer's Notebook Scoring Guide

Staple a copy into the front of your Writer's Notebook.

	4 Outstanding!	3 Wow!	2 So-so . . .	1 Oops!
Quality	Entries reflect real things, not chapters or "stories." I always attempt deeper thinking in my writing. There is often evidence of mini-lessons.	Entries include some real things but also lots of chapters or "stories." I usually attempt deeper thinking in my writing. There is some evidence of mini-lessons.	Entries do not often reflect real things. Sometimes I attempt deeper thinking in my writing. There is little evidence of mini-lessons.	My notebook has more drawing than writing. Entries are confused. They do not make sense. There is no evidence of mini-lessons.
Quantity of Entries	I always write in my notebook every day at school and at home.	I usually write in my notebook every day at school and at home.	I often write in my notebook at school. Sometimes I write at home.	I seldom write in my notebook at school. I hardly ever write in my notebook at home.
Neatness	My notebook looks like I truly treasure writing.	My entries are usually neat, clean, and well organized.	Some of my entries are clean and well organized.	My notebook is not neat. It looks like I do not treasure my writing.
Spelling and Punctuation	I reread my notebook with an editor's eye—paying attention to spelling and punctuation. Someone else can read my entries easily.	I often reread my notebook with an editor's eye—paying attention to spelling and punctuation. Someone else can usually read my entries easily.	Occasionally I reread my notebook with an editor's eye. It's often difficult for someone else to read my entries.	I do not reread my notebook with an editor's eye. It's very difficult for someone else to read my entries.

Independent Writing Scoring Guide Wall Chart

4 Outstanding!	3 Wow!	2 So-so . . .	1 Oops!
I wrote the whole time.	I wrote most of the time.	I wrote some of the time.	I wasted precious writing time.
I made my own writing decisions.	I made my own writing decisions.	I made my own writing decisions some of the time.	I did not make my own writing decisions.
I kept my pencil moving the whole time.	I kept my pencil moving most of the time.	I kept my pencil moving some of the time.	I did not keep my pencil moving.
I stayed in one good writing place.	I stayed in one good writing spot most of the time.	I changed writing spots.	I changed writing spots a lot.
I did not get distracted.	I did not get distracted.	I got distracted.	I got very distracted.
I crossed things out when I was revising and editing.	I crossed things out when I was revising and editing.	I forgot to cross things out when I was revising and editing.	I did not revise or edit my work.
I used what I know to help myself spell words.	I used what I know to help myself spell words.	I asked for help with spelling when I was writing.	I did not respect the writers around me.
			I played the "Pretend Game."

Persuasive Writing Checklist

_____ I clearly state my position or argument in the introduction.

_____ I begin with a lead/introduction that grabs readers' interest. For example, I

    _____ present interesting facts/statements;

    _____ tell a story related to my position or argument;

    _____ alarm the reader by presenting "what-ifs" or questions.

_____ I support my position or argument with some of these: relevant information, facts, expert opinions, statistics, quotes, and examples.

_____ I tell the readers everything they need to know to convince them of my position.

_____ I support and defend my position or argument in the body of the writing.

_____ I tell things in a logical order that makes sense. I place the most convincing evidence where it best supports my position.

_____ I use words that persuade readers to think or act in a certain way.

_____ I end with a strong conclusion that is interesting, convincing, and suggests action.

_____ I sound knowledgeable and authoritative.

Peer Conference Form

For future reference staple this form to the piece of writing.

Readers: _____

_____

Writer: _____

What the writing says:	I like:
What the writing says:	I wonder:
What the writing says:	My questions:

Plan of Action:

1. _____

_____

_____

2. _____

_____

_____

3. _____

_____

_____

figure A.1 *Veronica's first version of her story.*

Veronica   2-2-05

My First Communion
in Mexico

It Was a chilly morning I was awaked,I screamed

"oh my god I have to get ready for my first communion"
I was in a rush. I took a warm shower. I put on my white
dress,white tap shoes,and my white veil my mom said"put
on your Victorias Secret cream" my brother told me "did
you took a shower" I said "yes I did"Then my mom and
dad dropped me off at my aunt Leticia's house. They
had to because she knows how to do diffrent hair styles
she did my hair so beautiful. Then my mom and dad
picked me up I was at church my godmother was my
aunt Carmela. I loved the church because it's so quiet
after the church ended we had a party. It was so fun there
was food like pozole, tamales, rice,and my mom cooked
yummy Mexican beans. A lady came and delivered my
three milk cake. when it was time to eat cake a lot of
people eat it because it was so good.That was the best
day of my life.

figure A.2 *(continued)*

It was a chilly morning in Mexico. I woke up I
Said "oh my god I have to get ready for my
Communion."

①

figure A.2 *(continued)*

I was putting on my Pink dress then, I took
a warm Shower I was feeling so clean. when
I got out of the shower I Put on gliter on
my face and Victorias secret lotion the lotion
felt slimy as goo.

②

figure A.2 *(continued)*

Then my mom and dad droped me off at my aunt Leticias house.

③

figure A.2 *(continued)*

Her house Smelled like Rosemary herbs. Then
she asked me "what Kind of hair would hair
Style will you like meija". I told "her anything
you perfer". After my aunt Letica finished
brushing my hair my mom and dad took me to church.
(4)

The church was quiet as a forest. The pastor was speaking about the bible. The church smelled like flowers and herbs.

⑤

figure A.2 (continued)

After Church I had a party the was lots of foods like pozole, Rice, Beans, and Chicken. I also got so much presents. We were dancing because we had a sterio. At 7:00 P.M. My cake was deliverd the flavor was three milk. This was the best day of my whole entire life.

6